D0216557

POSTMODERN HOLLYWOOD

POSTMODERN HOLLYWOOD

WHAT'S NEW IN FILM AND WHY IT MAKES US FEEL SO STRANGE

M. Keith Booker

Westport, Connecticut
London

Library of Congress Cataloging-in-Publication Data

Booker, M. Keith.
   Postmodern Hollywood : what's new in film and why it makes us feel so strange /
M. Keith Booker.
      p. cm.
   Includes bibliographical references and index.
   ISBN-13: 978-0-275-99900-1 (alk. paper)
   ISBN-10: 0-275-99900-9
   1. Motion pictures—Philosophy. 2. Postmodernism—Social aspects. I. Title.
   PN1995.B613 2007
   791.430973′090511—dc22   2007023400

British Library Cataloguing in Publication Data is available.

Library of Congress Catalog Card Number: 2007023400

ISBN-13: 978-0-275-99900-1
ISBN-10: 0-275-99900-9

First published in 2007

Praeger Publishers, 88 Post Road West, Westport, CT 06881
An imprint of Greenwood Publishing Group, Inc.
www.praeger.com

Printed in the United States of America

∞™

The paper used in this book complies with the
Permanent Paper Standard issued by the National
Information Standards Organization (Z39.48-1984).

10   9   8   7   6   5   4   3   2   1

For Amy, Adam, Marcus,
Dakota, Skylor, and Benjamin

CONTENTS

Introduction:
Postmodernism and
Popular Film

Postmodernism, as both a historical and a cultural phenomenon, has been a central topic of academic discussions of culture and history in the past few decades. Partly because of the sometimes arcane nature of these discussions, the phenomenon of postmodernism has gained a reputation for complexity and inaccessibility, and it is certainly the case that some elements of postmodern thought, because they run counter to the dictates of what has come to be regarded as "common sense," are a bit difficult for the ordinary person to grasp. It is also the case that the specific films used by academic critics to illustrate the phenomenon of postmodernism in film have sometimes been difficult and abstruse, though most theories of postmodernism suggest that it is a far-reaching phenomenon that should have an impact on virtually every area of contemporary cultural production.

For example, the films of David Lynch, widely regarded as a director of confusing "art films," have been front and center in academic discussions of postmodern film. Thus, Lynch's *Blue Velvet* (1986) is one of the principal films discussed by Fredric Jameson as exemplary cultural products of the postmodern era in his seminal work *Postmodernism; or, The Cultural Logic of Late Capitalism* (1991). *Blue Velvet* is also a primary example cited by Norman Denzin in *Images of Postmodern Society*, his sociological discussion of the postmodern cultural terrain. Denzin notes in particular the film's refusal to identify its historical setting, freely mixing images that appear to derive from different historical periods: "This is a film which evokes, mocks, yet lends quasi-reverence for the icons of the past, while it places them in the present" (469). In addition, this film repeatedly states its central message ("It's a strange world") almost like a mantra, but this message is entirely trite, suggesting that Lynch is more interested in creating artistic images than in any sort of critical engagement with real-world issues. The catchphrase "It's a strange world" may go a long way toward explaining the tendency toward strangeness in Lynch's films, and thereby simply becomes mimetic.

Blue Velvet departs from Hollywood convention in a number of ways, but it is not really an inaccessible film. In it, teenage protagonists (played by Kyle MacLachlan and Laura Dern) discover their sexuality in their budding mutual passion, at the same time making the parallel discovery that the seemingly idyllic life of their town of Lumberton is underwritten by a dark world of crime and perversion that lies just beneath that placid surface. This is a film that openly invites Freudian readings—so much so that any such readings would be superfluous.

However, what Lynch's films represent is emphatically not reality but other representations of reality—which explains why they are sometimes so confusing to viewers who attempt to interpret them as being "about" the real world. Thus, the superficial tranquility of Lumberton— with its blooming flowers, singing birds, white picket fences, and friendly firemen—is quite transparently derived from nostalgic clichés of the American 1950s, with a look reminiscent more of a Disneyesque version of a town than any real town that ever existed in the 1950s or any other time. Meanwhile, the dark underside of Lumberton society seems equally stereotypical, deriving its material and look (cozy suburban homes suddenly replaced by stark urban red-brick buildings) from film noir—or what film noir might have been like without the Production Code. There are, actually, hints that the dark side of Lumberton might be a bit more authentic than the beautiful side, primarily in the way Lynch employs reminders of the tooth-and-claw nature of life in the animal kingdom, which, like Lumberton, can be both beautiful and violent—as signaled by the film's final image of a robin that lands on a window sill announcing the town's return to tranquility, but is at the same time eating an insect it has captured.

As noted by Denzin, *Blue Velvet* includes a number of inconsistent historical markers, though its principal historical roots lie between the mid-1980s, when the film was made, and the 1950s, from whence many of the characters seem to emerge and for which the film shows a certain nostalgia (another key tendency of postmodern culture), though quite vaguely defined. The 1950s are never overtly identified as an object of nostalgia, while much of the logic of the film seems specifically meant to undermine the kinds of idealized visions of small-town, nuclear-family life that are more typically associated with wistful visions of the 1950s. Much the same sort of hazy nostalgia informs *Twin Peaks*, the 1990–1991 television series in which Lynch was centrally involved, as it does Lynch's recent film *Mulholland Drive* (2001).[1] Indeed, the nostalgia of *Mulholland Drive* might be seen as especially postmodern in that the setting of the film is quite clearly contemporary with its making, yet its atmosphere and visual style show the clear influence of the noir films of the 1950s while it also draws upon a panoply of motifs from older films for its plot and characterization.

If postmodern films such as *Blue Velvet* and *Mulholland Drive* can, in fact, be understood by fairly broad audiences if approached properly, it is also the case that many extremely popular (and seemingly very accessible) films also epitomize the characteristics associated by critics such as Jameson and Denzin with postmodernism. Tim Burton's *Charlie and the Chocolate Factory* (2005), for example, is widely regarded as a children's film. It is, after all, a remake of a classic children's film, *Willy Wonka and the Chocolate Factory* (1971). But *Charlie and the Chocolate Factory* is far more than a children's entertainment. For one thing, it is a gorgeous film, filled with treats for the eyes and ears that are every bit as sweet as the confections whipped up in the factory of the title. It is also an exemplary postmodern film, both because of its emphasis on spectacular images and because of a playful tone underwritten by darkness. Among other things, the hints of darkness make the spirit of the film much closer to that of the source material in Roald Dahl's novel of the same title than was the original 1971 film adaptation. But all of Burton's films tend to contain dark elements, and *Charlie and the Chocolate Factory* is quintessential Burton, even if the previous works of Dahl and director Mel Stuart provided the basic materials with which he worked. In particular, the film epitomizes Burton's trademark focus on visual imagery over plot and characterization. In this case, of course, the production of impressive images is aided by the film's ultrahigh budget, though in many ways the film resembles nothing more than *Pee-wee's Big Adventure* (1985), Burton's first, relatively low-budget feature film. Indeed, the similarity between these two films may go a long way toward demonstrating the limitations in Burton's work, with its single clichéd message that imagination and creativity are the only antidotes to the crushing banality of day-to-day life in the late capitalist world.

In *Charlie and the Chocolate Factory*, the poverty of young Charlie Bucket (Freddie Highmore) and his family might represent one of the dark undertones in Burton's film, except that Burton seems little concerned with social commentary, and the entirely stylized depiction of it is clearly a mere simulation of poverty. We need not worry that anyone in the family will actually starve, and we are even invited to believe that the poverty of the family brings them closer together and makes their lives ultimately richer than those of the more economically fortunate. They live in a sagging, leaning, decaying home that seems a hybrid of Dickens and Disney, signifying poverty more as an idea than as a reality with real, human suffering attached.

The real darkness of *Charlie and the Chocolate Factory* resides in the factory itself, that traditional locus of sweaty, grimy capitalist misery, here transformed into a sort of brightly lit museum of luscious consumerist fantasy objects. In good postmodern (but also mythic) fashion, this factory resides in an entirely nonspecific location, as signaled by the fact that the denizens of the surrounding area speak with English accents but employ American currency. This factory, meanwhile, is no home to oppressed workers, its traditional labor force having been expelled years earlier. Instead, it is manned by hundreds of tiny, identical "Oompa Loompas," all played by the digitally multiplied Deep Roy, an actor from Kenya but of Indian descent, who thus serves as a sort of one-man embodiment of the former colonial world. Indeed, in the original version of Dahl's book, the Oompa Loompas were dark-skinned Pygmies from Africa, though they were made white in a 1973 revision that was released due to complaints that the original book was racist. The fact that all of the Oompa Loompas are identical invites comparison to both racist stereotypes about how members of nonwhite races all look alike and the way in which workers under capitalism are treated as interchangeable economic quantities, rather than human beings.

But there are no oppressed Third World workers here: we are apparently meant to believe that the Oompa Loompas genuinely love their work and revel (they frequently dance and sing) in the opportunity to inhabit the glorious factory, having been rescued from some horrid Third World locale by the factory's owner, renowned chocolateer Willy Wonka (Johnny Depp). Of course, it is also the case that the diminutive workers are held in thrall by the cocoa beans (their favorite delicacy) with which Wonka supplies them, almost like a pusher feeding drugs to an addict— or a First World corporation luring Third World workers with cheap wages. Burton pointedly ignores any possible metaphorical implications of this arrangement (in terms of colonialism, globalization, capitalism, or even slavery) and opts instead to ask us to take all of this at face value: the Oompa Loompas really *are* happy and better off in the factory.

The dark implications of the factory thus reside, for the purposes of the film, not in its workforce, but in its owner, whom Depp plays as a strange, creepy recluse of clearly questionable sexuality—inevitably triggering comparisons with Michael Jackson on the part of numerous critics. We are even given some psychological background to Wonka's strangeness, which is stipulated to be the result of his oppressive upbringing at the hands of his equally creepy dentist father (Christopher Lee), who sought in every way possible to stifle young Willy's budding creativity (and love of chocolate).

Wonka's response is to rebel by becoming as creative as possible and by channeling that creativity into the production of innovative candies (here obviously a metaphor for art), meanwhile paternally presiding over his domain of Oompa Loompas, who have replaced his former, more conventional workers because those workers were less tractable and posed more of a possible barrier to Wonka's creativity. But Depp's Wonka is hardly an unmitigated demonstration of the value of creativity. He remains psychically scarred by his childhood, so deeply alienated that he is unable to relate to ordinary human beings as anything other than the consumers of the goods produced by his factory or the workers who inhabit that factory but presumably never leave it and have no connection to the world outside of it. Depp's performance, widely derided by critics as entirely inappropriate for the presumably good-natured, pro-family film that he is inhabiting, thus presents us with a perfect postmodern character, all surface and no depth, his entire life consisting of his economic function as a designer and producer of sweets.

Indeed, given Depp's characterization of Wonka, there is something decidedly ominous about his project of attempting to lure Charlie to live with him in his factory, with the stipulation that he can never see his family again. The saintly Charlie, of course, turns him down, opting for family over riches, and by the end of the film the Buckets have taught even Wonka to value family, but this message has a sort of obligatory, tacked-on feel, as if Burton's heart wasn't really in it and he felt he had to include it only in order to secure the vast funding needed to produce the stunning array of images that constitute the interior of the factory. The other lessons presumably taught by the film are similarly half-hearted and obligatory, as the sad states of the children (other than the admirable Charlie) who tour the factory teach us that gluttony is bad for children, television is bad for children, it is bad to spoil children, and it is bad to push children to become overly competitive.

Here, however, the lessons, like the plot, are beside the point. Image is everything, and the unending barrage of spectacular images can match anything ever put on the screen in terms of their extravagant richness. In this and many other ways, *Charlie and the Chocolate Factory* is representative of postmodern film as a whole, its unabashed sense of itself as spectacle being perfectly in tune with the postmodern world, famously described by Guy Debord as the "society of the spectacle." The factory itself is a sort of Disney World of film images, each being more a representation of other images than of anything in reality. The film thus exemplifies Jean Baudrillard's vision of postmodern society as increasingly dominated by technologically generated forms of culture and experience, leading to the death of conventional reality and the growth of "hyperreality," in which all is simulation and all experience is mediated through images—particularly "simulacra," images that exist only in their own right, representing nothing in reality.

In fact, *Charlie and the Chocolate Factory* is a consummate postmodern film in a number of ways, though postmodernism is an extremely complex historical and cultural phenomenon that is still evolving and is therefore difficult to define. In the following readings of individual films, I will assume that postmodern culture is characterized by a number of basic attributes. For example, postmodernism participates in a general crisis of belief, of the kind indicated perhaps most famously by Jean-François Lyotard's influential suggestion that postmodernism is informed by a radical suspicion toward "totalizing metanarratives." This suspicion grows from, among other things, the fact that virtually all aspects of life in the postmodern era have experienced a dizzying and accelerating rate of change. This facet of postmodernism involves fundamental challenges to the Western philosophical tradition, but it often results in cultural products that are playful and lighthearted. In addition, the vapid nature of the messages delivered by films such as *Charlie and the Chocolate Factory* and *Blue Velvet* can be attributed to a half-heartedness that results from a lack of faith in the viability of *any* messages. Meanwhile, this distrust of totalizing metanarratives has led to a strong tendency toward pluralism in postmodern thought, which in the aesthetic realm often leads to the production of works that participate in multiple genres and styles within a single work. The tour of Burton's chocolate factory is, among other things, a tour of various film and television genres, thus exemplifying this side of postmodern culture as well.

The vertiginous pace of change in the postmodern era has also contributed to an increasing sense of the instability of personal identity, which accompanies the growing sense of alienation experienced by individuals during the era. After all, individual identity attains its stability through a perception of continuity of selfhood over time. But this perception is increasingly difficult to maintain in an age in which so many things have changed so radically over such short periods of time. Thus, Jameson, probably the single most influential theorist of postmodernism, has argued that the "psychic fragmentation" of the postmodern subject has become so radical that individuals no longer have a stable enough psyche to undergo the fundamentally modernist experience of alienation (*Postmodernism*, 90). Willy Wonka's seeming lack of any real identity epitomizes this phenomenon, as does Frank Booth's in *Blue Velvet*.

This schizophrenic sense of a loss of individual temporal continuity also contributes to a larger loss of any sense of historical continuity. Beginning in the 1950s, individuals in advanced Western societies have increasingly felt that they were living in unprecedented situations to which the experience of the past was irrelevant. For example, how could any lessons about history and politics learned before the nuclear bomb really apply to a world in which the bomb made sudden global annihilation a constant threat? Moreover, the pace of change was so rapid that the present also became disconnected from the future, which became more and more unpredictable. Thus, the totalizing systems that were called into question beginning in the 1950s included any and all scientific and theoretical models of history. *Charlie and the Chocolate Factory* takes place in a sort of timeless, fairy-tale world where history does not even occur, while Lumberton seems removed from history as well.

As I describe in my book *The Post-Utopian Imagination*, the loss of faith in historical metanarratives during the postmodern era has been accompanied by a weakening of the utopian imagination, and in particular by a loss of faith in the possibility that utopian dreams might actually be realized. If history did not make sense, how could it be expected to lead to an ideal conclusion? Thus, the postmodern era's sense of rapid and even terrifying change has been accompanied by an equally horrifying sense that, within the context of late capitalism, nothing ever really changes after all. *Charlie and the Chocolate Factory* and *Blue Velvet* contain a number of potentially utopian images, but they are all both dreamlike and thoroughly commodified. None seem meant as actual possibilities for the real world.

Also closely related to the collapse of belief in totalizing systems is the demise of the tradition of Aristotelian logic, through which Western society had long defined itself via a series of polar oppositions, the central of which were Good versus Evil and Us versus Them—both of which, in the Western tradition, ultimately amount to pretty much the same thing. Without such clear distinctions to rely on, postmodernist thought tends toward a radical relativism, in which no point of view can be maintained as absolutely superior to any other. The lack of any real message in films such as *Blue Velvet* and *Charlie and the Chocolate Factory* again comes into play here, as does the fact that so many aspects of the films don't really make sense from a logical perspective.

The collapse of belief in polar oppositions has a number of aesthetic consequences, including a growing sense of doubt about the distinction between art and reality. Of course, this particular crisis was furthered by the increasing aestheticization of life in the 1950s, as new communications and media technologies made it possible for culture to penetrate everyday life in an unprecedented way. The unstable boundary between fiction and reality is a key element of what Brian McHale has described, in his *Postmodernist Fiction* (1987), as a general postmodernist confusion of ontological levels and boundaries. Lynch's Lumberton clearly exists in a sort of alternative universe, where reality is constructed from fiction. Similarly, the children entering Burton's chocolate factory seem to enter an alternative reality, somewhat like Dorothy's arrival in Oz, except that the latter is ultimately recuperated as a dream.

Related to this confusion of levels is a questioning of the traditional distinction between high and low culture. Many critics, such as Andreas Huyssen, have seen this feature of postmodernism as a sign that it is more democratic than an elitist modernism. If nothing else, this deconstruction of the boundary between high and low art opened opportunities for popular culture, such as film, to assume a new importance in American society as a whole. *Charlie and the Chocolate Factory* is an avowedly popular cultural artifact, yet one would be hard pressed to find, in the annals of "high" art, images of superior aesthetic power. Similarly, *Blue Velvet* is an "art film" constructed from materials derived from the "lowest" forms of pulp culture.

The postmodernist questioning of traditional standards of aesthetic judgment leads to a general mode of playfulness and satire in which postmodernist art, often resorting to campy self-parody, seems to have difficulty taking itself seriously. *Charlie and the Chocolate Factory* again exemplifies this aspect of postmodernist art, which is related to the film's focus on superficial appearance rather than thematic depth. *Blue Velvet* seems more serious, but it is also campy, intentionally exaggerated in ways that tend to undermine any interpretation of the film as a serious examination of the issues upon which it seems to touch.

Of course, different observers have seen postmodernism in different ways. However, the very fact that highly popular films such as *Charlie and the Chocolate Factory* can illustrate so many academic conceptualizations of postmodern culture suggests that these conceptualizations have a much broader relevance. Indeed, even the most rarefied academic discussions of postmodernism, such as Jameson's *Postmodernism,* have often argued the usefulness of the concept of postmodernism for anyone who would attempt to come to grips with the complexities of day-to-day life in the contemporary world. Thus, while Jameson notes the importance to postmodernist culture of arcane works of performance art and experimental video, he also insists that postmodernism is now a cultural dominant and that even the most mundane products of popular culture are heavily conditioned by a postmodernist paradigm.

Jameson does not write for a popular audience, but his work certainly implies that such audiences could profit greatly from a better understanding of the phenomenon of postmodernism. Indeed, recent "beginner's guides" to postmodernism have been produced in an attempt to introduce the movement to broader audiences, though these guides are probably used most often as textbooks in college-level introductory courses on the subject. These texts include such works as *Introducing Postmodernism* by Richard Appignanesi and others (first published in 1995, but now available in a third edition, published in 2005), Tim Wood's *Beginning Postmodernism* (1999), and Kevin Hart's *Postmodernism: A Beginner's Guide* (2004). There is even an introduction in comic book format, in the form of James M. Powell and Joe Lee's *Postmodernism for Beginners* (1998).

Such primers can be useful for those who are attempting to get their bearings within the topic of postmodernism, though they provide very little in terms of the discussion of specific cultural texts as representative examples of postmodern culture. Works such as Brian McHale's *Postmodernist Fiction* (1987) and Linda Hutcheon's *A Poetics of Postmodernism* (1988) provide good introductions to the topic of postmodernism in fiction, especially the novel, though they are intended largely for academic audiences—just as the novels they discuss are, by and large, experimental literary efforts that are not necessarily intended to appeal to a mass audience. For the broader public, postmodernism resides primarily on television and in film. I myself have discussed postmodern television in my book *Strange TV* (2002), though much more work certainly remains to be done in that area, especially in terms of making discussions of postmodern television accessible to a popular readership. Postmodern film has received even less critical treatment. Many of the leading academic treatises on postmodernism—such as Jameson's *Postmodernism,* David Harvey's *The Condition of Postmodernity* (1990), and especially Denzin's *Images of Postmodern Society*—contain substantial discussions of film as an element of postmodern culture. The collections of essays edited by Cristina Degli-Esposti (1998) and by Peter and Will Brooker (1997) provide the most extensive discussions of postmodern film. However, these are again intended for academic audiences. Furthermore, essay collections, by their nature, do not provide comprehensive coverage but instead focus on spot coverage of specific films or phenomena.

The current volume is an attempt to contribute to the popular understanding of postmodernism as a cultural phenomenon by providing a comprehensive discussion of postmodern film that is accessible to a fairly broad audience—focusing on popular, accessible films in this discussion. My understanding of postmodernism derives most importantly from the work of Jameson, which, however difficult his work might be for most readers, is in many ways quite simple and straightforward. At the level of form and technique, for example, Jameson argues that postmodernist art (especially narrative art such as cinema or the novel) is characterized by two central tendencies: formal fragmentation and a reliance on styles that mimic those of earlier works or artists in a mode of pastiche.

For Jameson, however, these relatively straightforward formal characteristics are aesthetic symptoms of far more profound developments in postmodern society as a whole, caused by the fact that capitalism, in the wake of the dismantling of the great European colonial empires (primarily in the 1950s) has entered a new "late" phase characterized by the rapidly increasing global hegemony of consumer capitalism and capitalist modernization. Jameson's view of late capitalism builds primarily on the work of Ernest Mandel, though it is Jameson's particular contribution to suggest that postmodernism is the "cultural logic" of late capitalism, directly expressing its characteristics in aesthetic form. Thus, the formal fragmentation of postmodern texts is closely related to the increasing psychic fragmentation of individual subjects. Meanwhile, this psychic fragmentation itself implies that the mind of the individual artist is no longer stable enough to be the source of a unique personal style, resulting in the necessity of borrowing styles from others via pastiche. This tendency is further enhanced by the way in which the rapid rate of change in the postmodern era makes it virtually impossible for individuals to maintain any genuine sense of historical continuity. One result of this loss is a tendency for contemporary artists to regard the styles of the past as a sort of aesthetic cafeteria from whose menu they can nostalgically pick and choose without concern for the historical context in which those styles originally arose.

It is the reproduction of both the style and the content of earlier works from various periods that Jameson describes as "pastiche," which is,

> like parody, the imitation of a peculiar or unique, idiosyncratic style, the wearing of a stylistic mask, speech in a dead language. But it is a neutral practice of such mimicry, without any of parody's ulterior motives, amputated of the satiric impulse, devoid of any laughter and of any conviction that alongside the abnormal tongue you have momentarily borrowed, some healthy linguistic normality still exists. (*Postmodernism*, 17)

Among other things, Jameson sees this reliance on the styles of the past as an indication of the particular kind of nostalgia that is one of the defining characteristics of postmodern art. In addition, this "random cannibalization of all the styles of the past" reduces the past to a series of spectacles, a collection of images disconnected from any genuine sense of historical process.

An obvious implication of Jameson's reading of postmodernism is that, given the growing global hegemony of capitalism, postmodernism (as the cultural logic of late capitalism) should be hegemonic in the cultural sphere. As a result, a wide variety of cultural products should reflect the postmodern worldview in a number of different ways. This volume looks at the manifestations of postmodernism in a diverse array of films (mostly American) from the 1950s forward. Following Jameson's lead, chapter 1 examines the prevalence of narrative, formal, and thematic fragmentation in recent postmodern films, focusing on such examples as *Timecode, Moulin Rouge!, Run Lola Run, Zelig, Memento, Fight Club, Natural Born Killers*, and *Requiem for a Dream*. It also discusses the phenomenon of "hyperlink" cinema, of which Quentin Tarantino's *Pulp Fiction* may be the best-known example. The chapter also includes a discussion of the films of the Mexican director Alejandro González Iñárritu, who, in a series of films, has produced a sort of counterexample that employs the hyperlink form in ways that are more politically motivated than is typical of American postmodern films.

Chapter 2 focuses on nostalgia as a prevalent mode in postmodern film, with special concentration on the use of music both to evoke a nostalgic atmosphere and as an object of nostalgia in its own right. It includes discussions of such films as *Blue Velvet, A Midsummer Night's Sex Comedy, A Knight's Tale, Moulin Rouge!, American Graffiti, The Last Picture Show, Phantom of the Paradise, Grease, Hairspray, Cry-Baby, Back to the Future, Peggy Sue Got Married, Pleasantville, Austin Powers, Wayne's World, Sweet and Lowdown, Kansas City, O Brother, Where Art*

Thou?, *Pennies from Heaven*, and *Dancer in the Dark*. Chapter 3 also deals with postmodern nostalgia in recent films, this time as it is directed toward earlier motion pictures. In particular, it discusses the extent to which postmodern films borrow styles, motifs, and material from their predecessors—and are to an extent often *about* previous films, treating films and filmmaking as their principal objects of representation. Films discussed include the special case of Brian De Palma's numerous pastiches of Alfred Hitchcock's movies, Gus Van Sant's shot-by-shot remake of Hitchcock's *Psycho*, and the use of generic pastiche in the Coen brothers' *The Man Who Wasn't There*. Films that address the movie industry in various ways include *Blow Out*, *8½*, *Stardust Memories*, *The Purple Rose of Cairo*, *Barton Fink*, *O Brother, Where Art Thou?*, *Cecil B. Demented*, *Ed Wood*, and *The Player*.

Chapter 4 concludes my survey of pastiche in postmodern film with a discussion of the use of television and other media as a source of both style and content in recent American motion pictures. It includes a consideration of the phenomenon of the adaptation of television series to film, as well as movies that treat television as their subject matter, including *Stay Tuned*, *Wayne's World*, *Soapdish*, *Josie and the Pussycats*, *The Truman Show*, *Edtv*, *Being There*, *To Die For*, *Videodrome*, and *Click*.

The final chapter sums up the findings of the previous chapters, while also specifically addressing the implications of these findings in terms of the distinctive personal styles of postmodern filmmakers. It focuses on the films of Lynch, Burton, Tarantino, and David Cronenberg, all of whom are generally regarded as postmodern directors and all of whom are known for making films that bear their easily identifiable personal stamp. A look at the films of these directors suggests that they do indeed employ the strategies of fragmentation and pastiche associated by Jameson with postmodernism; however, it also demonstrates that their films show a new kind of postmodern creativity that goes beyond conventional notions of personal style. All in all, the extensive review of recent American cinema in this volume tends to verify Jameson's vision of both the aesthetic and ideological tendencies of postmodern film, while also demonstrating that a wide variety of recent American films can be considered postmodern.

Chapter 1

BREAKING UP IS HARD TO AVOID

FRAGMENTATION IN POSTMODERN FILM

In the distinctive opening sequence of Robert Altman's *The Player* (1992), Walter Stuckel (Fred Ward), security chief of a major film studio, complains that "the pictures they make now are all MTV: cut, cut, cut, cut. The opening shot of Welles's *Touch of Evil* was 6½ minutes long." Actually, the famous tracking shot that opens Orson Welles's *Touch of Evil* (1958) runs less than four minutes until the first cut, but Stuckel's point remains and is reinforced by his later references in this same scene to Alfred Hitchcock's *Rope* (1948), the entire length of which consists of a sequence of extended shots, each of nearly ten minutes in length (the maximum amount of film that would fit in a camera at the time). And Stuckel is certainly correct both that film editing in the late twentieth century was increasingly frenetic and that this editing was strongly influenced by the fragmented visual style of MTV music videos.

Of course, MTV is not the only fragmented form of popular culture in the late twentieth century, and this editing style also marks a more general characteristic of postmodern culture, as indicated by Fredric Jameson in his insightful *Postmodernism; or, The Cultural Logic of Late Capitalism* (1991). Indeed, films were becoming more and more fragmentary even before the founding of MTV in the early 1980s. For example, many of the editing techniques that have come to be associated with postmodern film were already prominent in the films of the French New Wave, as in the famous jump cuts of Jean-Luc Godard's *Breathless* (1959) or the whip pans, quick cuts, and fast zooms of François Truffaut's *Jules et Jim* (1961).

The Player itself seems to eschew such intrusive editing by opening with a complex tracking shot that runs more than eight minutes until the first cut, accompanied by music that alludes to the opening music of *Touch of Evil*. Yet *Touch of Evil* is hardly a paradigm of classic Hollywood film, and its whacked-out, excessive self-parody was already postmodern. In addition, the opening tracking shot of Welles's film is impressive partly because of the complexity with which it conveys a sense of fragmentation and frenetic activity even without cuts. The opening shot of *The Player* does much the same thing, managing to shift from character to character and scene to scene even within the same continuous shot. In any case, the opening tracking shots of both *Touch of Evil* and *The Player* call such attention to themselves as tours de force that they are every bit as intrusive (and, in a sense, fragmentary) as MTV-style quick cutting.

Much of the ironic humor of *The Player*, in fact, comes from the self-conscious way in which it continually exemplifies the very Hollywood stereotypes that it seems designed to criticize. As such, the film is largely about its own making, while at the same time declaring the inescapability of certain tendencies that it identifies primarily as being the result of the market forces that drive Hollywood film, but which might also be attributed at least in part to the growing cultural hegemony of postmodernism. Indeed, by Jameson's reading of postmodernism as the cultural logic of late capitalism, these two factors, in a sense, amount to essentially the same thing. The MTV-style editing mentioned by Stuckel is no doubt designed to attract young audiences to movie theaters, but surely there is a reason why such frenetic, fragmentary editing would appeal to young audiences at this particular point in history.

Then again, the increasing fragmentation of postmodern film can in many ways be seen as a logical extension of older montage techniques and indeed of the evolution of film itself as a medium. In his crucial essay "The Work of Art in the Age of Mechanical Reproduction," Walter Benjamin singles out film as the "most powerful agent" of the shattering of the traditional quasi-religious aura of the work of art by modern, mechanically reproduced art forms (223). Film, after all, is always already mechanically reproduced. There is no "original" film of which the various prints distributed are mere copies: each film exists *only* as mechanically reproduced copies. Further, film is inherently fragmented in both its construction and its presentation to audiences; each film is shot as separate scenes and presented as a montage in which these scenes are joined by a sequence of cuts that, for Benjamin, disrupt the sense of wholeness that gives traditional art much of its religious flavor. Unlike a painting, which is available for immersion and contemplation, the image constantly changes in film, leading to a "shock effect" that, in Benjamin's view, can increase perception and awareness on the part of the spectator (240).

According to Benjamin, this shattering of the aura, however unsettling, has the potential to make a major contribution to a revolutionary democratization of human societies, to "the adjustment of reality to the masses and of the masses to reality" (225). Unable to ignore the fragmentation of the film or to associate the film with the godlike hand of a single creating artist, audiences experience a kind of defamiliarization that fosters reception in a mode of thoughtful critique rather than admiring awe. In turn, this new form of engagement with art might help individuals better to question authority in their day-to-day political lives. Subsequent developments, such as the rise of the cultic *auteur*-director, suggest that traditional forms of artistic reception may be more difficult to overcome than Benjamin realized. In addition, the fragmentation of ordinary experience in the postmodern era removes much of the defamiliarizing power that Benjamin finds in the inherent fragmentation of film, which now becomes perfectly familiar and hardly shocking.

Benjamin's vision of film as a mechanically reproduced copy of which there is no original also foreshadows postmodernism in the way it resembles Jean Baudrillard's important concept of the *simulacrum* as a crucial element of postmodern experience. In addition, Benjamin's discussion of film anticipates Jameson's later characterization of postmodernism, even if Benjamin sees fragmentation in film as a potential challenge to capitalism, while Jameson sees such fragmentation as a reflection of the character of life in the late capitalist world.

For Jameson, one of the key markers of the postmodern condition is the psychic fragmentation of the individual subject. Drawing upon the work of Jacques Lacan, Jameson argues that, amid the increasing complexity and fragmentation of experience in the postmodern world, the individual subject experiences a loss of temporal continuity that causes him or her to experience the world somewhat in the manner of a schizophrenic who, Jameson says,

> is condemned to live in a perpetual present with which the various moments of his or her past have little connection and for which there is no conceivable future on the horizon. In other words, schizophrenic experience is an experience of isolated, disconnected, discontinuous material signifiers which fail to link into a coherent sequence. The schizophrenic does not know personal identity in our sense, since our feeling of identity depends on our sense of the persistence of the "I" and the "me" over time. ("Postmodernism and Consumer Society," 119)

Not surprisingly, Jameson suggests that this schizophrenic fragmentation in personal identity strongly influences postmodern narratives, in which the characters often experience fragmented, plural, and discontinuous identities. This schizophrenia, Jameson believes, can also be seen in the formal fragmentation of the narratives themselves, leading to the production of postmodern "schizophrenic" texts by authors such as Samuel Beckett.

Jameson's identification of pastiche and schizophrenia as key characteristics of postmodernist art directly echoes Benjamin's view that film disrupts its own aura both by undermining the association of the artwork with the activities of a godlike creating artist and by shattering the religious wholeness of the work of art itself. Jameson and Benjamin, in fact, may be describing very much the same cultural phenomena, though these phenomena had advanced much further and penetrated new areas of experience by the time Jameson was writing. However, while Benjamin sees the shattering of the aura as powerfully antiauthoritarian, Jameson's concept of postmodernism as the cultural logic of late capitalism suggests that postmodern fragmentation works in the interest of the status quo, depriving individual subjects of the kind of totalizing vision that is required in order to oppose capitalism in a genuinely effective way.

Put differently, the shattering of the aura leads to a reduction in the perceived gap between art (with its utopian sense of wholeness and completeness) and reality (with its dystopian sense of confusion and lack). For Benjamin, this reduced gap comes about from an increase in the utopian potential of reality; for Jameson, it derives from a reduction in the utopian energy of art. Writing in the 1930s, as the rise of fascism was moving the world inevitably toward the war that would drive him to his final despair, Benjamin was urging Marxists to politicize art and thereby oppose and reverse the fascist aestheticization of political reality. For him, the shattering of the aura in film is an important new tool in the battle to create an inherently political art. Jameson, writing on postmodernism in the 1980s and 1990s, argued that fragmentation works primarily toward the creation of an aesthetic perception of reality, thus aligning it with, rather than against, what Benjamin sees as the aesthetic tendency of fascism. However, by the time Jameson was writing, fascism itself had been superseded by late consumer capitalism as the primary global threat to human dignity and authenticity.

The opposed views of Benjamin and Jameson are largely the natural consequence of the fact that they were writing in very different historical times and describing very different kinds of films. To an extent, they can be read as an opposition between modernist and postmodernist visions of fragmentation. For example, Theo d'Haen discusses the use of collage techniques in both modernism and postmodernism, arguing that modernist collage suggests unity and simultaneity, while postmodernist collage acts to undercut any such unification of disparate images. He notes the "obstinate refusal of postmodern fragments to 'come together'" and claims that, unlike modernist works, in which "the unilinear functionalism of the work guarantees the possibility of a coherent reading emerging from the text itself, postmodern works do not offer . . . 'univalent' meanings" (222). Modernist formal fragmentation is centripetal—one might even say utopian—in its orientation, challenging audiences to reassemble the pieces into a coherent whole, while postmodernist fragmentation is centrifugal, denying the very possibility of wholeness—or utopia.

Of course, this distinction between centripetal and centrifugal fragmentation is not merely between the formal strategies of specific films or other artworks but also between the reception and interpretation of those works. Thus, Christopher Butler points out that modernist works like T. S. Eliot's *The Waste Land* and Ezra Pound's *Cantos* show the same sort of formal fragmentation that he sees as being a central characteristic of postmodernist works. However, this fragmentation tends to be read differently in such modernist works than in postmodernist ones. In particular, Butler argues that postmodernist theorists have tended to embrace centrifugal fragmentation, while the centripetal nature of the fragmentation of modernist works is not so much a property of the works as of modernist methods of reading them. For him, "the whole bent of modernist symbol-seeking and mythopoeic criticism has been to attempt to construct a unity and coherence for the works it analyzes" (*After the Wake*, 83).

Whether this quest for wholeness is conservative and authoritarian or utopian (and thus potentially radical) is not a simple question, however. Peter Bürger, discussing the possible political significance of fragmentation in modern art, warns that techniques such as montage may challenge the organic wholeness of the work of art, but that this challenge can have different implications in different contexts. Noting that artists of a wide variety of political orientations have employed montage-like techniques for very different purposes, Bürger concludes that "it is fundamentally problematical to assign a fixed meaning to a procedure" without a thorough consideration of the context in which that procedure is used (*Theory of the Avant-garde*, 78–79). Bürger, among other things, is concerned that the shock value of avant-garde artistic techniques is destroyed when those techniques are appropriated by institutionalized, commercial culture. From this point of view, the different attitudes of Benjamin and Jameson toward fragmentation in film can be understood in terms of the historical fact that techniques that were still shocking in the time of Benjamin had been comfortably absorbed by mainstream bourgeois culture by the time of Jameson, when the central examples of fragmented form were coming not from avant-garde art but from television commercials and MTV music videos.

Of course, the development of the classic Hollywood style of invisible editing in the 1930s and 1940s essentially removed the shock value that Benjamin had found in the inherently discontinuous nature of film editing, so that the increasingly intrusive cutting that marks films of the late twentieth century can be taken as a progressive attempt to recover some of the defamiliarizing effect of early montage films by directors such as Sergei Eisenstein. Here, the hyperkinetic editing of postmodern films resembles the extreme metafictional gestures of postmodernist authors such as Robert Coover and Gilbert Sorrentino, which can be thought of as an attempt to recapture some of the power of a modernist self-consciousness that had, by familiarity, lost much of its former punch. At the same time, the quick-cut style of many postmodern films serves a clear mimetic function as an expression of the increasing fragmentation of experience in the postmodern age. In addition, many postmodern films are so self-conscious about their formal fragmentation that this fragmentation itself becomes a metafictional commentary on postmodern conventions of film editing and narrative.

Stuckel's complaint in *The Player* about MTV-style editing in contemporary movies is another example of such self-conscious commentary, and it is certainly the case that music videos, identified by observers such as Anne Kaplan as a quintessential postmodern cultural phenomenon, have exercised a strong influence on contemporary film. Indeed, many emerging postmodern film directors—such as Spike Jonze and Michel Gondry—have started their careers as directors of music videos. But it is also surely the case that the increasing fragmentation of contemporary motion pictures has not simply been "caused" by the popularity of MTV-style music videos—both of these media respond to larger historical forces, including the increasing psychic fragmentation of individuals in the postmodern world. The disjointed style of some films seems intended as a protest against the fragmentation of experience under late capitalism, somewhat in the way Benjamin envisioned the antiauthoritarian potential of the inherent fragmentation of film as a medium. More often, however, it is clear that the fragmentation of most postmodern films merely reflects—or even celebrates—the fragmentation of contemporary life, more in the mode implied by Jameson in his vision of postmodernism as the cultural logic of late capitalism.

An exemplary case is Baz Luhrmann's *Moulin Rouge!* (2001), in which fragmented and frenetic MTV-style editing contributes to the production of a self-consciously dazzling postmodern spectacle (the exclamation point in the title is definitely appropriate) that looks like a cross between a music video and a video game, injected with a healthy dose of opera and adrenalin. But Luhrmann's film is all flash: its narrative is not just conventional but utterly banal (much like that of its operatic model, *La Bohème*), little more than a collection of sentimental bourgeois clichés, cloaked in the supposedly antibourgeois stance of the *fin de siècle* decadents.

Moulin Rouge! is a film set in France by an Australian director whose principal target audience is American. Both of its lead actors are major American film stars, though one (Ewan McGregor) was born in Scotland before rising to prominence in England, the other (Nicole Kidman) born in Hawaii and reared in Australia. Thus, among other things, the film nicely demonstrates the global nature of the film industry at the beginning of the twenty-first century. It also shows the universality of postmodernism itself. Indeed, even if one considers MTV music videos as the epitome of a postmodern editing style, it should be remembered that MTV itself is now a global phenomenon. Thus, it should not be particularly surprising that some of the purest examples of MTV-style editing come from films made outside the United States.

Representative here is Tom Tykwer's *Lola rennt* (1998, German, released in the United States as *Run Lola Run*). The full eighty-one minutes of this hyperkinetic film plays out like an extended music video, employing virtually every editing technique known to post-MTV man: Fast-motion, slow-motion, whip pans, fast zooms, super-quick cuts, jump cuts, flash frames, split screens, red tints, and occasional shifts from color to black-and-white or from live action to cartoon are all used to increase the film's sense of frantic action. It is, however, a film in which relatively little actually happens. Its simple plot—the title character (played by Franka Potente) rushes to try to save her boyfriend Manni (Moritz Bleibtreu) from his gangster boss after Manni loses 100,000 marks belonging to the boss—could easily fit into a music video. Indeed, the plot is so sparse that it can play out three times even in this relatively brief film, each time with a slightly different sequence of events that leads to a very different conclusion. Thus, the film potentially suggests the contingent and provisional nature of history and reality, à la the insights of chaos theory, though it mostly just shows the constructed nature of its own plot (and all film plots).[1]

The real story of the film, then, is not Lola running to save Manni, but rather Tykwer, both writer and director, playing with various narrative possibilities, with each version becoming more farfetched and less believable than the one before. The self-reflexivity inherent in this plot repetition, meanwhile, ironizes the third and final (happy) ending of the film, demonstrating the contrived nature of such endings. In any case, most of the action, as the title indicates, simply involves Lola running along the street, accompanied by a hard-driving, fast-tempo techno-rap soundtrack featuring Potente herself as the principal performer.

Lola rennt is an avowedly MTVesque experiment that seems set on demonstrating that considerable suspense can be generated from a minimal narrative core by the sheer tempo of the editing and soundtrack. In this, it declares itself a postmodern departure from narrative convention, though it also frequently alludes to earlier films—as when Lola's piercing, glass-shattering screams recall Günter Grass's *The Tin Drum* (1979), its frequent shots of the hands of a clock approaching noon recall *High Noon* (1952), or its scene of men carrying a large pane of glass across a street while a speeding vehicle approaches recalls who knows how many films. Nevertheless, *Lola rennt* clearly takes its style and form more from music videos than from previous feature films. It epitomizes both postmodern editing techniques and the minimization of narrative in postmodern film, recapitulating on a smaller scale the suspicion toward grand metanarratives that theorists such as Jean-François Lyotard have seen as central to postmodernism as a whole.

Films like *Moulin Rouge!* and *Lola rennt* indicate the way in which, in the postmodern era, fragmentation has largely become a fashionable formal experiment with no interest in achieving the shock effects associated by Benjamin with the fragmentation of film in the 1930s. One of the more interesting cases of fragmentation as a purely formal experiment is a film that is literally about filmmaking, Mike Figgis's *Timecode* (2000). This film, using quadruple split frames through its entire length, presents us with not one but four images at once, as if striving to get our attention by finally overloading us with more images than even postmodern subjects can process at once. *Timecode* would thus, in some ways, seem to be the quintessential example of fragmentation in postmodernist film. Each of the four frames shows separate simultaneous action that the audience must attempt to follow and piece together into something resembling a coherent whole. In this sense, the film is a fascinating technical experiment. Indeed, the experiment itself is the heart of the film, which is interesting to watch more because of the technical virtuosity with which its daring concept is realized than because of the four narratives of which it is composed. The split frames, in fact, clearly interfere with audience involvement in the narrative, potentially creating the kind of Brechtian estrangement effect that Benjamin associated with film in general, though here the effect is particularly postmodern to the extent that it calls attention to the relative decline of narrative drive in postmodernist film.

Among other things, this split-frame technique collapses the temporality of Eisensteinian montage into simultaneous spatiality, verifying the suggestion by Jameson (and numerous others, especially geographer David Harvey) that the imagination of postmodernist culture is primarily spatial, rather than temporal. However, the four-frame approach is only one aspect of the experimentation in this audacious film. For example, the action in each frame proceeds only according to a loose outline, leaving it up to the actors to improvise most their dialogue and much of the action. The film thus has a rather spontaneous and open-ended quality, calling attention to its own fictionality by reminding audience members (at least those who are in the know) that the narratives could easily have turned out otherwise. Indeed, the entire film was shot fifteen times (the last take was used for theatrical release), each of which was substantially different from the others.[2] Moreover, almost more technically daring than the split frames is the fact that each frame was filmed in one continuous take of approximately ninety-three minutes, an approach that leaves the long takes of *Touch of Evil*, or even *Rope*, far behind. *Timecode*'s long takes were made possible because it was shot not on conventional film (which allows continuous takes of a maximum of twenty minutes even with the technology available at the end of the twentieth century) but with state-of-the-art digital video cameras. Moreover, this technology is good enough that the image resolution is excellent, lacking the cheap look and feel of earlier video and suggesting that video may become increasingly important as a medium in future Hollywood films.

Of course, this use of continuous real-time takes, which would seem to be a major step toward the ultimate realization of Bazinian film realism, also runs directly counter to the postmodern fragmentation of the split-frame technique by removing cuts and editing altogether. Other aspects of the film, such as the improvised nature of the action and dialogue, create a sense of realism as well. Most importantly, the split-frame approach itself can actually be taken as a realist gesture, emphasizing that conventional filmmaking, by focusing on one scene at a time, is unable to convey the fact that, in reality, many different scenes occur in different places at the same time. In this sense, the split-frame approach succeeds in using new film technologies finally to get beyond the linear limitations of both oral and written narrative, which (despite experiments such as the counterpointing in Gustave Flaubert's *Madame*

Bovary or the "Wandering Rocks" chapter of James Joyce's *Ulysses*) are essentially confined to linear sequences and do a relatively poor job of representing simultaneous parallel actions. *Timecode*'s visuals achieve true simultaneous parallel representation, though even here, to avoid total incoherence in the audio, Figgis has to mix the four different audio tracks so that, at any given time, one of them is dominant, thus giving that frame precedence over the other three.

The individual split frames of *Timecode* contain realistic narratives, and the overall technique is actually quite conservative in the sense that the four different narratives are interrelated, ultimately fitting together to tell a fairly coherent story. The four frames are carefully synchronized (thus the title of the film), and, in many ways, the film's most impressive visual moments occur when characters occasionally move from one frame to another. But this movement also helps to tie together the overall narrative, which is a fairly conventional satire of greed, ambition, and pretentiousness in Hollywood, somewhat in the tradition of Vincente Minnelli's *The Bad and the Beautiful* (1952) or, more recently, *The Player*.

In one of *Timecode*'s story lines, Salma Hayek plays Rose, an aspiring Mexican actress desperately hoping to make it in Hollywood by looking for someone who will "discover" her. This story line intersects with the one featuring Jeanne Tripplehorn as Lauren Hathaway, Rose's wealthy (and insanely jealous) lesbian lover. She has good reason to be jealous, because Rose is, in fact, having an affair with the third protagonist, alcoholic producer Alex Green (Stellan Skarsgård), in the hope of gaining an opportunity to further her acting career. The fourth major protagonist is Green's frustrated wife, Emma (Saffron Burrows), completing the links among the different narratives.

Rose's meaningless copulation with Alex gets her nowhere, but, in the end, she is discovered anyway when she accidentally runs into fading director Lester Moore (Richard Edson), who is "big in Mexico" and who thinks Rose will be perfect for the lead role in his next film. Alex is less fortunate. Lauren, having bugged Rose's purse and thus learned of her affair with Alex, charges into the offices of Alex's production company in a jealous rage, pulls out a gun, and shoots him. He drops to the floor and lies bleeding to death as the film ends, with Emma walking along the street thinking she is headed for an attempted reconciliation with her husband.

This somewhat pedestrian basic narrative is made interesting only because of the experimental technique of the film, though it is also aided by superb improvisational performances from all of the lead actors as well as a hilarious turn by Julian Sands as a masseur sent to the production company to give free massages to everyone as a way of promoting the spa for which he works. The high comic moment of the film, however, occurs when artsy film director Ana Pauls (Mía Maestro) comes to the production company along with her lover, musician Joey Z (Alessandro Nivola), to pitch her latest idea for a film. The pitch itself involves a variety of quasi-sophisticated learned allusions and is accompanied by Joey Z's music, including an inspired hip-hop/reggae ode to the Russian Revolution. What makes the scene particularly funny, of course, is that the film being pitched is basically *Timecode* itself, including the split-frame technique, an idea Alex hilariously characterizes as "pretentious crap" when he hears it.

This self-referential humor saves *Timecode* itself from pretentiousness, while the entire pitch scene constitutes one of the film's most clearly postmodern moments—which is immediately disrupted by one of the film's most conventional moments when Lauren bursts into the meeting room to shoot Alex. This sudden shift from postmodern self-parody to conventional Hollywood realism is indicative of the way in which all of the film's postmodern gestures are held together by the basically realist matrix of the characterization and overall narrative structure. Meanwhile, this continuing reliance on conventions of character and narrative is typical of the way in which Hollywood films that might otherwise be characterized as postmodernist quite consistently maintain an underlying realism.

The split-frame technique of *Timecode* has hardly spurred a spate of imitators, though Figgis himself followed it with another film, *Hotel* (2003), that employs a similar technique. Here, however, most of the film's running time is spent in a conventional single-frame presentation that breaks into multiple frames only sporadically. Yet *Hotel* oddly seems *more* fragmentary than *Timecode*, partly because the framing changes throughout the film and partly because the plot of the film itself is more disjointed, involving several different subplots, each of which belongs to a different genre. The main plot involves the efforts of a film crew in Venice to shoot (in the style of the Danish *Dogme* filmmaking group) a film adaptation (entitled *Malfi*) of John Webster's *The Duchess of Malfi*. In addition, this crew is being followed around Venice by another crew that is shooting a documentary about the making of the first film. Meanwhile, they all stay at a Venice hotel that is run by cannibalistic ghouls, adding a horror-film subplot. None of these plots really go anywhere (and several fragments don't really contribute to any subplot), but none of them are really the point. *Hotel* is not ultimately about the making of *Malfi*; it is about the making of *Hotel* and the construction of postmodern cultural artifacts in general.

In a sense, the split frames of *Timecode* and *Hotel* are a special case of what critic Alissa Quart has called "hyperlink cinema," in which multiple narratives intertwine in a single film, allowing (and requiring) viewers to jump about in time within a story and from one story to another much in the way they jump about among websites on the Internet. Referring specifically to Don Roos's *Happy Endings* (2005), Quart notes that Roos's film,

> like hyperlinking itself, is irremediably relativist. Information, character, and action co-exist without hierarchy. And we are always one click away from a new life, a new story, and new meaning, all equally captivating but no better or worse than what we have just left behind. ("Networked," 51)

Quart is particularly enthusiastic about the way *Happy Endings* engages our contemporary "information-processing proclivities" (48). However, she also notes that the film is only one among many recent additions to the "new genre" of hyperlink cinema, including Roos's own *The Opposite of Sex* (1998) and *Bounce* (2000). Other direct precedents are Paul Thomas Anderson's *Magnolia* (1999) and Robert Altman's *Short Cuts* (1993), and indeed one could identify Altman as the genre's founding father, with his *Nashville* (1975) as its real founding text. For Quart, however, Roos is considerably hipper and more contemporary than Altman, taking the latter's narrative techniques "into web territory" (50). For example, Roos periodically adds touches such as captions that add an extra dimension to the narratives, providing in quick capsule form extra information about the pasts or futures of the characters that supplement the parts of their experience that are actually shown.

Still, it is not at all clear that Quart's analogy between the experiences of watching films like *Happy Endings* and of surfing the Web is really appropriate. After all, the latter gives users much more control over where they go, even if they are likely to encounter unexpected information along the way. Nevertheless, her identification of hyperlink cinema as a distinct film phenomenon that requires viewers to process multiple information streams seems to be catching on. For example, Roger Ebert cites the genre in his reviews of Mark Bamford's *Cape of Good Hope* (2004) and Stephen Gaghan's *Syriana* (2005). In fact, Ebert himself was using the hypertext analogy as early as 1998 in his review of Steven Soderbergh's *Out of Sight* (1998), a stylish thriller that demonstrates that nonlinear plotting need not be confusing or conflict with entertainment value. One might also include in this category such films as Todd Solondz's *Happiness* (1998) and *Storytelling* (2001), Soderbergh's *Traffic* (2000, written by Gaghan), the recent Academy Award–winning *Crash* (2004, directed by Paul Haggis), and virtually all of the films of Guy Ritchie, including *Lock, Stock, and Two Smoking Barrels* (1998), *Snatch* (2000), and *Revolver* (2005). Ritchie's films give the genre of hyperlink cinema a particular British inflection, but—with their reliance on strategies such as over-the-top violence and ultra-hip soundtracks—they also show the heavy influence of the films of Quentin Tarantino, whose landmark *Pulp Fiction* (1994) probably did more than any single film to popularize the hyperlink narrative form in film.

Pulp Fiction, indeed, was a landmark film in more ways than one. One of the most self-consciously cool films ever made, *Pulp Fiction* was so commercially successful that it virtually demolished the boundary between independent and Hollywood cinema. Tarantino's film, with its fragmented narrative and patchwork construction from bits and pieces of the cultural past, is a leading example of postmodernism in a highly commercial film, so it should come as no surprise that the film exemplifies the postmodern appropriation of elements from the popular culture of the past. Indeed, the very title of Tarantino's film explicitly announces the film's roots in a cultural form often regarded as "low" even in comparison with other forms of pop culture.

If most of the distinctive elements of Tarantino's style were already present in *Reservoir Dogs* (1992), they emerged fully formed in the smoother, more accomplished, and substantially hipper *Pulp Fiction*, the film that truly made Tarantino a star, the kind of director whose devoted fans eagerly await the appearance of his next product. After *Pulp Fiction* they had a substantial wait, but the appearance of *Jackie Brown* in 1997 further solidified Tarantino's position as a major new director, even if it lacked the intense coolness of its predecessor. Though still employing the hyperlink form, *Jackie Brown* is an altogether more mature and accomplished work, much more conventional (and less overtly postmodern) than *Pulp Fiction*. Based (somewhat loosely) on the Elmore Leonard novel *Rum Punch*, it presents an essentially continuous narrative, its primary deviation from classic Hollywood form being a number of scenes that overlap in time, so that events just related are told again, but from the point of view of a different character. The soundtrack of *Jackie Brown* again includes a wide variety of music from different sources, much of it diegetic, played on car radios and even (in one key instance of musical nostalgia) on an old-fashioned record player. The majority of the music again comes from the 1970s, this time with an emphasis on Motown music by such artists as the Supremes and the Delfonics.

Jackie Brown looks back to the past in other ways as well, as in one scene in which the forty-four-year-old title character (played by Pam Grier) muses sadly to even older bail bondsman Max Cherry (Robert Forster) about growing old. The casting of Grier and Forster itself gives the film a nostalgic flavor, as does the casting of Robert De Niro as Louis Gara, an aging criminal who has decidedly lost his touch. "What happened to you?" asks his long-time partner in crime Ordell Robbie (Samuel L. Jackson). "You used to be beautiful." This reference to Gara's more dashing younger self cannot help but evoke memories of De Niro's earlier roles as well, and Gara comes off as something like a decaying version of the small-time hoods played by a younger De Niro in such films as Martin Scorsese's *Mean Streets* (1973) or Sergio Leone's *Once upon a Time in America* (1984). De Niro's young Vito Corleone, from *The Godfather: Part II* (1974), meanwhile, serves as the small-time hood made good, a sort of counterpoint to the failed Gara. On the other hand, while De Niro's character in *Jackie Brown* is genuinely pathetic (and played brilliantly that way by De Niro), Brown and Cherry emerge triumphant, proving that age has only sharpened their abilities, even if Jackie's ass is a little bigger and Max's hair a little thinner than in earlier years.

In the same way, *Jackie Brown* nostalgically looks back on a number of predecessors in film, beginning with its opening airport sequence, a pastiche of the opening of *The Graduate* (1967). *Jackie Brown* especially echoes films from the golden years of the 1970s, yet seems confident in its ability to hold its own among such illustrious predecessors as the entire tradition of film noir (inflected through the 1970s rise of neonoir). The most obvious predecessors, however, are the blaxploitation films of the 1970s, of which *Foxy Brown* is the most relevant example— a fact to which the title of Tarantino's film calls attention. (The character in Leonard's novel was named Jackie Burke, so the change to Brown has an obvious allusive effect.)

Such allusions place *Jackie Brown* in a long line of pop cultural works, even if this film aspires to a seriousness that most of those works never even attempt. Ritchie's Tarantino-inflected films, with their focus on a dark world of crime and violence, build on some of the same "low" materials, but similarly lack real seriousness. They also indicate the usefulness of hyperlink editing techniques for conveying the confusion of this world, even if they have the tendency to make life in it seem a bit more hip and cool than it really is. Other films influenced by *Pulp Fiction* have focused on similar subject matter, as in Doug Liman's *Go*

(1999), a sort of teenage version of *Pulp Fiction*, or Paul McGuigan's stylish crime thriller *Lucky Number Slevin* (2006). The latter illustrates particularly well the efficacy of hyperlink techniques for presenting the bits and pieces of a mystery, though the fact that these pieces all come neatly together in the end suggests an ultimately conservative orientation in this film.

Hyperlink crime films, perhaps because of the influence of *Pulp Fiction*, tend to be presented in a self-consciously hip mode. As a result, many of the films influenced by Tarantino (including Ritchie's) have been regarded as shallow and superficial, far more interested in style than in substance. On the other hand, the intertwining plots of hyperlink films are particularly good at presenting the complexities of convoluted interpersonal dramas (as in *Magnolia*, *Crash*, and *Happy Endings*). At times, however (one might cite *Magnolia* again here), such films verge on pretentiousness, as if their directors feel that complex narrative forms automatically make their films sophisticated and profound enough to address fundamental philosophical and eschatological issues. Hyperlink films seem better suited to the exploration of more down-to-earth political, social, and economic relationships (as in *Nashville*, *Traffic*, *Syriana*, and *Crash* again), which often involve precisely the kinds of intricate webs of interconnections that underlie hyperlink cinema itself.

Among those who have used the hyperlink form to construct weighty and serious explorations of both social and personal relationships, one might single out the work of Mexican filmmaker Alejandro González Iñárritu (in conjunction with screenwriter Guillermo Arriaga), beginning with *Amores perros* (2000). Stylistically, *Amores perros* is a typical example of hyperlink cinema. Its complex, nonlinear narrative, with multiple plot strands that only vaguely intersect, seems highly reminiscent of *Pulp Fiction*, as does the subject matter, which deals heavily in graphic violence and criminal activity. *Amores perros* also recalls Tarantino in its frenetic pace and editing style, enhanced through the use of a loud, trendy soundtrack to support the action. Particularly prominent here is the extensive use of rapid, jerky camera movements to reinforce the sense of frantic activity. In fact, the camera seems virtually never to be still; even when it is not rapidly panning from one spot to another it tends to be a bit unsteady—as do the characters.

The characters, however, set *Amores perros* dramatically apart from predecessors such as *Pulp Fiction*. In contrast to the waning of affect that seems to flatten characters such as Tarantino's Vincent Vega and Jules Winnfield into comic book figures, the characters of *Amores perros* are richly realized human beings, all flawed, all damaged, but all decidedly able to feel, even if the conditions in which they live make it impossible for them to convert those feelings into rewarding human relationships. In the first of the film's three major plot strands, Octavio (Gael García Bernal) is desperately in love with Susana (Vanessa Bauche), the wife of his own brother, Ramiro (Marco Pérez), a street tough and small-time drug dealer. Octavio plans to run away with Susana, accumulating money to do so by entering his beloved dog, Cofi, in the dogfights that constitute a large part of the illegal economy of the Mexico City slum in which they live. Susana seems to have strong feelings for Octavio as well, but she is mostly just trying to find a way for her and her infant child to survive amid the brutalizing poverty and violence that mark the underclass world in which they live.

In the second plot, top model Valeria Amaya (Goya Toledo) seems also to have found true love, though the object of her affection, Daniel (Álvaro Guerrero), a magazine editor, is again already married to someone else. In this case, however, Daniel leaves his wife to be with Valeria, and the two set up housekeeping in a relatively pleasant (though not lavish) middle-class apartment. This plan is interrupted when the first two plot lines intersect as Octavio, driving with Cofi at high speeds in flight from some thugs who have just shot and badly wounded the dog, crashes his car into Valeria's. Octavio is seriously, but not fatally, hurt in the crash. Valeria's principal injury is a badly broken leg.

Valeria returns from the hospital seemingly on the road to recovery in her love nest with Daniel. Unfortunately, things go from bad to worse at this point. One day, Valeria's small dog, Richie (whom she seems to love perhaps even more than Daniel), disappears into a hole in the flooring of the apartment. He remains there for days; Daniel and Valeria occasionally hear him underneath the flooring, while also becoming aware that the area is infested by rats. Tensions grow between Valeria and Daniel, and he begins to dream of returning to his wife and daughters. Meanwhile, Valeria's leg becomes gangrenous and has to be amputated. Eventually, Richie is recovered, but Valeria returns from her amputation a broken woman, her career as a model ruined, her relationship with Daniel in serious jeopardy. If poverty is the key to the suffering of Octavio and Susana, the story of Valeria and Daniel demonstrates that middle-class affluence is no guarantee of happiness.

The third plot line of *Amores perros* features a protagonist who has, in fact, lived in both worlds. Simply identified as El Chivo (The Goat, played by Emilio Echevarría), this figure floats through the first two plot lines looking like a harmless street person. Accompanied by the pack of stray dogs that he has taken in, El Chivo wanders about going through garbage looking for items of value. He and his dogs live in squalor in a run-down building, and he at first seems like a much older version of Octavio, the pathetic old man that Octavio might someday become.

On the other hand, El Chivo, with his long hair and bushy gray beard, also looks something like a Karl Marx gone to seed, and it turns out that he is, indeed, a figure of the fallen Left. Eventually, we learn that he had once been a college professor with a wife, daughter, and comfortable life. But, unhappy with the world as it was, he decided to dedicate himself to changing it, hoping to build a better world in which eventually to live with his family. He went underground and became a notorious leftist guerrilla. He was not, however, able to change the world. Instead, he was captured and sent to prison for twenty years, emerging a broken old man to find his ex-wife remarried and his daughter believing that he is dead.

It is under these conditions that El Chivo becomes a scraggly street person trailed by numerous dogs, though it turns out that he is still not what he appears. He is, in fact, still very dangerous, a highly efficient hit man who performs occasional jobs for Leonardo, the corrupt cop who earlier captured him. In this way, he has accumulated a considerable amount of money, vaguely hoping to use it somehow to reestablish contact with his daughter, whom he begins to follow around at a distance. Meanwhile, he intersects the first two plot lines primarily in that he observes the accident between Octavio and Valeria, retrieving Cofi from the scene and nursing him back to health.

This step once again changes El Chivo's life. One day, when he is out, the wounded Cofi, apparently attacked by the other dogs, kills all of them. El Chivo returns to find his ruin of a home strewn with blood and carcasses. Profoundly affected by this event, El Chivo is unable to go through with his latest contract killing (in which each of two half-brothers has tried to pay him to kill the other, thus echoing the conflict between Octavio and Ramiro). El Chivo, meanwhile, cuts his hair and shaves off his beard, putting on a respectable suit and donning the glasses he had stopped wearing because there was nothing worth seeing. He steals into the home of his daughter and leaves a considerable sum of money for her; he also leaves her with a recorded promise that he will return once he feels able to look her in the eye without shame. Then he and Cofi (now called Blackie) set out on foot across a barren landscape, hoping to rediscover the sense of hope that had once enabled El Chivo to dream of a better world.

This lingering element of utopian hope, however feeble, sets *Amores perros* apart from most postmodern films, as does the depth of emotion and (especially) pain experienced by the characters. Though radically estranged from those around them and often reduced to loving dogs because of their inability to maintain meaningful relations with other human beings, they at least still *want* to establish such relations. However, damaged, these characters seem less like the fragmentary nonsubjects associated by Jameson with postmodernism and more like Jameson's high modernist subjects, still stable enough in their own subjectivity to experience the anxiety and alienation attributed by Jameson to such subjects.

One is, in fact, tempted to attribute the difference between *Amores perros* and *Pulp Fiction* to the fact that the former maintains strong vestiges of modernism while the latter is more thoroughly postmodern. On the other hand, the realism-modernism-postmodernism model of cultural history refers primarily to developments in Western Europe and the United States, and it is important not to ignore the Mexican origins of *Amores perros*. González Iñárritu has himself suggested, in an interview with Bernardo Pérez Soler, that his film should be "placed in the category of 'non-western cinema'—certainly it has nothing to do with either Hollywood or what's being made in Europe" (Pérez Soler and Edward Lawrenson, "Pup Fiction," 30). *Amores perros* thus perhaps illustrates Jameson's occasional suggestions that Third World culture offers a sense of unity and authenticity no longer available in the mainstream postmodern culture of the West. In his somewhat notorious essay "Third-World Literature in the Era of Multinational Capitalism," Jameson urges First World scholars to study Third World culture to find examples of individual characters who are still organically connected to their social worlds. Similarly, he argues elsewhere that Third World cinema might be particularly interesting because the Third World is "the last surviving social space from which alternatives to corporate daily life and social relations are to be sought" (*Geopolitical Aesthetic*, 188).[3]

On the other hand, González Iñárritu seems to protest too much that his film is completely unrelated to trends in Hollywood, especially given its hip stylistic echoes of Tarantino and other postmodern filmmakers. Jameson himself suggests that, while Third World cinema might still pose some sort of alternative to Hollywood, the West has at this point been so successful at eradicating radical opposition to capitalism in the Third World that, even there, forms of postmodernism are becoming dominant (*Geopolitical Aesthetic*, 188). *Amores perros* does indeed show the impact of the global spread of postmodernism, but it also maintains a lingering humanism and utopianism that would seem to bear out Jameson's vision of Third World culture as a bastion of authenticity.

Of course, much of the difference between *Pulp Fiction* and *Amores perros* derives from the very simple fact that consumer capitalist culture is more powerful in the United States than in Mexico, where (as the case of the Zapatistas in Chiapas amply illustrates) legitimate radical opposition to the prevailing order is still more than a vaguely remembered fantasy. At the same time, much of the similarity between *Pulp Fiction* and *Amores perros* no doubt arises from the increasing global reach of consumer capitalism and, in particular, the increasingly global nature of the movie industry. Thus, if Western films were growing more and more postmodern from the 1950s to the beginning of the twenty-first century, then postmodernity has also slowly extended into the non-Western world during this period, with an understandable lag brought about by the continuing viability of alternative cultural forces indigenous to those regions and by the fact that socialist ideas still have some purchase in certain parts of the world.

The surprising success of *Amores perros* enabled González Iñárritu himself to move into more mainstream Hollywood filmmaking, illustrating, among other things, the growing difficulty of even drawing a distinction between American and "foreign" films in the era of postmodern globalization. *21 Grams* (2003), for example, features a big-time Hollywood cast headlined by Sean Penn and including Benicio del Toro and Naomi Watts, both of whom gained Academy Award nominations for their roles in the film. This film again employs the hyperlink form. In typical hyperlink form, *21 Grams* presents the lives of its main characters as separate narratives that gradually merge and intermingle. Thus, while it focuses on the private lives of its characters, it ultimately insists that no one lives a life that is entirely separate from the lives of others, so that even the most private of experiences must be understood in social context. In a similar way, the chronologies of the narratives in *21 Grams* are particularly scrambled, but everything comes together in the end, suggesting that it is still possible to make sense of life in a conventional narrative way.

In this sense, many hyperlink films could be seen as exercises in what Jameson calls "cognitive mapping," or the process of making sense of one's world and one's place in it, a process that Jameson sees as being particularly difficult in the complex and fragmented reality of the postmodern world. This is particularly the case for a film like *21 Grams*, however, because it is so deadly serious (literally, as most of the characters find themselves in life-or-death situations at some point) and completely eschews the hipness of a movie like *Pulp Fiction*. The film does unfortunately seem to dip into pop metaphysics in the end (perhaps recalling *Magnolia* or a similar film), revealing (without mentioning him by name) that the title is a reference to the dubious research of early-twentieth-century physician Dr. Duncan McDougall, who undertook the scientifically silly project of measuring the weight of the human soul by attempting to determine the amount of weight lost at the moment of death. Granted, this reference may be metaphorical and does not really imply a belief in McDougall's research, but it is also pointless, attempting to lend the film a metaphysical dimension that it hardly needs to make its points.

Haggis's much-admired *Crash* strives for seriousness without resorting to this pop-metaphysical quality, adding a social (almost allegorical) element to the intersection of the lives of its diverse protagonists by having each of them represent different ethnic backgrounds. In so doing, the film makes a number of important points about ethnic and cultural stereotyping, while at the same time effectively demonstrating that human beings are complex and multidimensional, not easily described by stereotypes. Thus, a jaded, racist policeman (played by Matt Dillon) fondles a black woman during a traffic stop, then later risks his life to save that of the same woman; meanwhile, an idealistic young policeman (played by Ryan Phillippe) complains about racism in the police force, then shoots and kills a black youth when he wrongly assumes that the youth is reaching for a gun. The film also drives home some important lessons about the way in which viewing others through stereotypes further increases the radical alienation that separates us from each other as individuals in postmodern American society, of which the Los Angeles setting (its denizens sealed off from one another by the steel and glass of the cars that they typically inhabit) is the paradigm. Unfortunately, the film's message (racism is bad, stereotyping is simplistic) is itself something of a cliché, while the film tends to reduce all social differences to ethnic ones, ignoring other important elements, especially those based on class.

Postmodern cognitive mapping, of course, is made particularly difficult by the global nature of late capitalism, so that even films like *Crash* or *21 Grams*, which interweave so many different ingredients of a local reality, consider only a tiny portion of the global system. More overtly political hyperlink films such as *Traffic* and *Syriana* sometimes encompass a more international scale, though, while González Iñárritu addresses this concern by extending his own narratives to a global scale in *Babel* (2006). This film consists of four parallel narratives: one set in Mexico, one in Japan, and two in Morocco. The film is still hyperlink cinema in that it frequently switches between narratives. However, each individual narrative is told in an essentially linear fashion, though the stories are slightly out of temporal sync with one another. Ultimately, the four narratives are all interrelated in what might be regarded as an exercise in cognitive mapping, reminding us that the lives of different people on different continents can be extensively interconnected in the contemporary era of globalization.

On the other hand, *Babel* has relatively little to say about global politics, other than to point out the Babelian dangers of cross-cultural miscommunication, with a strong suggestion that Americans (and, even more so, the U.S. government) are particularly bad at this kind of communication due to their inability to view events from anything other than their own perspective. Instead, the film focuses on the intricacies of global interconnectedness, suggesting (reminiscent of chaos theory) how seemingly minor events can have major ramifications even on faraway continents. Thus, Yasujiro, a wealthy Japanese businessman (played by Kôji Yakusho) comes to Morocco on a hunting trip and gives a rifle to his Moroccan guide as an expression of appreciation. The rifle later falls into the hands of two young Moroccan boys who, on a lark, irresponsibly fire at a tour bus in the desert. Susan Jones (Cate Blanchett), an American woman on the tour bus, is hit and seriously wounded, far from adequate medical facilities. She and her husband Richard (Brad Pitt) take refuge in a small Moroccan village, waiting for help that is delayed because the American authorities, declaring the shooting to be the work of terrorists, refuse to allow her to be transported by a Moroccan ambulance because that would be "inappropriate." Meanwhile, the two small Jones children are back home in San Diego with their Mexican nanny Amelia (Adriana Barraza). With the return of the Joneses delayed by the misfortune in Morocco, Amelia reluctantly takes the children with her to her son's wedding just across the border in Mexico. Near catastrophe ensues. The children are ultimately saved (as is their mother), but Amelia, an illegal immigrant in the United States for the past sixteen years, is detained by border authorities for deportation to Mexico. At the same time, the two Moroccan boys are being hunted by Moroccan police, and one of them is apparently killed. Yasujiro, whose well-meaning act initiated all of this trouble, has his own troubles back in Japan. His wife has committed suicide, and his teenage daughter Chieko (Rinko Kikuchi), her adolescent angst heightened by her mother's death, her father's emotional distance, and her own deafness, embarks on a series of sexual misadventures in a desperate attempt to make some sort of human connection.

Chieko's dramatic alienation (or perhaps psychic fragmentation) is in many ways a dramatization of a central irony of the postmodern condition: in a world in which globalization has made the lives of individuals all over the planet increasingly interrelated, these same individuals find it harder and harder to feel any genuine sense of connection to anyone. Indeed, most of the characters in the film, not just the literally deaf Chieko, have a great deal of difficulty really hearing others when they speak. Ultimately, however, the film's emphasis on these connections once again makes it an exercise in cognitive mapping—and a kind of cry of protest against the fragmentation of experience in the postmodern world, despite its own formal fragmentation.

If films such as those of González Iñárritu address—and potentially seek to counter—the social breakup of the postmodern world, other films have sought to address more directly the fragmentation of the individual postmodern subject. Especially interesting examples of this in relation to individual psychic instability can be found in the later work of David Lynch, beginning with *Lost Highway* (1997), which is a sort of transition between the camp noir aesthetics of *Blue Velvet* (1986) and *Wild at Heart* (1990) and the somewhat more mature noir-inflected aesthetics of *Mulholland Drive* (2001). Like the earlier Lynch films, *Lost Highway* again features stereotypical images, this time especially focusing on a fast-tracking shot of a highway as seen looking forward from a speeding car. This same image also appears in both *Blue Velvet* and *Wild at Heart*, but is here more central, resonating as it does with the film's title—while once again evoking (with an irony that emanates from the clichéd nature of the image) the American road narrative tradition. *Lost Highway* also includes some of the same strange characters as its predecessors in Lynch's work, though this time they are generally less gratuitously weird and contribute more to the film's plot. At the same time, certain elements of the plot itself are even weirder than those of the earlier films, in ways that themselves might be taken as gratuitous weirdness for its own sake.

This film begins with a relatively conventional noir segment in which jazz saxophonist Fred Madison (Bill Pullman) and wife Renée (a brunette Patricia Arquette) seem to be drifting through their lives so estranged from one another that they are apparently able to speak to each other only in short whispered sentences, devoid of affect. A hint of the strangeness to come occurs when Fred awakes and sees Renée looking at him in bed, her face momentarily replaced by that of a strange, eerie-looking man. Meanwhile, someone comes to the front door of the Madisons' sterile, modernistic home (which seems to reflect their relationship) and whispers over the intercom that "Dick Laurent is dead." Fred, however, apparently doesn't even know Laurent, though we aren't sure about

Renée: there are very vague hints that she may have a secret life of her own. Soon afterward, the Madisons begin to receive videotapes left on their doorstep. These tapes (including one that includes a shot of the two of them asleep in their bed) indicate that someone (or something) has them under surveillance and has even entered their home. Police are called, and the two detectives who come to the scene add an element of offbeat strangeness with their oddly aloof deadpan behavior, reinforcing the film's enactment, in the marriage of the Madisons, of what Jameson calls the waning of affect in postmodern culture.

At this point, we are uncertain what kind of film we are watching. Is it a ghost story? A film noir? Matters take an even stranger turn when the Madisons attend a party at the home of a sleazy-looking man by the name of Andy (Michael Massee), who it seems may be having an affair (or some sort of clandestine relationship) with Renée. At the party, Fred meets the mystery man (played by Robert Blake) whose face he had earlier thought he saw on Renée. This man appears periodically throughout the film, usually when someone is about to be killed or something weird, perhaps supernatural, is about to happen. Whether he is meant to be the Grim Reaper or Satan or something else is never made clear, just as many mysteries about this film are never solved. After a creepy encounter in which it appears that the mystery man is simultaneously at Andy's party and at the Madisons' house, the Madisons return home to see fleeting lights and flitting shadows inside the house. Fred goes in to check out the house and is then followed by Renée, though the two seem to be unable to locate one another within the house. Then Fred finds another videotape that shows a murdered Renée with a blood-covered Fred at her side, confused and apparently unaware of what has happened. The film then quickly cuts to Fred's questioning by the police detectives who appeared earlier, followed by his conviction of first-degree murder for Renée's killing. Sentenced to death, he begins his life in prison, awaiting execution.

At this point the film undergoes a dramatic break. One night, Madison, suffering from excruciating headaches, sights the mystery man inside the prison, followed by a surreal sequence of nightmarish visions. The next morning, guards (exclaiming that "this is some spooky shit we got here") find that Fred has somehow been transformed into (or at least replaced in his high-security cell by) young Pete Dayton (Balthazar Getty). Dayton, clearly not the man sentenced to die, is released from prison. The film then drifts into what seems to be a completely separate noir narrative in which Dayton, an auto mechanic, has no connection with Madison, though he does hear what is apparently Madison playing sax on the radio at one point, becoming visibly upset.

Another connection between the film's two segments occurs when Dayton becomes involved in a dangerous clandestine sexual relationship with Alice Wakefield, the mistress of sadistic crime boss Mr. Eddy (Robert Loggia). Sparks fly when the two first see each other, with Lou Reed's version of "This Magic Moment" playing on the soundtrack. But this is far from conventional Hollywood magic. Wakefield, like Renée Madison, is played by Arquette, though this time as a blonde, furthering the film's investigation of the instability of identity in the postmodern world. The steamy relationship between Dayton and Wakefield predictably leads to trouble. For one thing, Mr. Eddy quickly becomes suspicious of their relationship. For another, Wakefield, in classic film noir femme fatale fashion, seduces Dayton into the robbery and murder of Andy (apparently the same Andy as in the first part of the film), who is somehow involved with Mr. Eddy (and Wakefield) in a dark world of prostitution and pornography, possibly including the making of snuff videos.

During their last sexual encounter, Wakefield warns Dayton that "you will never have me," then walks away, naked, and literally vanishes—as if she had been a ghost. Soon afterward, Renée inexplicably reappears, this time having sex with Mr. Eddy at the Lost Highway Hotel. Meanwhile, Dayton morphs back into Madison and the film veers off into a surreal sequence (punctuated by several appearances of Blake's mystery man) in which Madison and the mystery man kill Mr. Eddy, whom we eventually learn is (in one sense or another) the same person as Dick Laurent. Madison then drives Eddy/Laurent's Mercedes back to the Madison home from the first part of the film, where he goes to the front door and announces over the intercom that "Dick Laurent is dead," thus looping us back to the beginning of the film. Madison then flees in the gangster's car, with police in hot pursuit as he veers down the lost highway, presumably the highway to Hell.

Lost Highway is liberally sprinkled with clues concerning the bizarre goings-on in the film, but none of these clues really do much to help explain the film's strange turns and shifting identities. Part of the explanation may simply be that Lynch is reminding us of his godlike power as the film's creator and of his ability to institute any strange turns that he wishes, whether they make sense or not. Still, the film seems to want to make a very postmodern statement about the instability of individual identity, a theme that is reinforced by the film's own identity crisis as it shifts freely back and forth among genres in the course of its running time. All in all, though, *Lost Highway* tends toward strangeness for the sake of strangeness, perhaps as a condemnation of the banality of the typical Hollywood product. As such, *Lost Highway* again anticipates

Mulholland Drive, which makes the censure more explicit in that much of the film is literally about the movie industry. Indeed, the earlier film appears in many ways to be a sort of rehearsal for the later one, which is more accomplished in almost every sense, though the somewhat rough-hewn quality of *Lost Highway* is quite appropriate to its atmosphere and subject matter. In particular, *Lost Highway*, like *Mulholland Drive*, exhibits a very postmodern aesthetic of mixture: not only does it contain two seemingly inconsistent narrative segments and a variety of different generic elements, but it mixes individual scenes that don't quite cohere in the manner of the typical Hollywood film. Thus, while *Lost Highway* is a highly unusual film in the way it mixes these different elements, none of the elements are in themselves genuinely new.

It is in *Mulholland Drive* that Lynch seems finally to perfect this mixing technique. Here, almost every scene is a minor masterpiece of its kind, but the individual scenes do not necessarily fit together in any conventional fashion. The film rejects the realistic conventions of Hollywood movies far more thoroughly and effectively than do most other postmodernist examples, while nevertheless relying on its own deviations from realistic conventions to generate energy and interest. Indeed, though it actually began as a pilot for a proposed television series, *Mulholland Drive* is highly filmic. It draws upon numerous classic Hollywood motifs to construct a narrative that situates itself within a number of traditional Hollywood genres (especially film noir and movies about Hollywood) but then explodes the conventions of those genres. Indeed, it deconstructs the notion of narrative altogether, representing a key example of postmodern fragmentation in the way it is assembled from a series of highly compelling scenes but refuses ever to allow these scenes to come together to tell a coherent story. For three-fourths of its running time, the film seems almost on the verge of making sense, inviting audiences to accompany the characters in their attempts to piece together clues that will help them to make sense of their own lives. Then, however, the film's detective-story plot completely unravels; characters suddenly switch identities, facts and situations established earlier in the narrative abruptly change, and the film veers off into a surreal series of episodes and images that are clearly designed to operate independently of conventional logic and sense-making.

The central plot of the first three-quarters of *Mulholland Drive* is, in itself, fairly standard Hollywood fare. As the film begins, a sultry beauty (played by Laura Elena Harring) is about to be killed execution style, on a remote section of Mulholland Drive in the hills above Los Angeles. Then a carload of joyriders tears around a corner and crashes into the car bearing the woman and her two would-be killers. She somehow survives (the film's first deviation from verisimilitude), while all others in both cars are killed. Dazed and confused by the impact, she staggers back to civilization and takes refuge in an apartment she finds open, realizing by now that the accident has caused her to lose all memory of her past and identity. Then, Betty Elms (Naomi Watts), a perky fresh-faced blonde, arrives at the apartment, which belongs to her actress aunt. The aunt is out of town making a film, and Betty, newly arrived from small-town Canada and dreamy-eyed at the glitter of Hollywood, is to occupy the apartment while she attempts to break into the movies in her own right.

Betty encounters the strange woman from the auto accident, who identifies herself as "Rita," having taken the name from a poster for the Rita Hayworth film noir *Gilda* on a wall in the apartment. She indeed has some of the sultry sexiness of Hayworth, while Betty has the innocent beauty of the typical Hollywood ingénue, with a dash of the blonde Hitchcock heroine thrown in for good measure. The two then play amateur detectives as they attempt to discover "Rita's" real identity, eventually concluding that the key to the mystery lies somewhere on Mulholland Drive, perhaps in the personage of one Diane Selwyn, whose name Rita suddenly remembers and whom they then attempt to track down. The very title of the film encourages audiences also to assume that Mulholland Drive holds the key, while also perhaps suggesting a link to Billy Wilder's *Sunset Boulevard*, a link reinforced by a shot of a street sign for the actual Sunset Boulevard early in *Mulholland Drive*.

This evocation of *Sunset Boulevard* hints at a number of possible interpretations for *Mulholland Drive*. For example, the fact that the events of *Sunset Boulevard*—like those of the later *American Beauty* (1999)—are narrated posthumously by the film's protagonist suggests the possibility that "Rita" was in fact killed in the auto accident but somehow did not realize she was dead and continued to walk among the living, much in the mode of the protagonist of the cult horror film *Carnival of Souls* (1962). However, such tantalizing interpretive possibilities never quite come together in *Mulholland Drive*, which seems specifically designed to evade interpretation. For example, a number of subplots provide scattered puzzle pieces that we naturally assume must hold some sort of clues, though some scenes (as when a young man dreams of meeting a horrible-looking man behind a Winkie's restaurant, then goes there and in fact encounters the man—or perhaps demon) don't seem to have anything to do with the main plot or, for that matter, to make sense at all.

As the plot proceeds, oddities accumulate, while every scene seems just slightly out of kilter, partly due to Angelo Badalamenti's offbeat score. Meanwhile, the various subplots tend to veer off just as they seem about to join up with the main plot. For example, one subplot involves a movie director, Adam Kesher (Justin Theroux), who is being pressured by gangster types to cast Camilla Rhodes (Melissa George), a fresh-faced blonde actress, in his upcoming film, which the gangsters are financing. Just as he is auditioning the actress (who clearly resembles Betty), Betty herself shows up on the set. Betty's eyes meet with Kesher's and Hollywood sparks magically fly. We all know what will happen next: Kesher will fall in love with Betty, then defy the gangsters by casting her instead of Camilla. But that isn't what happens. Betty all of a sudden remembers an appointment with Rita and rushes off without ever even meeting Kesher. Soon afterward, the plot unravels altogether, with Watts suddenly assuming the role of Diane Selwyn and Harring the role of Camilla Rhodes. The new Selwyn and Rhodes may or may not be lesbian lovers (as Betty and Rita had earlier become), and Rhodes may or may not be shifting her romantic allegiance from Selwyn to Kesher, possibly in a bid to further her acting career. Ultimately, the scenes get weirder and weirder and finally just stop, apparently concluding with Selwyn's suicide after a mental breakdown.

All of this is not quite as incoherent as it sounds. For example, the final especially weird and surrealistic scenes can be recuperated as emanating from Selwyn's breakdown. Moreover, the switches in identity occur just after the new Selwyn awakes from a sleep, leaving open the interpretation that all of the film that has come before was actually just her dream, the identity shifts representing precisely the sort of displacement that Freud identifies as a key strategy of the dreamwork. Many early reviewers, in fact, opted for this explanation, though it is surely simplistic and doesn't really explain numerous aspects of the film. The new Selwyn encounters one after another of the characters (now, except for Kesher, with shifted identities) who had appeared in the earlier part of the film, in a motif that is surely meant to recall the experience of Dorothy after she awakens from unconsciousness in *The Wizard of Oz* (1939), a film that serves as important background to much of Lynch's work. However, far from reinforcing the interpretation of the early part of the film as Selwyn's dream, this link suggests that we look to the world of cinema, rather than the world of dreams, for an explanation.

Betty, in one early scene, surveys with amazement her aunt's classic Hollywood apartment, describing it as a "dream place." However, she also notes slightly later that the experiences she is having are "like something from a movie." Indeed, virtually all of the action of Mulholland Drive is self-consciously filmic, the suggestions of dream imagery only serving to remind us that dreams and movies operate according to many of the same principles. Hollywood, in this film, is very much a dream factory, even if the dreams are sometimes nightmares.

Much of the weirdness in *Mulholland Drive* can be read as a comment on the formulaic construction of Hollywood narratives. However, somewhat in the mode of *The Player*, *Mulholland Drive* can never quite escape the Hollywood stereotypes it is criticizing. Lynch's film is constructed from precisely the same formulaic elements that it seems to want to critique, gaining distinctiveness not from a rejection of formulas but from the combination of numerous different formulas, stirred together into one big cinematic stew. It is, once again, these formulas as modes of representation that the film is really about, giving it a reflexive quality that is, to an extent, directly illuminated by at least two sequences in the film. In one of these, Betty practices with Rita for an upcoming audition. In the run-through, the script seems terrible and Betty doesn't seem much better. Then, in the actual audition (which also features Chad Everett as an aging movie star), Betty is suddenly transformed into a virtuoso performer, and the banal script magically becomes steamy and powerful. The resulting comment on movie magic and on the power of actors and directors to produce differing emotional effects from the very same scenes is fairly clear. Later, in an even more telling scene, Rita suddenly awakes at 2 A.M. and begs Betty to go with her to Club Silencio, where a bizarre live show is under way. All of the performances in this decidedly weird show turn out, however, to be pantomimes. As the emcee explains, "It's all an illusion. A recording." The same, of course, applies to *Mulholland Drive* itself, and the film makes abundantly clear its status as a filmed object under the direction of a director who can make the action move in any direction he wants. That direction, in Lynch's case, is centrifugal and anticonventional, and the plot ultimately explodes in all directions, while at the same time denying the desire of audiences to make realistic sense of it all.

As a film about Hollywood, *Mulholland Drive* is often cynical about the movie business, as when shady financial backers attempt to apply pressure to force Kesher's hand in casting the film he is making in the first part of Lynch's film. Similarly, even if Betty is not taken literally as a character in the second Diane Selwyn's dreams, it is still easy to see that the two function as a sort of before-and-after pairing. Betty is the wide-eyed innocent who comes to Hollywood with dreams of fame and aesthetic achievement; Selwyn is the older and wiser version who knows the cruelty of the Hollywood system. As Maximilian Le Cain puts it, "*Mulholland Drive* is a film about the death of dreams."

Still, with its almost loving re-creation of various Hollywood stereotypes and its careful attention to artistic detail in the construction of the film's look and sound, *Mulholland Drive* can also be taken as an homage to the aesthetic possibilities of cinema if it can only break free of the most formulaic of plot and character stereotypes. Indeed, there is a clear element of nostalgia in the film's look and feel, which continually evoke the 1950s in much the same vague and nonspecific way that earlier Lynch works, such as *Blue Velvet* and the television series *Twin Peaks*, had already done. Again, however, this nostalgia is postmodern both in its nonspecificity and in its tendency to concentrate not on the historical memory of the 1950s but on cultural products of the 1950s, such as film noir.

Given that Hollywood films are among the central cultural projections of the ideology of consumer capitalism, one might suspect that Lynch's subversion of narrative forms might also function as a challenge to capitalism, somewhat along the lines of Linda Hutcheon's argument that postmodern "historiographic metafictions" challenge official versions of narrative history. However, Lynch has no interest in posing socialism (or anything else) as an alternative to capitalism. As a result, *Mulholland Drive,* however aesthetically brilliant and genuinely surprising, is politically inert and does little or nothing to produce the politicization of art espoused by Benjamin. The film, with its scenes that don't quite link together to tell a coherent story, does serve the diagnostic function of commenting on the fragmentation of experience in the postmodern world, but it neither attributes that fragmentation specifically to capitalism nor suggests an alternative that might lead to a more logical form of experience. *Mulholland Drive* is thus a perfect illustration of the fact that, even when they seem effectively critical of the capitalist status quo, postmodern films seldom offer effective alternatives, making their critique relatively innocuous.

Lynch's films, nevertheless, are a special case of postmodern cinema in that they draw in significant ways on avant-garde precedents, attempting to renew the techniques of the avant-garde for a new generation. Of course, one might argue that, like the film being made by the protagonist Anselmi in Federico Fellini's *8½*, *Mulholland Drive,* by eschewing politics and depending so heavily on stock Hollywood motifs, has all of the drawbacks of an avant-garde film with none of the virtues. Nevertheless, Lynch's film does support Andreas Huyssen's argument that there is a continuing avant-garde strain in postmodernist culture, even as the dominant strain in postmodernist culture seems to derive from the pop art movement.

The films of Tim Burton are among those that most effectively combine these two strains in postmodern aesthetics. Burton's films are almost like slide shows, fragmented streams of images, and in this sense might be said to employ avant-garde montage techniques. Yet the actual content of these image streams is derived almost exclusively from pop cultural materials. Typical here is the decidedly strange *Edward Scissorhands* (1990), a film that brings new meaning to the notion of "cut-cut-cut" as the central technique of postmodern film. Reportedly Burton's personal favorite among all of his pictures, *Edward Scissorhands*—like his earlier short film *Frankenweenie* (1984)—essentially retells the Frankenstein story, this time through the optic of the fairy tale.[4] *Edward Scissorhands* also looks back to Burton's *Vincent* (1982) by casting Vincent Price as a mysterious inventor who lives in a mysterious mansion atop a mountain overlooking a typical American suburban community.

As *Edward Scissorhands* begins, the Frankensteinian inventor has converted a piece of machinery into an artificial man (the title character, played by Johnny Depp) but has died before completing the project, leaving the man with scissors (part of the original machinery) for hands.[5] Left alone in the dark and decaying mansion, Edward is eventually discovered by Peg Boggs (Diane Wiest), a kindly Avon lady who comes to the mansion hoping to make a sale. Peg then takes Edward back to live with her family in their suburban home, setting up the main content of the film, which involves the inability of Edward, because of his difference, to fit in with the residents of the Boggses' conformist community.

This far-fetched narrative turns out to be much more entertaining than it sounds, partly because *Edward Scissorhands* again depends more on images than narrative to achieve its effects. One of the film's central images, of course, is the character of part-man-part-machine Edward, made sympathetic by Depp's effective portrayal, though he still seems not quite human. Also striking are the "artworks" Edward produces with his unusual hands, especially the spectacular topiary with which he eventually decorates the entire community. Ultimately, however, the most striking image in the film is the community itself, which serves as a vehicle for a thoroughgoing, though rather gentle, satire of American suburban life.

Burton's vision of this community was based on his own memories of growing up in suburban Burbank, California, but the depiction of it has an extremely nonspecific quality that makes it impossible to locate this community in any particular time or place. Though the neighborhood scenes were shot on location in an actual suburb outside of

Tampa, Florida, the film nevertheless has a vaguely retro look that evokes the 1960s, which is appropriate given that the story is being told by one of the characters from a much later perspective, while at the same time giving the film the look of the era of Burton's own childhood. On the other hand, the story is being told by this character from the perspective of at least 50 years later than the action, which would place that action in the 1940s, rather than the 1960s, unless the storytelling actually occurs well into the twenty-first century. Meanwhile, many of the automobiles, appliances, and other devices in the film seem to date from an era later than the 1960s, making the historical setting of the action entirely indeterminate.

This lack of historical specificity is typical of postmodernist film, though, in this case, it also enhances the film's fairy-tale atmosphere. This atmosphere is further reinforced by the fact that the houses in the neighborhood were repainted for the shooting in an array of improbably bright and varied colors. And this color scheme extends beyond the houses to the mise-en-scène of the entire film, which is consistently decorated in a similar palette. Thus, the locals wear preposterously tacky clothing in the same colors as their houses, making them look like escapees from a John Waters film. In addition, the local stores and even the set of a local television talk show are decorated in these hues as well. The point seems clear. At first glance, the brightly painted houses might seem to be declarations of individualism, allowing the local residents to escape the conformism that has been associated with suburbia, especially by its critics. But given the brightly colored nature of *everything* in this world, the painted houses are merely another form of conformism. Each house may be a different color, but each color is similarly and therefore conventionally garish, and all of the residents have painted their houses in like styles.

The herd mentality of the locals is also demonstrated in their attitude toward Edward. At first, he becomes an object of fascination to the gossipy neighbors, who flock to the Boggs home hoping to get a look at the new curiosity. Much in the mode of a Hollywood film director, when Edward's hot, he's hot, and everyone wants a piece of him. When he trims the Boggses' bushes into spectacular topiary, the neighbors all want their bushes trimmed. When he gives one neighborhood dog a stylish trim, everyone wants him to coif their dogs. When he gives one woman an unusual haircut, they all want interesting haircuts. And in the end, when he falls out of favor and is proclaimed dangerous, everyone declares him dangerous, chasing after him in the mode of the enraged villagers of *Frankenstein*.

Thus, as in *Charlie and the Chocolate Factory*, the bright colors of *Edward Scissorhands* disguise a film with a dark core, though in the end Edward does manage to escape back to his mansion, where he lives in isolation, creating beautiful artworks that no one will ever see. In particular, he carves giant ice sculptures, the by-products of which are the periodic snowstorms that occasionally strike the area as a reminder of Edward's continuing existence. The film thus updates *Frankenstein* with a happier ending and with the figures of the monster and the creator ultimately collapsed into one.

Indeed, Edward Scissorhands is a hybrid figure in more ways than one, most obviously in the way he is part human and part machine. Edward's status as an artist allows Burton to address a number of issues, though all of them are of course complicated by the fact that Edward himself is also an artwork. For example, the film repeatedly poses (but never answers) the question of whether Edward would be better off if he had "normal" hands or as he is, with the scissorhands that make him unique. In other words, would he be happier attempting to pursue an ordinary life or as an artist, even if his art makes him a danger to all of those around him and makes genuine intimacy with others (those scissors are really sharp) virtually impossible?

In its obviously autobiographical treatment of such themes, *Edward Scissorhands* recalls nothing more than *8½*, and it may be no coincidence that Burton has identified Fellini (another former cartoonist) as one of his favorite directors and fundamental role models, precisely because of Fellini's own concentration on images rather than narrative. Thus, asked in an interview about criticism of his narratives as fragmented and incoherent, Burton responded, "Do Fellini movies have a strong narrative drive?" (Salisbury, *Burton on Burton*, 114). Further, Burton noted in the interview, "The thing I liked about Fellini was that he created images that even if you didn't know what they meant literally, you *felt* something" (51). "It's not creating images to create images," Burton went on to say. "And even though I didn't fully understand a lot of what he was saying, I could feel a heart behind it" (51).

One might question whether there is such a heart behind Burton's images, which are both visually flashier and emotionally flatter than Fellini's. After all, if the outlook of an early Burton film such as *Pee-wee's Big Adventure* (1985) is overtly childish, then the sentimentalism of *Edward Scissorhands* is more than a bit trite, although this fact may speak less to Burton's lack of emotional depth as an individual artist than to the emotional flatness of experience in the postmodern world. The comparison between Burton and Fellini thus has something in common with Jameson's comparison of Andy Warhol's postmodernist "Diamond Dust Shoes" to Van Gogh's high modernist "A Pair of Boots," the former, for Jameson, being marked by a relative superficiality and "gratuitous frivolity" that marks the "waning of affect" in postmodern culture (*Postmodernism*, 10).

Actually, Fellini's film, while retaining strong modernist characteristics, is far from "high modernist," but tilts toward the postmodern with its basic playfulness and its tangled confusion of ontological levels. Nevertheless, the point remains, waning of affect (and all other postmodern phenomena) presumably having advanced considerably in the three decades between *8½* and *Edward Scissorhands*. Fellini's Anselmi may be unable to love, but he seems to feel genuine emotions (and is a genuinely tormented human artist), while Edward Scissorhands (anticipating Depp's portrayal of Willy Wonka), almost entirely lacking in emotional depth, is all surface. The word for Anselmi's predicament, of course, is alienation, and here it is relevant that Jameson sees alienation as the key trope for the transition from modernist to postmodernist emotional experience. According to Jameson, "concepts such as anxiety and alienation (and the experiences to which they correspond) . . . are no longer appropriate in the world of the postmodern." He adds, "The shift in the dynamics of cultural pathology [between modernism and postmodernism] can be characterized as one in which the alienation of the subject is displaced by the latter's fragmentation" (*Postmodernism*, 14).

The aural and visual resources of film are ideal for conveying changes in character, so the medium is especially well suited to the portrayal of discontinuous identities of the kind Jameson associates with postmodernism. Of course, characters who literally suffer from schizophrenia or various forms of multiple personality disorders have often been portrayed in American cinema. Among other things, such films offer opportunities for actors to display their versatility by playing several roles in one. For example, Nunnally Johnson's *Three Faces of Eve* (1957) won a Best Actress Oscar for Joanne Woodward in the title role of a woman suffering from multiple personality disorder.

There is nothing inherently postmodern about such films, which, by presenting fragmented personalities as symptoms of mental illness, serve largely to reinforce the notion that "normal" people have stable, unitary personalities. This is especially true when, as in the case of *Three Faces of Eve*, the narrative is presented in a conventional, realist form. On the other hand, when a fragmented personality is presented as the protagonist of a fragmented narrative, the congruence between the condition of the character and the form of the story makes the character seem far less abnormal. Thus, even films that identify multiple personality as an illness can suggest that their protagonists are more representative of the postmodern condition than of mere pathology.

For example, the protagonist of Woody Allen's *Zelig* (1983) would seem to epitomize the kind of discontinuous postmodern subject described by Jameson. An outcast all his life and thus desperate to fit in and be liked, Leonard Zelig (played by Allen himself) has developed a chameleonlike ability unconsciously to take on the appearance and personality of those around him. He thus takes on an unending sequence of different personae but essentially has no real identity of his own. From scene to scene, he might be a white gangster, a black jazz trumpeter, an Orthodox rabbi, or a German Nazi. As Robert Stam puts it, "His random cannibalization of the personalities of others turns his own into an aggregation of pastiches, a blank postmodern collage of available styles" (217).

After this ability is discovered at the end of the 1920s, Zelig quickly becomes a media sensation in a way that seems anachronistic, more typical of the postmodern 1980s than the 1920s or 1930s. But this film, despite its mock documentary style, is hardly concerned with historical accuracy. Indeed, much of Zelig's subsequent career seems to be located in the midst of the 1920s, well before his discovery in 1929, a tactic that makes no narrative sense but that allows the film to produce a number of nostalgic images of the 1920s as a wild and carefree Jazz Age. *Zelig* refers to the culture of the 1930s as well, featuring several scenes from *The Changing Man*, a fictional 1935 film detailing Zelig's life and career that recalls the Warner Bros. "prestige" biopics of the 1930s, even as *Zelig* itself serves as a postmodern commentary on the biopic genre.

In any case, Zelig's identity ultimately stabilizes when psychiatrist Eudora Fletcher (Mia Farrow) diagnoses and cures his malady, allowing him to live a long and relatively normal life (in married bliss with her). Zelig's attempts to fit in comment on, among other things, the assimilation of Jewish immigrants into American society in the early twentieth century. However, as Stam notes, Zelig is actually at his most assimilationist after his cure, when he becomes a "bland All-American, an acritical parrot of the reigning ideology" (217). Rather than becoming a true individual, he merely spouts individualist clichés. "Be yourself," he tells an admiring group of youngsters. But Zelig *has* no true self, epitomizing a postmodern predicament in which proclaiming oneself a unique individual is the ultimate form of conformism. Zelig, in short, becomes a representative postmodern Everyman rather than a pathological freak, but with a hint that his new normality is even more freakish than his earlier pathology.

The formal fragmentation of *Zelig*, though striking, is similarly contained. Noting the "fragmentation" of both *Zelig* and *Radio Days* (1987), Foster Hirsch cites these films as examples of Allen's delight in the ability of the film medium to "juggle shards of visual and aural information" (223). *Radio Days*, indeed, consists merely of a series of nostalgic anecdotes, with no continuous narrative thread at all. *Zelig* is even more fragmented, consisting mostly of a series of visual jokes involving Zelig's various transformations and showing him as he comically interacts with various historical personages, thus anticipating the technique of *Forrest Gump* (1994). However, the biographical form of the film (however parodic) gives *Zelig* a certain narrative coherence, while, as Hirsch also points out, Allen's use of a voiceover narrator helps to "suture his narrative fragments" (224). The formal fragmentation of the film is thus relatively bland, lacking the impact of the fragmentation in many postmodern films.

Christopher Nolan's *Memento* (2000) also focuses on the pathologically fragmented nature of the identity of its protagonist, who even shares a first name with Zelig. However, *Memento* takes the condition of protagonist Leonard Shelby (Guy Pearce) much more seriously, while also using this condition as the basis for a much more radical (and postmodern) disintegration of its narrative structure. Still, this film provides a realistic explanation for its fragmentation by attributing it to a brain injury suffered by Shelby. Due to this injury, Shelby is unable to retain memories for more than a few minutes, though he still (apparently) has a normal memory of everything that happened before the injury. Thus, while Shelby has knowledge of his identity and personal history, he now lives in a perpetual present, with no sense of temporal progression from one moment to the next. As such, his condition, even though it has a physiological explanation, serves as a sort of literalization of the fragmented and schizophrenic experience of time that Jameson associates with postmodernism.

In order to capture Shelby's disjointed movement through time better, the plot of *Memento* proceeds essentially in reverse chronological order. The very first scene of the film actually runs backward, a fact that is made clear by the fact that it features a Polaroid photo in the process of undeveloping. The rest of the film consists of a series of brief narrative segments, each of which proceeds in normal chronological fashion but is then followed by a sudden jump to another scene earlier in time. The audience is thus forced to do a considerable amount of detective work to gain an understanding of the story, which differs so dramatically from the plot. Here again, however, the experience of the audience

parallels that of Shelby, who is also involved in detective work. In particular, he is attempting to track down and kill the assailant who gave him
his injury after having just raped (and apparently killed) Shelby's wife.
Of course, Shelby will not be able to remember having extracted his
revenge, but that, as we realize in a final twist at the end, is just as well.
This quest for revenge is the only reason Shelby has for living, so he
prefers to continue the quest endlessly, even after its presumably successful completion.

Standard Hollywood editing tends to produce an illusion of continuity by effacing the fact that movies consist of a sequence of separately
filmed scenes. By placing these scenes in reverse chronological order,
Memento calls attention to the way all films are constructed, although
this foregrounding of the inherent fragmentation of film also helps to
create a sense of the disjointed nature of Shelby's experience, even
though his sense of time does not flow in reverse order. Of course, one
could argue that the film's emphasis on the pathological nature of
Shelby's experience suggests that, by contrast, "normal" experience is
not so fragmented—just as the emphasis on the fragmentation of film
emphasizes the fact that time flows more smoothly in the real world. In
addition, the unusual structure of *Memento* forces audiences to think
consciously of each scene as part of the history of the scenes that came
before it. Thus, if one accepts Jameson's definition of a genuine historical sense as "the perception of the present as history" (*Postmodernism*,
284), then the film's structure actually tends to help audiences to learn
to think historically.

One might also compare here Nolan's recent film *The Prestige*
(2006), a stylish period piece that features Christian Bale and Hugh
Jackman as two rival magicians in Victorian England. The film's sleight
of hand sometimes rivals that of its major characters, but all mysteries
are solved in the end, when it is revealed that the two have used different paths to achieve the same magical effect. In the case of Alfred Borden (Bale), apparent teleportation has been achieved through the use of
a double, a second man who looks and sounds exactly like Borden. In
fact, both men *are* Borden, sharing a single identity and living a single
life. Robert Angier (Jackman) also uses a double to accomplish the same
trick, but his version involves a science fiction device (made for him by
famed scientist Nicola Tesla) that literally creates a double of him
(whom he then murders) every time the trick is performed. The film's
complex, nonlinear plot thus echoes the complex, multiple identities
of the two main characters, making it very much a postmodern film,
despite the nineteenth-century setting.

Less formally inventive (or perhaps gimmicky) than *Memento*, David Fincher's *Fight Club* (1999) nevertheless occasionally employs techniques such as rapid cutting to reinforce the sometimes extreme action that it conveys. In addition, *Fight Club*, which features a protagonist who suffers from a type of multiple personality disorder, quite overtly and specifically attributes this malady to the effects of consumer capitalism. The film also attempts to explore certain utopian alternatives to the capitalist system. However, these alternatives (which essentially involve male bonding through mutual participation in violence) are so debased and problematic that they tend to overwhelm the anticapitalist message, leading Roger Ebert to declare the film "the most frankly and cheerfully fascist big-star movie since *Death Wish*."

As *Fight Club* begins, the unnamed narrator/protagonist (played by Edward Norton) is the quintessential nerdy alienated yuppie, a slave to his white-collar office job and to the commodities he works the job in order to buy. The tedious routine of his life has driven him to extreme insomnia, to which he attributes a growing sense of the unreality of his life. "Nothing seems real," he tells us as he works over a copy machine. "Everything's a copy of a copy of a copy." His condition, however, is due not so much to insomnia as to late capitalism and postmodernity, in which, at least according to Baudrillard, everything is indeed a copy of a copy.

The narrator is at least to some extent aware that capitalism is the source of his malaise. For one thing, he is well acquainted with the ruthlessness of the capitalist system. Employed by a major automobile manufacturer, he works as a recall coordinator, whose job it is to do cost-benefit analyses to determine whether it will be cheaper to recall and fix defective automobiles or merely to pay the damages resulting from lawsuits when people are killed or maimed in accidents resulting from the defects. Further, commenting on the penetration of consumer capitalism into every aspect of life, the narrator envisions the colonization of deep space by U.S. corporations, with everything renamed for corporate sponsors: "the IBM stellar-sphere, the Microsoft Galaxy, Planet Starbucks." He also comments on the proliferation of "single-serving" products, acknowledging an awareness that such products both respond and contribute to the alienation and loneliness of individuals in the modern world.

The narrator is also cognizant of his own addiction to commodities, especially tasteful, reasonably priced home furnishings ordered from the IKEA catalog. IKEA catalogs, he suggests, have now replaced pornography as the objects of lustful gaze. In one early scene, the camera pans about his commodity-filled apartment, labeling each item with an overlay of the catalog description on the screen. He acquires these items compulsively, hoping that somehow they will help to fill the emptiness of his life. They don't, of course, because consumerist desire can never be fulfilled but must merely trigger additional desires in an endless chain that keeps the whole capitalist machine rolling.

Seeking other forms of solace, the narrator begins attending meetings of support groups for various serious diseases, such as testicular cancer, which he pretends also to have. At these meetings, he finds a kind of community in shared suffering (though his own suffering is entirely bogus), and this brief glimpse of utopian possibility for a time cures his insomnia. Then he encounters a woman, Marla Singer (Helena Bonham Carter), who, he realizes, is also attending the meetings as a "tourist." This discovery destroys the authenticity of the experience, and his insomnia returns.

Soon afterward, however, he meets one Tyler Durden (Brad Pitt), who gradually introduces him to another sort of utopian community. Durden is everything the narrator is not. Dazzlingly handsome, superbly muscled, and an astonishing sexual athlete, Durden is a totally free spirit who has opted out of the capitalist system. He lives in a large abandoned house (the look of which seems to have been modeled on the distinctive visual style of *Blade Runner*) and has no interest in tasteful furnishings. He dresses in complete bad taste and absolutely doesn't care. He works odd jobs, at which he spends most of his time sabotaging his employers, for example, working as a waiter and urinating in the soup. On another occasion, he works as a projectionist and splices single frames of pornography into family films, creating disturbing effects in an audience on whose brains the frames register without their awareness.[6]

Soon after they meet, the narrator's apartment and all those IKEA furnishings are destroyed in a mysterious explosion, and he goes to stay with Durden in his derelict mansion. Durden then encourages the narrator to join him in founding a secret "fight club" at which men would gather to engage in fierce bare-knuckle combat, thus taking out the frustrations that arise from the routinization of their day-to-day lives but also achieving a sense of community and belonging. The brutal and bloody fight scenes that accompany this motif are among the film's most memorable—and are responsible for its reputation as a testosterone-drenched endorsement of male violence. Actually, the film does not specifically endorse this violence, but neither does it actively criticize it. Indeed, it is during these moments of combat that the narrator and the other characters achieve, if only for a few moments, a utopian authenticity of experience that has been denied them by their commodity-saturated lives.

Durden (for reasons that ultimately become clear) shares the narrator's awareness of the evils of capitalism but is able to articulate this knowledge in a more vivid way. He is also well aware that it is precisely the soul-numbing effect of consumer capitalism that the fight club is designed to overcome. "The things you own end up owning you," he tells the narrator. Then, addressing a gathering of the fight club, he expresses his sympathy for their frustration, noting that they have all been encouraged by television to expect to become "millionaires and movie gods and rock stars" but instead find themselves mired in meaningless dead-end jobs to make money to buy useless commodities. "Advertising has us chasing cars and clothes, working jobs we hate so we can buy shit we don't need."

Soon, fight clubs begin to spring up nationwide. Moreover, Durden gradually turns the club members into a private militia, developing a plan not merely to take out their capitalism-induced frustrations on each other but to initiate a guerrilla war against the capitalist system. At first, this plan involves mostly pranks (though sometimes violent ones), but ultimately Durden conceives a plan to blow up the headquarters of a number of credit-card companies and of TRW, the credit reporting company. He hopes thereby to destroy debt records and throw the capitalist system into chaos.[7]

It is at this point that the narrator begins to realize that Durden is not a separate individual, but merely a manifestation of his own frustrations and fantasies. He then struggles to prevent the bombings, eventually ridding himself of Durden by shooting himself in the mouth—which, oddly, seems to "kill" Durden but not the narrator. The narrator then joins Marla as they look out over the city as the bombs begin to explode and buildings begin to drop one by one. In the wake of the September 11, 2001, destruction of the twin towers of the World Trade Center, this final scene becomes far more chilling than it had originally been, even though we are told that the guerrillas have carefully ensured that nobody is in any of the buildings and that no one will be killed by the explosions. In the film, in fact, this destruction is played essentially for comedy. As the film ends, the narrator sardonically tells Marla that she met him "at a very strange time in my life."

Despite its embedded critique of capitalism, the portrayal in *Fight Club* of the anticapitalist guerrilla force seriously diminishes any potential impact of that critique. For one thing, the bloody violence of the fight clubs hardly seems feasible as a means of transcending the antagonistic social relations of capitalism. Nor does this fighting really seem preferable to the acquisition of IKEA furnishings. Furthermore, the guerrilla force that arises in opposition to capitalism seems to have no ideological agenda other than pure destruction. This devastation, meanwhile, is less anarchist than fascist. The guerrillas themselves obey a discipline so iron-clad that they seem almost like mindless robots, or perhaps brainwashed cult members, and the "utopian" alternative to capitalism that they represent is clearly of a right-wing, rather than socialist, variety.

Of course, the utopian alternative presented in *Fight Club* is not meant to be taken seriously. Ultimately, in fact, the failure of the utopian imagery in the film should probably be attributed less to its own specific shortcomings than to the tremendous difficulty involved in presenting a utopian alternative to capitalism that audiences *can* take seriously. Indeed, almost all utopian images in postmodern film are of a similarly debased and problematic variety, their collective impact being to suggest the impossibility and unavailability of alternatives to a late capitalism that seems in such total control at this late juncture in history. About the most that any film seems able to do is to express contempt for capitalist values, often through the portrayal of characters who opt out of the system either by turning to violent crime or through the consumption of mind-altering substances. These alternatives are hardly desirable and are utopian only in the weakest sense. In fact, they are no alternatives at all: violence and crime are merely a consequence, or perhaps special case, of capitalist competition, while drug addiction is just an extension of the raging desire to consume that drives the economy of late capitalism.

Such themes are often closely associated with the fragmentation of postmodern film, and cinematic presentations of violence or drug use are often accompanied by particularly frenetic editing or disjunctive narratives, which serves a mimetic function and helps to reinforce the themes of these films. David O. Russell's *Three Kings* (1999), for example, uses fragmentary postmodern editing techniques to help convey the confusion of war and its aftermath—while also suggesting that U.S. foreign policy may be equally confused. Meanwhile, the violent tendencies of American society as a whole are addressed in Oliver Stone's *Natural Born Killers* (1994), released in the same year as *Pulp Fiction*. Stone's film is a case study in MTV-style quick-cut editing and indeed represents some of the most spectacularly intrusive editing in American cinema. It also has a rousing soundtrack, although the music (especially the crucial songs by Leonard Cohen) is generally much darker than that in *Pulp Fiction*. More importantly, *Natural Born Killers* puts its violence up front and demands that audiences think seriously about it, rather than simply treat it as cool. In fact, though itself based on a story by Tarantino, *Natural Born Killers* might be taken as the anti–*Pulp Fiction*, the latter representing precisely the kind of glorification of violence that Stone's film seeks to condemn. Indeed, numerous critics have seen the cool violence of *Pulp Fiction* as a key marker of the moral vacuity of postmodernist culture as a whole.[8]

Natural Born Killers details the careers of lovers Mickey and Mallory Knox (Woody Harrelson and Juliette Lewis), a sort of postmodern Bonnie and Clyde who go on a cross-country murder spree, beginning with her own parents. It then follows their capture, imprisonment, and escape in the midst of a spectacularly violent prison riot. Indeed, the entire film is spectacularly bloody and violent, a fact that brought considerable criticism when it was released, despite the fact that the film (unlike *Fight Club* or *Pulp Fiction*) is quite clearly meant as a bitter denunciation of the violent tendencies in American culture.

Stone's intrusive, quick-cut editing is designed precisely to create the effects described by Benjamin, distancing audiences from the violent subject matter and presumably preventing the film from becoming just another celebration of violence of the sort it is meant to condemn. Indeed, the film is so heavily edited that it becomes more of a postmodern image stream than a coherent narrative. Stone seems to have attempted to use every possible effect in the editor's toolkit to interrupt audience identification with the plot. The story is continually intercut with jarring images derived from film, television, and even cartoons, while secondary scenes from various sources are often projected into the background of the scenes of the main narrative. The film frequently switches back and forth between color and black-and-white and between conventional film and video. Weirdly tilted camera angles; strange, erratic camera movements; extreme close-ups; colored tints; slow-motion; and fast-motion all help to create disorienting effects, while the radically eclectic compilation soundtrack also adds to the sense of chaos and fragmentation that informs the film.

One might want to describe these intrusive effects as Brechtian, as they certainly are in a technical sense, though Stone's film lacks Bertolt Brecht's vision of socialism as an alternative to the capitalist corruption and chaos he describes. Indeed, Stone seems intentionally to suggest that there is no viable alternative to the debased media-induced values of contemporary American society. Even the spectacular crimes of the Knoxes are safely absorbed by the spectacle-loving American society, which makes them media idols. Indeed, much of Stone's message seems to involve the suggestion that the Knoxes are products of America's media-driven society, not reactions against it, and he depicts them as no more murderous or violent than the authority figures who battle against them.

In the end (in a chilling parody of the typical happy ending of Holly-wood films), the soulless Mickey and Mallory end up as typical subur-banites, driving along in their Winnebago with two kids fighting in the back and another on the way. The mindset of bourgeois suburbia appa-rently matches their own quite well. Meanwhile, somewhat in the man-ner of *The Player* (but in a more disturbing way), *Natural Born Killers* itself seems unable to transcend the phenomena it criticizes. Stone's elaborate editing style is ultimately more MTV than Brecht and seems derived from the very media he is criticizing, suggesting the difficulty of escaping media indoctrination.

Whereas *Natural Born Killers* connects the media and violence, Dar-ren Aronofsky's *Requiem for a Dream* (2000) connects the media with drug culture. Stone's film suggests no contradiction between bourgeois values and mass murder, while Aronofsky's (based on the novel by Hubert Selby Jr.) sees drug use as an extension of, rather than an alter-native to, mainstream capitalist behavior. Aronofsky's film also exempli-fies the MTV editing style disparaged by Altman's Stuckel, while, as the title indicates, it uses both the psychic fragmentation of characters and the formal fragmentation of the editing style to comment on the loss of utopian energy in postmodern America. The dream for which the film serves as a requiem is nothing less than the American dream itself, here depicted as reduced by the logic of consumerism to a debased and com-modified vision of better living through increased consumption, whether it be of sex, food, drugs, or more conventional consumer goods. *Req-uiem for a Dream* is also, for a postmodern film, unusually powerful emotionally, which combines with the anticonsumerist theme to make it one of the few genuinely postmodern films that is also truly political. On the other hand, the politics of the film consist almost entirely of a denunciation of the destruction of utopian dreams by the logic of con-sumerism; it does not offer any alternative vision of utopia that might effectively counter this logic or its dire consequences.

Requiem for a Dream has an essentially dualistic plot structure. In one story line, Sara Goldfarb (Ellen Burstyn), an aging widow, battles loneliness and despair by watching massive amounts of television and consuming large amounts of sweets. She is particularly addicted to watching the *Tappy Tibbons Show*, a sort of postmodern hybrid of the game-show, talk-show, and inspirational self-improvement genres. Unfortunately, Sara's two addictions clash when, believing she has a chance to appear on her favorite show as a contestant, she discovers that she has grown too fat to fit into her favorite red dress, which she hoped to wear on the show. Failing to lose weight by her own resolve, she turns to diet pills liberally dispensed by a callous doctor, which helps her to break her addiction to food, only to find that she has now developed an even more damaging addiction to the pills.

In the other plot line, Sara's son, Harry (Jared Leto) pursues his own happiness with girlfriend Marion Silver (Jennifer Connelly) and friend Tyrone Love (Marlon Wayans). Here, there is a vague glimmer of utopia in the genuine friendship between Harry and Tyrone and in the seemingly genuine love between Harry and Marion. Unfortunately, all three pursue their dreams of happiness and prosperity largely in a heroin-induced haze, their dependence on illegal drugs paralleling in a fairly obvious way the addiction of Sara to television, food, and legal prescription drugs.

Not surprisingly, both plot lines spiral relentlessly downward as the various characters grow increasingly desperate in their quest to feed their addictions and thus to gain a few moments of respite from the overall emptiness of their lives. Sara gradually begins to lose touch with reality, experiencing various hallucinations and eventually losing all sense of a distinction between the actuality of her life and the events she sees on television. She first begins to project herself into the *Tappy Tibbons Show*, then finds the show invading her apartment, experiencing a confusion of ontological levels that completely lacks the playfulness of postmodern metafiction. It is, in fact, so terrifying that it leads to a complete mental breakdown that leaves Sara lying in a mental ward where she is subjected to shock treatments and other forms of harsh treatments.

If Sara's story becomes, among other things, a powerful commentary on the soul-destroying effects of American pop culture, the story of Harry, Marion, and Tyrone becomes an allegory of capitalism itself. Harry and Tyrone become drug dealers and meet with considerable initial success. Cash piles up in a shoebox in their closet. Living the capitalist dream, they begin to make plans for a grand future. But capitalist competition has its downside as well, just as capitalist economies tend to have highs and lows. A war between Italian- and African-American drug lords competing for the same market leads to an almost complete disappearance of the local heroin supply, and Harry and Tyrone soon find that their cash is gone. The two head south seeking a new supply of drugs, but they never reach their Florida goal. Tyrone ends up in a Southern jail, where he is brutalized daily, while Harry (paralleling the situation of his mother) lies hopelessly in a Southern hospital, his arm amputated due to an infection caused by his repeated heroin injections. Back in New York, Marion is reduced to performing shockingly degrading sexual acts in order to find the means to feed her drug habit. Each of the four major characters is shown, as the film closes, curled up in a fetal position, retreating inward in an attempt to shut out the cruelty of external reality.

This story is an inherently powerful one, but it is significantly enhanced by Aronofsky's editing style, which reflects the disjointed psychic states of the characters through the use of weird, disorienting camera angles and movements. Particularly important to this effect are rapid cutting and fast-motion action that emphasize moments of intensified experience, as when the younger characters shoot up with heroin or when Sara feeds her own addictions with food or diet pills. Aronofsky also makes extensive use of split screens, which serves to emphasize the characters' sense that they are surrounded by a confusing world beyond their grasp. Thus, split-screen editing can emphasize the fact that many different things are going on at once and that the characters are unable to assemble all of these events into a coherent vision of the world. However, perhaps the most effective use of a split screen occurs early in the film in a scene in which Harry and Marion experience what is probably their most tender and intimate moment in the film. Though the two lie together, side by side, they are shown in split screen, each character occupying a separate frame, making clear the gap that remains between them. Each is far too empty and unstable to have any hope of making a genuine and lasting connection to the other.

While such complex, speeded-up, quick-cut editing often seems, in postmodern films, designed primarily to make the movie appear hip (Guy Ritchie's films come to mind), Aronofsky's use of such techniques makes an important contribution to the message of *Requiem for a Dream*, the formal fragmentation of the film effectively supporting his portrayal of the psychic fragmentation of his characters. In addition, while the story of the heroin addicts might suggest that this fragmentation is the abnormal effect of illegal drug use, the parallel story of Sara makes it clear that the psychic destruction of these characters is part of a far more general and pervasive effect in contemporary American society. Thus, the insatiable need of Harry, Tyrone, and Marion for heroin becomes merely a special case of the insatiable need to consume that is fostered by a capitalist system that offers the consumption of commodities (both material and cultural) as compensation for the impossibility of authentic intersubjective experience within a system that drives inexorably toward the commodification of anything and everything, including human relationships and human beings. Marion's turn to prostitution marks her commodification in a particularly overt way, but it is not, within the logic of *Requiem for a Dream*, all that fundamentally different from Sara's seduction by the *Tappy Tibbons Show*.

This suggestion of the commodification of human relationships is not in itself new. Indeed, this commodification is essentially nothing more than an aspect of the great modernist theme of alienation. However, the frenetic and fragmented editing of *Requiem for a Dream* suggests that we are dealing with something more radical here: not only are the characters unable to reach beyond their own subjectivity in order to relate to others as subjects, but they in fact have little or no subjectivity to begin with, their very selves having been shattered by the commodity-saturated environment in which they live. In short, the film perfectly exemplifies Jameson's conclusion that alienation was a "modernist experience," while the postmodern experience is one of a more radical "psychic fragmentation" that leaves individual subjects with too little stability and substance even to be able to experience alienation in the classic, modernist sense (*Postmodernism*, 90).

Unfortunately, *Requiem for a Dream* as a movie so perfectly mirrors the psychic fragmentation of its characters that the film itself acquires a certain hollowness and emptiness that mutes its anticapitalist message. Or, alternatively, one could argue that contemporary audiences are too fragmented to be able to process the message properly. In any case, most reviewers missed the anticapitalist theme altogether, seeing the film essentially as a "drug movie."[9] David Walsh, reviewing the picture on the World Socialist Web Site, complains that the film presents no explanation of "the pressures, economic and psychological, that might drive people to seek relief in drugs," though he also quotes author Selby to the effect that his novel (to the spirit of which Walsh claims the film is all too faithful) is about "the great American dream: prosperity, property, prestige, etc. And the fact that it'll kill you dead. Striving for it is a disaster. Attaining it is a killer."

If *Requiem for a Dream* is in danger of becoming an enactment of that which it seeks to criticize, a film like *Natural Born Killers* includes so much violence that it is constantly in danger of becoming a violent spectacle in its own right—a peril that may be exacerbated by the fact that audiences *want* such spectacles and therefore focus on that aspect of the film. Meanwhile, the violence in *Fight Club* becomes such a focus that it obscures the anticonsumerist theme of that film. In all cases, however, the problem may partly be that American audiences, conditioned as they are by the constant barrage of consumerist messages that constitutes their daily discursive environment, are simply not receptive to anticapitalist messages and so ignore them—or at least process them in only the most superficial of ways.

Contemporary American popular culture is, in fact, filled with criticism of capitalism, and indeed cultural objects are almost obliged to carry an anticapitalist message in order to appear "cool." This phenom-enon is surely the result not of the overwhelming power of anticapitalist ideas in our contemporary context but of their overwhelming impo-tence. Furthermore, capitalism itself is informed by a revisionist ideology that demands constant change and reform, in line with the drive for innovation that drives the consumer economy. Thus, a simple criticism of the evils of capitalism, without proposing socialism as a legitimate alternative, is perfectly consistent with capitalism itself and poses no ideological threat. The message of such criticisms is generally clear: We all know things are bad, but the beauty of the system is that it has the capacity to make things better.

The various ostensible critiques of capitalism that can be found in postmodern cinema are thus in no way inconsistent with Jameson's vision of postmodernism as the cultural logic of late capitalism, just as the various instances of fragmentation in postmodern film are clearly more in line with that vision than with Benjamin's earlier notion that fragmentation in film had a powerful subversive potential. It is certainly the case that recent "anticapitalist" movies fail to present socialism or anything else as a serious alternative to capitalism. After all, films such as *Fight Club*, *Natural Born Killers*, and *Requiem for a Dream* are so thoroughly "about" the impossibility of utopia that they can offer little in the way of utopian alternatives to the contemporary America they present as such a psychic wasteland.

Socialism, meanwhile, has simply become something of a joke in post–Cold War American culture, so much so that no American film-maker would dare propose it seriously as a possible cure for what ails us at this time. One thinks here of the comic ode to the Russian Revolution in *Timecode*, but representations of socialists in American film had already started to become jokelike even while the Cold War was still under way—think of the amusingly anachronistic socialist agitator who appears in *Monty Python and the Holy Grail* (1975), the socialist ideo-logue in *Zelig* who ludicrously declares the title character to be part of a capitalist plot to exploit workers, or the UFO nut in *Stardust Memories* (1980) who proclaims his assurances that any intelligent inhabitants of other planets are sure to be Marxists. This inability to treat socialism seriously exemplifies Jameson's complaint that, amid the fragmented vis-tas of postmodern experience, genuinely meaningful themes almost inevitably appear "corny" (*Postmodernism*, 90). Thus, in capitalism's greatest ideological victory, socialism has, at the beginning of the twenty-first century, become the corniest theme of all.

Chapter 2

AS TIME JUST SITS THERE

THE MUSIC OF POSTMODERN NOSTALGIA

One of the key sequences in Quentin Tarantino's *Pulp Fiction* (1994)—widely regarded as the epitome of popular postmodern cinema—occurs when Vincent Vega (John Travolta) and Mia Wallace (Uma Thurman) dine out at Jack Rabbit Slim's, a restaurant/club that is a living tribute to the culture of the 1950s. As Vincent says when Mia asks him what he thinks of the club, "It's like a wax museum with a pulse." In the club, the ambient music is all from the 1950s, whether it comes from the jukebox or from live performers doing imitations of stars from the fifties such as Ricky Nelson. The walls are decorated with posters for 1950s films, and the booths are made to resemble classic cars of the decade. The host is an Ed Sullivan imitator, the waiters are dressed to look like such fifties icons as Buddy Holly and Marilyn Monroe, and the items on the menu are named after various figures from 1950s pop culture.

Of course, the very title of *Pulp Fiction* evokes the fifties, when the pulp fiction phenomenon was at its peak, while numerous aspects of the movie itself reference the film noir tradition of the 1940s and 1950s.[1] There is, however, little genuine nostalgia for the 1950s in *Pulp Fiction*, which is very much a hip film of the 1990s. Similarly, the atmosphere of Jack Rabbit Slim's is informed less by a wistful desire to return to the 1950s than by a very 1990s attempt to appropriate the fifties for commercial use as campy spectacle. The club, then, merely simulates nostalgia, rather than evoking genuine longing for the past. As such, Jack Rabbit Slim's is the perfect postmodern setting, drawing on images from history in a purely ahistorical way, showing little real sense of the pastness of the past or of past history as the antecedent of the present. Meanwhile, the potential nostalgia of the sequence at Jack Rabbit Slim's is further complicated by the fact that the highlight of the evening is a twist contest in which Mia and Vincent dance to the music of Chuck Berry's "You Never Can Tell." They win, of course, as Travolta proves that he is still Travolta, even after all the years and all the pounds he has put on since his appearances in *Saturday Night Fever* (1977) and *Grease* (1978), some of the most memorable dance performances in American film since the days of Fred Astaire and Gene Kelly.

In this sense, the dance contest sequence at Jack Rabbit Slim's is more an example of nostalgia for the 1970s than for the 1950s, bringing back memories of the heyday not of Chuck Berry but of John Travolta himself. Of course, without any real historical sense, temporal boundaries slide around freely in this sequence—and in *Pulp Fiction* as a whole. For one thing, "You Never Can Tell" was released in 1964, and the twist itself was a phenomenon of the early sixties, not the fifties. Such details, of course, are unimportant in a film that flaunts its lack of historical moorings, for a director not born until 1963, or in the midst of a soundtrack that runs the gamut of popular music from the 1950s to the 1990s. Even the title music is a composite, beginning with the California surfer music of "Misirlou" by Dick Dale and the Del-Tones (1962), then abruptly switching styles and decades (the transition marked by a sound effect like the turning of a radio dial) to the cool urban seventies funk of "Jungle Boogie" by Kool and the Gang.

In any case, the real point to Travolta's dance performance in *Pulp Fiction* may not be to remind us of the way he was, but to demonstrate that he's *still* that way (sort of)—that the pop culture icon of the 1970s can still do it in the 1990s. *Pulp Fiction*, in short, suggests that its star, like the film itself, has defied the passing of time. Indeed, one might argue that one of the secrets to the enormous success of *Pulp Fiction* was the fact that, by proving that he still had some of the old moves, the aging baby boomer Travolta provided a boost to aging baby boomers everywhere. But the film was even more popular with younger audiences, and what was really crucial to the success of *Pulp Fiction* was the thorough hipness with which the film gleefully combined various periods, genres, and styles, producing the perfect postmodern cinematic stew. *Pulp Fiction* was, in fact, one of the signature postmodern films of the 1990s and almost certainly the one that most influenced other filmmakers.

The heteroglot soundtrack is a crucial part of both *Pulp Fiction*'s sense of postmodern plurality and its particularly nonspecific postmodern nostalgia. It was also crucial to the film's commercial success, and the soundtrack itself remained on *Billboard*'s Top 200 albums chart for more than 100 weeks, selling more than three million copies. Jeff Smith, in fact, sees the soundtrack album for *Pulp Fiction* as the "most notable" example of soundtracks in the 1990s that were so commercially success-ful that they caused many film companies to open their own music divi-sions specifically for the distribution of soundtracks (195).

It is not surprising that the soundtrack of *Pulp Fiction* should be so important to both its nostalgia effect and its commercial success, post-modern nostalgia itself being a commodity that, like all commodities, is largely produced and marketed by capitalist enterprises in search of profit. Meanwhile, the hugely successful marketing of soundtracks such as that of *Pulp Fiction* is a key indicator of the more commodified nature of postmodern nostalgia, as opposed to the nostalgia Caryl Flinn has located in the use of classical music in the Hollywood films of the 1930s and 1940s.

Flinn notes that films of these decades quite often employed scores based on the classical works of nineteenth-century Romantic composers to create an "impression of perfection and integrity in an otherwise imperfect, unintegrated world" (9). Indeed, Flinn argues that this prac-tice was so widespread that film music came to be associated quite gen-erally by both filmmakers and critics with "the idea of anteriority and idealized pasts" (3). Flinn here builds directly on Richard Dyer's influen-tial 1977 essay "Entertainment and Utopia," which notes the "Utopian sensibility" that informs such cultural products as the Busby Berkeley musicals of the 1930s. Dyer's focus is on production, in that he locates the utopian energies of such films in attempts to overcome a perceived lack of wholeness and perfection in the time of the films' production. Flinn, on the other hand, locates these utopian energies in reception, arguing that they are produced by audiences (and critics) and that "the utopias mounted to redress these apperceived lacks are created at the moment of reading, even if those utopias are then simply thrown back-ward" (155).

For both Flinn and Dyer, music is associated with a utopian desire for wholeness, combined with a rather nostalgic tendency to locate this wholeness in an idealized past. In this sense, their arguments seem to ask for comparison with Fredric Jameson's identification of a particular form of nostalgia as a crucial aspect of postmodern experience, and of the "nostalgia film" as a key phenomenon of postmodern culture. Indeed, while focusing on the classic films of the 1930s and 1940s, Flinn notes that "music continues to play a key role in triggering this wide-scale yearning for yesterday" in more recent movies, such as George Lucas's *American Graffiti* (1973), a key example of the postmodern nos-talgia film. Flinn does grant, however, that more recent motion pictures (and more recent critics) differ from their predecessors in that the films of the thirties and forties (and their music) have themselves become objects of nostalgia in the later films and the work of later critics (153). Still, Flinn seems to see no fundamental difference in the utopian nostalgia associated with movie music in the 1930s and 1940s and that associated with later films of the postmodern era. Nostalgia, in short, is nothing new.

I think, however, that it is important to stipulate some ways in which postmodern nostalgia is distinct from other forms of nostalgic engagement with the past, even though it is also important to acknowledge the continuity that Flinn cites. That is, as I have argued in *Strange TV*, postmodernism should not be seen as the product of a radical historical break but as the cumulative effect of a number of continuous historical processes associated with the gradual globalization of capital and the increasing penetration of consumerist practices into every aspect of daily life. As Raymond Williams reminds us in the early pages of *The Country and the City*, virtually all periods of Western history have been informed by a certain sense that the present world is in the throes of a fall from an older, more organic, and more authentic social order. Williams thus traces nostalgic visions of "Old England" backward in time from the 1970s through the Middle Ages, concluding that this nostalgic "escalator" finally comes to rest only in Eden (12). Indeed, Williams's evocation of the Edenic myth reminds us that visions of a lost golden age have been central to Western civilization at least since the days of the Old Testament. Moreover, Greek myth traces such a fall back even earlier.

Nostalgia, then, is thoroughly ingrained in Western culture, no doubt partly because of a tendency to project personal history onto public history, which Williams acknowledges when he notes the suspicious tendency of nostalgic visions to be located in the childhoods of their authors. On the other hand, Williams also grants that nostalgia is a complex phenomenon that cannot be easily dismissed as personal fantasy or useless longing for spilt milk. Indeed, Williams's entire project is embedded in a post–World War II British cultural studies movement in which historians such as E. P. Thompson and Eric Hobsbawm have attempted, in various ways, to find progressive potential in nostalgic visions of a past in which working-class culture played a more vital role in English society.

What, then, is new about postmodern nostalgia? For one thing, historians such as Thompson have emphasized that the progressive nostalgia of which they write must have at least some basis in authentic experiences, so that nostalgia becomes part of an effort to recover a usable past. Postmodern nostalgia, it would seem, requires no such basis in historical truth. In addition, postmodern nostalgia is more mediated by culture than are earlier forms of nostalgia. Thus, nostalgic memories of the 1950s tend to focus not on the historical reality of the decade (which was largely grim) but on the culture of the decade (which contained exciting new energies in the form of the emergent phenomenon of rock 'n' roll music). By focusing on culture, postmodern representations of the past tend to be doubly mediated because they are representations of remembered representations.

Further, postmodern nostalgia is a far more commercial phenomenon than were its earlier forms; like everything else in the postmodern world, postmodern nostalgia is thoroughly commodified. As consumer capitalism runs at higher and higher speeds, cultural styles change more and more rapidly, thus encouraging the consumption of new cultural artifacts at an increasing pace. Yet, even as the market system renders culture obsolete more and more rapidly, it also attempts to maximize profits by recycling earlier culture styles as nostalgia products. Postmodern nostalgia is largely a product of this attempt.

What's more, this conversion of nostalgia into a marketing strategy disengages it from memories of any specific historical past and allows it to float freely through different periods. Like all commodities, commodified visions of the past are completely interchangeable. Thus, as Jameson has emphasized, postmodern nostalgia is thoroughly spatialized. The past, in the postmodern imagination, is no longer figured as part of a process that makes it the prehistory of the present, but is instead a mere museum of static images, a "set of dusty spectacles" (*Postmodernism*, 18). Postmodern nostalgia is historically nonspecific and can easily shift from one period to another. Indeed, because all time periods become interchangeable commodities, postmodern nostalgia need not even focus on the past at all but can focus on the present or even the future. In short, the postmodern version of nostalgia, more profoundly than earlier forms, involves memories of something that never was, much in the manner that the postmodern simulacrum of Jean Baudrillard involves reproductions of a nonexistent original. Thus, postmodern nostalgia films produce fantasy images of, say, the 1950s that have little or no basis in actual historical memories of the decade. In addition, postmodern nostalgia is a primarily stylistic movement, a sort of imitation of earlier forms of nostalgia that lacks the utopian longing for a better world that seems to be the motivation of the nostalgia in such works as the classic Hollywood films discussed by Flinn.

On the other hand, music may be even more central to the phenomenon of postmodern nostalgia than it is to Flinn's "classical" nostalgia. The films of David Lynch immediately come to mind here. Thus, the oddly nonspecific nostalgic tone of both *Blue Velvet* (1986) and *Mulholland Drive* (2001) is enhanced by Angelo Badalamenti's scores, which range over various styles that one might associate with a variety of periods, but produce a vaguely old-fashioned feel. Meanwhile, in both films Badalamenti's often-jazzy original score is supplemented by well-known popular music, usually from the 1950s and early 1960s. Roy Orbison, for example, looms large in both films, his own performance of "In Dreams" being key to the soundtrack of *Blue Velvet*, while a crucial scene in *Mulholland Drive* features a Spanish-language performance of Orbison's "Crying." On the other hand, Dean Stockwell's weird pantomime of "In Dreams" in *Blue Velvet* is decidedly creepy and anything but nostalgic.

The performance of "Crying" in *Mulholland Drive* is also a pantomime, though it features Rebekah Del Rio lip-synching her own emotionally compelling Spanish-language rendition of the song. In addition, the film-within-a-film that is being made in *Mulholland Drive* seems to be a musical featuring music from around the beginning of the 1960s, well within the period of the long 1950s. In one decisive scene, director Adam Kesher (Justin Theroux) auditions actresses for the lead role in his film. The auditions consist entirely of lip-synching recordings of Connie Stevens's 1960 hit "Sixteen Reasons" and Linda Scott's 1961 pop update of the 1932 Oscar Hammerstein and Jerome Kern show tune "I've Told Every Little Star." This scene can thus be taken as *Mulholland Drive*'s acknowledgment of its own construction from preexisting materials, though the nature of this scene also leaves open the possibility that *Mulholland Drive* is criticizing the tendency of more conventional Hollywood films to recycle such materials, thus presumably proclaiming its own relative creativity.

Music is also crucial to Lynch's *Wild at Heart* (1990)—in this case, the music of Elvis Presley, perhaps the quintessential American musical icon. In particular, one of the central characters, ex-con Sailor Ripley (Nicholas Cage), is an Elvis Presley lover who essentially keeps up a running Elvis impression through the entire film—complete with several Elvis-like musical performances. Like *Blue Velvet*, *Wild at Heart* makes significant use of Lynch's trademark shots of raging flames (accompanied by exaggerated sound effects) to punctuate moments of passion or violence, a symbol that would, like Lynch's general penchant for clichés, be almost embarrassingly hackneyed were it not for the possibility of reading the cliché as an intentional commentary on the poverty of symbolism available to the postmodernist artist. Here, in fact, the flame images are especially foregrounded (and even integrated into the plot), though, if anything, this foregrounding makes the symbolic use of this image seem even more of a cliché.

Blue Velvet was excoriated by some reviewers as pornographic and by others as just plain stupid, but it made Lynch a major figure in American film, winning him a National Society of Film Critics award for best director and garnering an Oscar nomination in the same category. *Wild at Heart* then won the Palme d'Or at the Cannes Film Festival, announcing Lynch's arrival as an "art" director of international repute. Yet *Wild at Heart*, despite its continuing gestures toward avantgarde style, is even campier than *Blue Velvet*. The film's plot is simple. Ripley is released from prison after doing nearly two years for manslaughter, having beaten a man to death for insulting his girlfriend, Lula Fortune (Laura Dern). He immediately returns to his torrid relationship with Lula, over the objections of her witchlike mother, Marietta Fortune (Diane Ladd), who responds by hiring two different hit men (both apparently lovers of hers) to kill Ripley. Ripley and Lula then decide to embark on a cross-country joyride, thus breaking the terms of his parole. They make it as far as the town of Big Tuna, Texas, with the two hit men in hot pursuit, though one arranges to have the other killed in a weird voodoo-like ritual along the way. Ripley and Lula then encounter a third man who has apparently also been contracted to kill Ripley, in the person of the spectacularly sleazy Bobby Peru, played by Willem Dafoe in a preposterously over-the-top turn that fits in perfectly well with the string of other bizarre characters the two lovers have encountered in the course of their travels. Ultimately, Peru is killed by police while in the process of trying to kill Ripley, but he has also gotten Ripley involved in an armed robbery that results in the latter's return to prison for another six-year term. All ends well, though: the film closes with a pastiche of the typical happy Hollywood ending as Ripley is again released, rejoining Lula (and their now five-year-old son) and declaring his love by singing to her (with vocal backgrounds and musical accompaniment that come from out of nowhere) his rendition of Elvis's *Love Me Tender*—which he had earlier promised to sing only to the woman with whom he planned to spend the rest of his life.

Wild at Heart provides us with an internal statement of its "theme," this time in Lula's declaration "This whole world's wild at heart and weird on top," which is pretty much the same theme as *Blue Velvet's* mantra-like "It's a strange world," though in this case the protagonists are more worldly and already wild themselves, even before they encounter the weirdness and perversion that meets them in the film. Whereas *Blue Velvet* draws on genres such as the erotic thriller, the coming-of-age story, and the noir crime story, *Wild at Heart* is a sort of combination of the quest narrative and the couple-on-the-run narrative, in the mode of *Bonnie and Clyde* (1967), though its real predecessor (and the one to which it continually and overtly refers) is *The Wizard of Oz* (1939). This latter connection creates tremendous irony, given the "adult" subject matter of *Wild at Heart*, while *The Wizard of Oz* is often considered the archetypal American children's film. However, it is also a film with considerable dark undertones, which are highlighted through the intertextual dialogue with *Wild at Heart*. Meanwhile, this dialogue also connects *The Wizard of Oz* with the tradition of the "road" narrative, perhaps the quintessential American genre.

The *Wizard of Oz* is also a musical, and its importance to Lynch suggests the importance of music to Lynch's continual filmic echoes of the past. It is certainly the case that, as with the classical films of the 1930s and 1940s, music is quite often central to the nostalgic visions embedded in postmodern films. However, while the earlier movies located the sounds of an idealized past in works of high culture, postmodern nostalgia films tend to draw upon the popular music of earlier eras, suggesting another form of the breakdown of the boundaries between high and low culture that has so often been cited as a key aspect of postmodernism. Of course, some postmodern films have used the same romantic nineteenth-century music as their classic predecessors. For example, Woody Allen's *A Midsummer Night's Sex Comedy* (1982) features the music of Felix Mendelssohn (whose first major composition was the Overture to *A Midsummer Night's Dream*) to help create atmospheric effects for its fin de siècle setting. On the other hand, Mendelssohn's music is actually too old for the period involved, while Allen himself disrupts the period atmosphere by going through the whole film playing pretty much the same character he plays in all of his contemporary works. As a result, the romantic music is somewhat destabilized, giving its use an ironic quality that the use of such music does not have in the films of the 1930s and 1940s. In addition, Allen's film is overtly based on a combination of Shakespeare's *A Midsummer Night's Dream* and Ingmar Bergman's *Smiles of a Summer Night* (1955), mixing Renaissance and modern sources to create a sense of timelessness, or at least ahistoricity.

Allen's films often feature nostalgic references to the period from the 1920s to the 1940s. In fact, Allen is virtually never nostalgic about the

1950s, so his films as a whole constitute an important reminder that post-modern nostalgia need not necessarily be focused on that particular decade. Indeed, Allen's most direct thematization of fifties musical nostalgia is highly ironic. *Broadway Danny Rose* (1984) centers on the attempts of a struggling agent (played by Allen) to cash in on the nostalgia craze in promoting the career of has-been lounge singer Lou Canova (Nick Apollo Forte), who had scored one minor hit twenty-five years earlier, back in the 1950s. Not surprisingly, Allen, one of America's most nostalgic film-makers, does not particularly criticize nostalgia itself, though he does comment on its ruthless exploitation for commercial purposes by having Canova jump to a different agent just as his career is about to take off thanks to the boost it has received from the nostalgia boom. Meanwhile, this view of fifties nostalgia as a commercial enterprise may help to explain Allen's tendency to locate his own nostalgic visions in the thirties and forties, a presumably less thoroughly commodified age.

Sometimes Allen even uses music or other images from those decades to lend a nostalgic tone to films that are set in the present, as in the Gershwin score and black-and-white photography of *Manhattan* (1979). In fact, in a clear indication of the spatialization of history in the post-modern imagination, the use of music in postmodern film is so historically nonspecific that it can slide freely around from one time frame to another. In one recent phenomenon, ironic effects are created through the anachronistic use of contemporary popular music in films set in the past. Such films at first seem antinostalgic, suggesting a preference for contemporary culture over that of the past, but they really just indicate the reversibility of postmodern nostalgia and the interchangeability of past and present in a cultural vision that converts all of history into a cafeteria line of commodified images.

A Knight's Tale (2001) represents a telling example of this sort of use of popular music in postmodernist film. Set in the Middle Ages, the film makes absolutely no pretense to historical accuracy but instead revels in its own projection of modern attitudes and psychologies into the past. It thus represents a classic example of the phenomenon Georg Lukács describes as "modernization," by which the bourgeois historical novel of the late nineteenth century gradually lost touch with a genuinely historical past by increasingly treating it as identical to the present, except more violent and colorful. Thus, for Lukács, novels such as Gustave Flaubert's *Salammbô* (1862) represent an attempt to "escape from the triviality of modern bourgeois life" by depicting an exotic past in which "inhumanity, cruelty, atrocity and brutality become substitutes for the lost greatness of real history" (Lukács, 192–93).

A Knight's Tale, then, attempts to escape the triviality and routinization of life under late capitalism by locating its thoroughly modern story
in the presumably more heroic world of the Middle Ages. The film
focuses on William Thatcher (Heath Ledger), a poor boy whose anachronistically ambitious father taught him not to accept the limitations of
his class but to strive to attain more in life. Thatcher takes full advantage
of this life, seizing an opportunity to pose as a nobleman so that he can
compete as a knight on the European pro jousting circuit, culminating
in the world championships in London. Along the way, he wins the love
of a beautiful princess and the respect of an unconventional prince, who
dubs him a legitimate knight near the end of the film. Needless to say,
Thatcher also wins the world championship, then prepares to live happily ever after with his princess.

A Knight's Tale is thus not a medieval story at all but a modern
sports movie intended for modern audiences. As such, it is even more
disengaged from history than is *Salammbô*. Not only is the film peopled
by thoroughly modern individuals but, unlike the depiction of ancient
Carthage in *Salammbô*, it does not even bother to depict the Middle
Ages as especially violent. Granted, violence is the very heart of the film,
and the numerous scenes of jousting and swordplay are its crucial
scenes. But these scenes are not especially bloody by the standards of
contemporary cinema. Moreover, by containing its violence within sport,
rather than genuine combat, the film significantly limits the level of
bloodshed that actually occurs. Thus, rather than depict a past that is
like the present, only bloodier, *A Knight's Tale* presents a past that is like
the present, period.

In addition, *A Knight's Tale* presents its anachronistic treatment of
the Middle Ages as a sort of running joke for the amusement of its audience. Thus, one of the central characters is Geoffrey Chaucer (Paul Bet-
tany), an aspiring author who travels about Europe seeking grist for his
literary mill. He is presented as a sort of huckster and public relations
expert, suggesting that, even in the Middle Ages, the most lucrative use
for his facility with language would be to go into advertising. Even more
overt is the use of music, which dramatically announces the film's own
awareness of its ahistoricity. In an early scene, for example, the crowd
awaiting a jousting tournament sings and claps along to the strains of
Queen's "We Are the Champions," just as the crowd at a modern
American football game might do. Later, when William dances with his
princess for the first time, he does so to the strains of David Bowie's
"Golden Years," and the film ends with AC/DC's "You Shook Me All
Night Long."

The entire soundtrack of *A Knight's Tale* is made up of classic rock tunes, which leaves no doubt that the film is uninterested in an authentic account of medieval experience. Here the use of classic rock, rather than absolutely contemporary popular music, does give the soundtrack an air of pastness, but it also flattens history, treating the past as a homogeneous period that runs from the Middle Ages to the 1980s. Of course, this soundtrack has strong economic motivations as well. For one thing, it joins the modernized plot and characters in an attempt to attract young audiences, who would likely be uninterested in a genuine depiction of the Middle Ages. For another, it creates opportunities for the marketing of a soundtrack album.

Music is also crucial to the impact of Sofia Coppola's *Marie Antoinette* (2006), a historical biopic that follows the life of its title character, beginning with her betrothal to the dauphin of France at age fourteen. It then tells the story of her rise to the throne and her life as queen, up to her arrest, along with her husband, then King Louis XVI, during the French Revolution. It stops short, however, of their subsequent beheadings. *Marie Antoinette* is at first glance an authentic period piece, with lavish costuming and elaborate settings. The film was shot on location in Paris, including shooting in the actual palace at Versailles. However, a closer look shows that the film is just slightly out of kilter. In addition to slight historical inconsistencies, the colors of the film are not quite right; they are, in fact, extremely bright, as is the lighting, which gives the film an oddly contemporary look, despite the period settings and costumes. Similarly, Kirsten Dunst's performance in the title role makes Marie (who is a teenager during much of the film) seem very much like a young woman of the early twenty-first century. Jason Schwartzman similarly plays Louis as a sort of clueless modern youth, who would seem more at home playing video games than ruling a nation. The effect of the lighting and performances is fairly subtle, though it is reinforced by less subtle moments, as when a pan shot showing us Marie's extensive collection of expensive, custom-designed shoes reveals that the young woman owns a pair of very modern-looking tennis shoes. Finally, the music is again a very big part of the blurring of historical setting that is so crucial to this film. While much of the soundtrack has the classic, romantic feel that one might expect from a period piece, this conventional music is also interlaced with a liberal dose of modern pop and punk music, again suggesting, in a very postmodern way, the interchangeability of Marie's historical setting and our own.

The anachronistic music is also crucial to Baz Luhrmann's *Moulin Rouge!* (2001), for which a crucial advertising strategy was the release of a popular music video featuring a collection of contemporary female pop stars reprising Patti Labelle's classic "Lady Marmalade" while dressed in costumes intended to suggest the dress of can-can dancers at the original Moulin Rouge in Paris. The musical choice was appropriate for this highly theatrical film, Labelle's song having been introduced in her own highly theatrical performance at the Metropolitan Opera House (the first performance there by an African-American act) in 1974. The strategy of marketing the film via a music video was appropriate as well. The film takes its own editing style largely from music videos, epitomizing the use of postmodern editing techniques. As such, it employs a panoply of contemporary devices to produce a cinematic spectacle that supposedly reproduces for contemporary audiences the spectacular experience that was what audiences in the real Moulin Rouge would have experienced at the end of the nineteenth century—and at the beginning of the modern age.

Though set in Paris in the late 1800s, *Moulin Rouge!* takes its music—and even much of its dialogue—from late twentieth-century sources. To an extent, the anachronistic music and dialogue are merely a running joke, though the film also seems to want to suggest that the anachronism is not as severe as it appears; it goes out of its way to present fin de siècle Paris as a crucial historical turning point when the postmodern sensibilities represented in the film were first born among the bohemian "Children of the Revolution." Exactly what these sensibilities are, however, is a bit confused, as the film itself is a weird mixture of old-fashioned romanticism and overtly trendy postmodern spectacle.

In fact, *Moulin Rouge!* is confused in all sorts of ways. Like all of the films in Luhrmann's "Red Curtain" trilogy,[2] it is built on a central opposition between sincere youthful innocence and stodgy bourgeois conformism. However, in this case, youthful "innocence" is represented primarily by a collection of supposedly idealistic Parisian bohemians, headed by painter Henri de Toulouse-Lautrec (played to great comic effect by John Leguizamo), himself historically an aristocratic icon of decadence and debauchery.[3] Meanwhile, the principal representative of the bourgeois establishment is not a bourgeois at all, but another aristocrat, the evil Duke (Richard Roxburgh, in another hilarious comic turn). The over-the-top performances of both Leguizamo and Roxburgh give their characters a cartoonish quality, but then *Moulin Rouge!* never pretends to realism or psychological depth. The main actual bourgeois figure in the film is impresario Harold Zidler (Jim Broadbent), owner and operator of the Moulin Rouge (based on a real-world figure). The film's Zidler, however, is a figure not of conformism but of innovation, as he hopes to convert his establishment from a seedy club to a respectable modern theater, though in fact the club seems lavishly spectacular from the very beginning, looking almost more like Studio 54 than a turn-of-the-twentieth-century club. The historical Zidler, incidentally, was also a modernizer, the newfangled electric lights with which he was fascinated and with which the club was liberally adorned reportedly having been for some almost as big an attraction as the famous dancing girls. Indeed, the historical Moulin Rouge was a combination of art, technology, and pure sex—much like the cinema that was, at the very same time, being born, with Parisians like the Lumière brothers on the forefront. Luhrmann's focus on the club can thus be read as a reflexive commentary on filmdom itself.

The main plot of *Moulin Rouge!* is pure cliché, focusing on the attempts of two young lovers to get together despite the obstacles placed in their way by a society that does not share their youthful passion and disregard for convention. In this, Luhrmann again reproduces the plots of his earlier films, especially *William Shakespeare's Romeo and Juliet* (1996), which updated an old literary chestnut for the MTV generation, complete with a modern setting and rock soundtrack. In *Moulin Rouge!*, however, the two lovers are themselves even more clichéd than the plot. One is Satine (Nicole Kidman), a whore with a heart of gold who happens also to be the star of the Moulin Rouge stage show, where she flaunts her availability for purchase by wowing the audience with elaborately produced performances of numbers such as Marilyn Monroe's "Diamonds Are a Girl's Best Friend" and Madonna's "Material Girl." The other lover is Christian (Ewan McGregor), a fledgling writer who can see through the gaudy surface to recognize Satine's inner goodness.

Or something like that. Actually, the plot of *Moulin Rouge!* is pretty much beside the point. In fact, as if to make sure that plot is secondary, Luhrmann gives away the ending by beginning the film in 1900 as Christian looks back on and attempts to write about events of the year before. The rest of the film is then shown in flashback, and attentive viewers know from the very beginning that the love of Christian and Satine is doomed by her impending death. The attempts of Christian to win Satine away from the evil Duke (while still managing to get the Duke to finance the embedded show—appropriately titled "Spectacular Spectacular"—that he is writing as a star vehicle for Satine) are thus rather pointless.

Everything about *Moulin Rouge!*, in fact, is avowedly pointless, except for the spectacle itself. But the spectacle is dazzling, and the film is an impressive visual achievement, embracing its postmodern look in a way that differs dramatically from the intentionally retro look of the postmodern nostalgia films discussed by Jameson. Still, *Moulin Rouge!* is a quintessential postmodernist film, epitomizing both Guy Debord's notion of the "society of the spectacle" and Jameson's view of postmodern culture as flat and superficial. Moreover, despite its modernization of the fin de siècle setting and its complete disavowal of a nostalgic aesthetic, the film remains nostalgic in its obvious longing for a time when romance of the kind embodied in the plot was still possible as something other than a joke or a mere frame on which to hang spectacular visuals.

Luhrmann's location of this time at the end of the nineteenth century participates in a far-ranging postmodern tendency to recycle the monuments of Victorian culture as the stuff of postmodernism. *Bram Stoker's Dracula* (1992), Francis Ford Coppola's contribution to the vampire genre, is one of the leading examples of this phenomenon, its title calling attention to its Victorian source, somewhat in the same nostalgic way Luhrmann's *William Shakespeare's Romeo and Juliet* announces its source—except that Luhrmann's identification of Shakespeare is surely unnecessary, although it does suggest the faithful way in which most of the dialogue is taken directly from Shakespeare's original script. Yet this script is now placed in such a foreign environment (a kind of modern-day urban dystopia) that one could argue that this film takes more liberties with its Shakespearean original than any of the other various film adaptations of the play, at least until Andrzej Bartkowiak later made it into a modern martial arts film in *Romeo Must Die* (2000).

Despite such examples of free-roaming nostalgia and even reverse nostalgia, it is certainly the case that the most prominent nostalgic visions in recent American culture have focused on the 1950s, though one needs here to extend the "fifties" to the period of 1946–1964. For example, one of the most prominent examples of fifties nostalgia in American pop culture is the long-running *Happy Days* television series (ABC, 1974–1984), which is, in fact, set in the early 1960s. *Happy Days*, meanwhile, was essentially a spin-off of *American Graffiti*, which Jameson sees as perhaps the best example of the attempts of American cinema to capture the "mesmerizing lost reality of the Eisenhower era" (*Postmodernism*, 19). Yet *American Graffiti* is actually set in 1962, midway through the brief Kennedy presidency. Nevertheless, postmodern nostalgia is a complex and historically ambiguous phenomenon, so Jameson is not necessarily wrong here. He is, in fact, surely right.

Indeed, *American Graffiti* often goes out of its way to evoke the feel of the Eisenhower years, as in its use of the 1955 classic "Rock around the Clock" as its title music. Still, this "fifties" film is really more about the end of the 1950s than the 1950s proper. It details the experiences of four recent high school graduates and their friends during one night at the end of the summer of 1962. It is an eventful night, but the actual events are largely irrelevant. *American Graffiti* is all about evoking the atmosphere of the time, which is accomplished with significant aid from a soundtrack loaded with hits from the 1950s by such stars as Bill Haley and the Comets, Buddy Holly, the Big Bopper, Chuck Berry, Frankie Lymon, and the Platters. There is also a smattering of distinctively 1960s-style music by artists such as the Beach Boys, used to indicate the coming of new times.

One of the main characters, hot-rod king John Milner (Paul Le Mat), angrily dismisses this new music as "shit." Milner is intensely aware of changing times, already waxing nostalgic for the good old days of the 1950s, though he declares that he, unlike friends Steve Bolander (Ronnie Howard) and Curt Henderson (Richard Dreyfuss), will not miss high school at all. Steve and Curt, meanwhile, are headed for even more obvious changes. Good students in high school, they are to leave town the next day, headed east to start college. By placing its action on this particularly pivotal night, *American Graffiti* makes quite clear that it seeks, in an almost allegorical fashion, to parallel the transition of its protagonists from the simpler days of childhood to the more complex days of adulthood with the concurrent shift in American society from the sureties of the fifties to the more uncertain times of the sixties.

American Graffiti clearly portrays this transition as a loss, as one might expect a nostalgia film to do. As Jeff Smith notes, "The particular selection of songs serves to romanticize the late fifties and early sixties as a lost Golden Age" (177). Further, we learn from on-screen text inserts at the end of the film that Milner would be killed by a drunk driver in 1964, while another of the major characters, Terry "the Toad" Fields (Charles Martin Smith), would soon be lost in Vietnam. Steve, the dreamer who envisions an exiting life of adventure and achievement beyond the bounds of small-town life, succumbs to bourgeois routine and ends up in the banal position of a small-town insurance agent. The only character who might conceivably be going on to bigger and better things is Curt, who, we are told, becomes a writer. We are also informed that he will be living in Canada, but not whether he is a successful writer nor whether he moved to Canada to avoid the draft. Still, it is clearly possible to infer from this information that, within the troubled environment of the 1960s, one must leave the United States altogether to have any hope of success.

By 1962, as Milner notes, the good old days, even of rock music, are over. Thus, complaining about the new surf music, he concludes that "rock 'n' roll's been going downhill since Buddy Holly died." Of course, Milner's vision of the death of Holly as the end of an era is hardly unique. Holly's premature death, at age 22, in a February 3, 1959, plane crash has functioned ever since as one of the mythic moments in rock-and-roll history, "the day the music died." Not surprisingly, given the nostalgia therefore attached to Holly, his brief but incredibly influential career itself became the subject of a nostalgia film, the 1978 biopic *The Buddy Holly Story*. That film includes few details about the 1950s as a decade, though there are a few iconic moments, as when Holly and his wife-to-be attend the screening of a movie at which the audience wears 3-D glasses, one of the trademark images of the 1950s. The focus of the film is on Holly's music, which star Gary Busey memorably and abundantly performs in what can only be described as a simulation (rather than imitation) of Holly's own sound. That is, Busey does not attempt to sound like Holly actually sounded but to capture the spirit of Holly's music in a way that might resemble the way audiences might recall Holly having sounded.

Jameson describes *American Graffiti* as the "inaugural film" in a new wave of cinematic nostalgia, and the film's success certainly gave nostalgia a tremendous marketing boost. The film also gave it a new hipness as compared, say, to Peter Bogdanovich's much bleaker *The Last Picture Show* (1971), a nostalgia film that locates the end of the good old days as early as the film's setting in 1952 and 1953, associating (albeit in a subtle and indirect way) this end not with the premature death of Buddy Holly in 1959 but with the premature death of Hank Williams Sr. on January 1, 1953, at the age of twenty-nine. As the title indicates, motion pictures are also an important source of nostalgia here. For one thing, the impending death of the small Texas prairie town in *The Last Picture Show* is crucially marked by the closing of the town's only movie house. For another, one of the last films seen in the movie house is Howard Hawks's classic western *Red River* (1948), which details the vital frontier days of the nineteenth century, when Texas was moving toward the future, as opposed to the early 1950s, when the frontier is closed and the heroic Texas is receding into the past.

Still, the music of Williams, which completely dominates the soundtrack of *The Last Picture Show*, is the principal source of the film's air of nostalgia. The bulk of the film is set in 1952 (when many of the main characters are in their last year of high school), and the songs of Williams play constantly on radios, jukeboxes, and record players. Then, in the last segment of the story, set in 1953, Williams's music disappears, marking the fact that he has in the meantime died, though his death is never specifically mentioned in the film. As Jeff Smith argues, Williams's self-destruction via substance abuse can itself be read as a commentary on the decadence of the American society represented in the film as past its prime and already in an advanced state of decay, leaving the movie's young protagonists nothing to look forward to but "a life of quiet desperation, desolation, and death" (171). On the other hand, one can also read Williams's music in the film as an emblem of a more authentic folk-based culture that would soon be destroyed by the advancing commercialization of American music. After all, Williams died seven days before the eighteenth birthday of Elvis Presley, which would make Elvis approximately the same age as the principal characters in the film and his music the music of the fallen world in which they will live their adult lives.[4]

By 1974, the fifties nostalgia craze was so well established that it had already become an object of film parody. In particular, Brian De Palma, in *Phantom of the Paradise* (1974), is bitterly (if comically) critical of nostalgia itself as a pure marketing ploy. Essentially a rock remake of *Phantom of the Opera*, *Phantom of the Paradise* also includes a strong dose of Goethe's *Faust* with side glances at Oscar Wilde's *The Picture of Dorian Gray*, Alfred Hitchcock's *Psycho* (1960), and John Frankenheimer's *The Manchurian Candidate* (1962), all combined in a complex postmodern intertextual and intergeneric stew. In the meantime, the film satirizes not only the greed and ambition that pervade the music business (and show business in general) but also the lust of audiences for spectacular entertainment, especially if it involves violence and death. The film, while it has its moments of comedy and camp, is thus considerably darker and more bitter than the better known *The Rocky Horror Picture Show*, which followed it a year later, even though it anticipates so many of the themes and motifs of the later film. *Phantom of the Paradise* is a kind of explanatory prologue to the spectacular violence that would inform most of De Palma's subsequent films (suggesting that this violence is supplied in response to audience demand), while also serving as a predecessor to such later satirical films as Oliver Stone's *Natural Born Killers* (1994).

Phantom of the Paradise begins as Swan (Paul Williams), an ultra-successful rock impresario, is introduced in a voiceover by Rod Serling, thus alluding to *The Twilight Zone* and immediately evoking a form of 1950s nostalgia. Among other things, this voiceover informs us that Swan is the guiding force behind the Juicy Fruits, a manufactured musical group that, we are told, "singlehandedly gave birth to the nostalgia wave in the 1970s." Later, when profits from the fifties nostalgia craze begin to wane, Swan transforms the Juicy Fruits into the Beach Bums, a Beach Boys retread, hoping thereby to cash in on sixties nostalgia.

If *American Graffiti*, *Phantom of the Paradise*, and, to an extent, *The Last Picture Show* are all about the music, the same, oddly enough, cannot be said for the most important example of the 1950s nostalgia musical. *Grease*, released in 1978, is clearly set in the 1950s, though apparently very late in the decade, as evidenced by the fact that *The Blob* (first released in 1958) is playing at a drive-in in the film and that diegetic music such as Ritchie Valens's "La Bamba" (released at the beginning of 1959) is heard.[5] On the other hand, the music of *Grease* is somewhat problematic in terms of dates. Though the film is a legitimate, old-style musical, its major musical numbers, performed by pop icons Olivia Newton-John and John Travolta, are very much in the style of the 1970s, as is the well-known title song, sung by Frankie Valli. Indeed, the contemporaneity of the music (along with the popularity of the stars) largely accounts for the fact that the film and its soundtrack album were such big hits at the time and that the film was rereleased in 1998, this time amid a wave of nostalgia for the 1970s—or perhaps of nineties nostalgia for seventies nostalgia for the fifties, a phenomenon of which *Pulp Fiction* was a key founding text in 1994, though Tarantino's earlier *Reservoir Dogs* (1992) used a soundtrack that came primarily from the 1970s as well and even featured a radio program devoted to seventies nostalgia.[6]

The only major musical number in *Grease* that is even vaguely in the style of the 1950s is Travolta's campy rendition of "Grease Lightnin'," a paean to the old car that he and his fellow "T-Birds" plan to transform into a sexy hot rod. Even here the risqué lyrics (the car, we learn, will be a real "pussy wagon" once it is fixed up) would be entirely out of place in the world of 1950s rock (though maybe not in the blues music from which rock evolved), but the sound is reasonably authentic for the time, especially as Travolta does Elvis even more overtly in this number than in the rest of the film. Tellingly, however, the number is transformed midway into a dream sequence, with a pure white background and exaggerated costumes, presumably to underline the boys' fantasies about the car, but also indirectly acknowledging the way in which the version of the 1950s presented in the film is pure fantasy.

Despite its status as a musical (and a prominent appearance in the film by Sha-Na-Na, the ultimate fifties nostalgia group), *Grease* is, as a 1950s nostalgia film, more about the look (especially the eponymous greased hair) than the sound, and even the look is highly stylized, representing an obvious, rather campy, simulacrum of 1950s teen style rather than an attempt at authentic representation of the sort that appears in *American Graffiti*. Meanwhile, numerous motifs (such as the crucial drag race and the basic image of high school delinquents) in *Grease* seem lifted directly from 1950s films such as Nicholas Ray's *Rebel without a Cause* (1955) or Richard Brooks's *The Blackboard Jungle* (1955), but aspects of these earlier films that had been serious or even tragic are now played for light comedy. In *Grease*, all of the problems encountered by the youthful protagonists are easily solved and largely without consequences, though this light tone has less to do with a genuine sense of the late 1950s as a simpler time than with the youth and innocence (they may be delinquents, but they are benevolent ones) of the main characters, who are all in their senior year at Southern California's Rydell High.

Then again, postmodern nostalgia is always a matter of fantasy, not reality, even when it is a matter of personal, rather than historical, memory. In their portrayal of the end of the 1950s within the context of coming-of-age stories, both *Grease* and *American Graffiti* make obvious at least one major reason for the seeming desire of the 1970s to be nostalgic for the 1950s: the large first generation of baby boomers, who grew up in the long 1950s and graduated from high school at the end of that period, had now spent ten years or so in an adult world punctuated by the Vietnam War, Watergate, and the difficult economic times of the 1970s.[7] Little wonder that they looked wistfully back on their own childhood years in the 1950s as simpler and easier times—or, more accurately, wished that they could. This nostalgia opened up a wide variety of marketing and merchandising opportunities for U.S. corporations, which correspondingly invested heavily in advertising designed to stimulate nostalgia for the 1950s, even as much American advertising in the 1960s had overtly rejected the 1950s as a gray time of mind-numbing conformism.[8]

That this literal sort of nostalgia was somewhat at odds with the logic of consumer capitalism, with its demands for incessant innovation and forward movement, merely indicates the contradictory nature of capitalism itself. Capitalism is nothing if not contradictory, and the same can certainly be said for postmodern nostalgia films. Thus, if *American Graffiti* focuses on the end of the 1950s as a fall from grace, Martin Davidson's rather obscure *Eddie and the Cruisers* (1983) is much more ambivalent about this transition. Set in 1982, it centers on the nostalgic revival of the music of a fictional rock group that hit the top of the rock charts with a fifties-style album in 1963, then recorded one more (unreleased) album in early 1964, shortly before the (apparent) death of their leader, Eddie Wilson (Michael Paré), in an auto accident. The new interest in the group's music spurs television journalist Maggie Foley (Ellen Barkin) to do a feature on the band, and most of the film's narrative involves her interviews with the surviving band members. She also seeks to recover the tapes of the unreleased album, which disappeared shortly after Eddie's death—and after the record company refused to release the album because it was nothing like the band's earlier music.

Placing the band's one big moment in the turning-point year of 1963 puts them on the cusp of history. Indeed, when the tapes of the missing album (entitled *Season in Hell*) are finally discovered and released, it becomes clear that the album, rather than repeating the band's earlier success in 1950s-style music, looked forward to the new music of the 1960s. As Foley describes it in her feature report, "The innocence of the fifties was over, and so was rock 'n' roll as we knew it. We were entering a new age, an age of confusion, an age of passion, of commitment. Eddie Wilson saw it coming. *Season in Hell* is a total innovation for its time. It was a signal of greatness to come."

Eddie and the Cruisers views the 1950s as a simpler and more innocent time, partly because the band members were young then and are now, in the early 1980s, fast approaching middle age. It thus uses the motif of personal aging and maturation to mirror the coming of age (and growing cynicism) of America at the end of the 1950s. At the same time, the film is less nostalgic for the 1950s than for the *end* of the 1950s. That is, it seems to yearn for a time when it was still possible to envision, and even participate in, a crucial turning point that might lead to fundamental changes in the world.

John Waters's *Hairspray* (1988) also uses music to identify the year 1963 as the end of an era, in this case as the end of the era of racial segregation in Baltimore. In particular, *Hairspray* makes the integration of a local teen dance show (an *American Bandstand* look-alike) the key to the integration of Baltimore as a whole. Music and dancing are, in fact, the heart of *Hairspray*, in which Waters tones down the outrageousness of his earlier films to produce a relatively mainstream work that is only lightly campy in its presentation of the attempts of "chunky" teenager Tracey Turnblad (Rikki Lake) to win a place on the *Corny Collins Show* and, subsequently, to contribute to the integration of the show.

Tracey succeeds, of course, thus marking a turning point in Baltimore history, a moment that is clearly identified as the end of the 1950s and beginning of the 1960s. For example, Tracey, complaining of the conservatism of her mother (played by famed cross-dresser Divine), says, "You're so fifties." Later, the mother, eventually surrendering to the inevitability of the changes going on around her, later declares the birth of the 1960s: "It's the times. They're a changin'. Somethin's blowin' in the wind." Among other things, this string of Dylan quotes suggests that one change under way involves an increasing tendency to experience reality through the mediation of culture. It also suggests the ability of modern consumer capitalism to convert seemingly subversive cultural statements into cliché.

On the other hand, the change remarked by Mrs. Turnblad is figured in *Hairspray* as a moment of genuine liberation and as a victory for the downtrodden of all kinds. Thus, while race is the central issue in the film, Tracey's success also announces the availability of new horizons for women, even if they do not meet conventional standards of beauty. In addition, Waters, whose films collectively celebrate lower-class (in every sense of the word) culture, even makes class an issue here by making Tracey's success a sign of the triumph of her "upper lower class" family over the haughty, bourgeois Von Tussles (played by pop icons Sonny Bono and Debbie Harry, in an instance of inspired casting), whose daughter is ousted by Tracey as Miss Auto Show 1963. Indeed, the Von Tussles, who had earlier declared the Turnblads to be "white trash, plain and simple," wind up in disgrace, while the Turnblads and their African-American allies are triumphant, marking the arrival of the 1960s as the coming of a new age of opportunity for those who had formerly been disadvantaged by their race, class, gender, or even body type.

There is, it should be emphasized, nothing that is necessarily progressive in such celebrations of positive social and political change. Especially in a comedy such as *Hairspray*, vexing social problems are made to seem all too easily addressed, which does little to encourage viewers to want to participate in the difficult work of genuine political change. Indeed, by seeming to indicate that the problem of race was "solved" in the 1960s, *Hairspray* announces to contemporary audiences that they no longer need even to worry about racial injustice. On the other hand, *Hairspray* does suggest the possibility of an ongoing struggle in that the film's principal villains, the Von Tussles, remain unrepentant at the end of the film. They may have been rejected by most of the other characters, but they still regard themselves as superior to others on the basis of race and class. Furthermore, although they may be forced to integrate the amusement park they own, this will no doubt serve merely to increase their profits and provide them with additional resources to carry out their struggle against progress.

In *Hairspray*, Waters comically poses rock music as a subversive force that helps to break apart the repressive structure of 1950s society. In the even lighter *Cry-Baby* (1990), he does much the same, though this time locating the film in the midst of the 1950s, rather than at their end. *Cry-Baby* places even more emphasis on class than does *Hairspray*: if Tracey Turnblad is upper lower class, then Cry-Baby Walker (Johnny

Depp) is lower lower class, and damn proud of it. Meanwhile, the lower-class "Drapes" (Baltimore slang for greasers) are presented as benevolent and good-hearted white trashers who just want to be left alone but are constantly harassed by the upper-class squares, who hope to drive such trashy elements out of Baltimore altogether. As the two sides tangle, good-girl square Allison Vernon-Williams (Amy Locane) switches sides and finds true love with Cry-Baby, thus essentially traveling the arc taken by Sandy Olsen (Newton-John), who must become a bad girl in order to win the heart of bad boy Danny Zuko (Travolta) in *Grease*.

The class conflict of *Cry-Baby* is all in fun, of course: the squares are cartoonishly evil, while the Drapes are comically trashy but good-hearted: Confederate flags are a crucial part of their décor, but some of their best friends are black. The representation of the Drapes is aided by the inspired casting of Iggy Pop and Susan Tyrrell as Cry-Baby's grandparents and guardians (his parents having been executed in the electric chair). Among other things, the inclusion of these grandparents ensures that, here, the battle between Hip and Square, between liberation and repression, is couched purely in terms of class, whereas the normal 1950s scenario involves a more generational conflict between free-spirited teens and repressed, hypocritical oldsters. Meanwhile, the plot of *Cry-Baby* (what there is of it) is used merely to create an opportunity for presenting various light-hearted images of the two opposed cultures of stuffiness and trashiness. This opposition is also played out in the music, which, unlike in *Grease*, is all fifties-style, with the squares performing light, slow, elevator-music tunes, and the Drapes going in for down-and-dirty rock, with a clear "Negro" influence. Depp, in fact, does Elvis through the whole film—a much better and funnier Elvis than Travolta had in *Grease*, though Depp doesn't dance much and doesn't do his own singing, instead lip-synching to the voice of James Intveld.

The overall result in *Cry-Baby*, as in *Grease*, is a comic fantasy version of the 1950s, though this time it is even campier, especially given that it is populated by Waters's trademark oddball characters and kitschy mise-en-scène. The fifties again come out as a simpler time when problems could be solved with just a little effort and a good guitar, though the film does have a sort of dark undertone that carries reminders of the carcerality and injustice that were rampant in American society in the 1950s. Thus Cry-Baby (like *Hairspray*'s Tracey) is unfairly sent to reform school but (also like Tracey) wins his release rather easily, here winning the heart of Allison in the process. The 1950s also figure here as a time in which marginal groups such as the Drapes already embodied the countercultural impulses of the 1960s, thus exemplifying, though in comic form, Jameson's observation that some fifties nostalgia films—Coppola's much more serious *Rumble Fish* (1983) is his example—saw the 1950s as the time of "the first naïve innocence of the countercultural impulses of rock and roll and youth gangs" (*Postmodernism*, 19).

If films from *American Graffiti* to *Cry-Baby* allow audiences to look back on their own younger days, other fifties nostalgia films allow characters from later periods literally to travel back to the 1950s. Indeed, one of the most telling means of representing the 1950s in postmodern film involves the phenomenon of time travel, in which a character or characters from the film's present is transported back to the 1950s. Time-travel films have, in fact, become an important genre of postmodern science fiction, but movies such as Robert Zemeckis's *Back to the Future* (1985) and Coppola's *Peggy Sue Got Married* (1986) are hardly science fiction at all. These films are concerned very little with the imaginary technology of time travel or with the philosophical enigmas that it poses. Instead, they merely posit time travel of various sorts as a possibility in order to allow them to transport characters from their own present time into the setting of the 1950s.

Among other things, this tactic of placing a modern character in a past setting again represents a literalization of the phenomenon of "modernization" described by Lukács. One might, then, want to consider the possibility that the fascination with time travel (almost always involving travel into the past) in postmodern film might be taken as a sign of this same sort of loss of historical sense, taken to a more extreme level. One would not, of course, wish to place too much weight on the assumptions of a film such as *Back to the Future*, which uses the time-travel motif mainly to create opportunities for light comedy. In this film, mad scientist Dr. Emmett Brown (Christopher Lloyd) invents a time machine (a souped-up DeLorean, actually) that 1980s teenager Marty McFly (Michael J. Fox) inadvertently uses to travel back to 1955. In this case, the depicted difference between McFly's hometown of Hill Valley in 1955 and 1985 is relatively small, though telling. In particular, everything in the small town seems new, neat, and clean in 1955, while in 1985 it all seems to be in a state of both physical and moral decay, with an adult movie theater operating right off a town square that now seems dingy and diminished relative to its 1955 version. There is, however, a vague suggestion of political progress in that the town mayor of 1985 is a black man who had been scoffed at as a teenager in the 1950s when he first announced (acting on a suggestion from the time-traveling Marty) his ambition to become mayor.

Otherwise, the main interest in this film is generational, rather than historical, and the main plot involves Marty's encounters with his parents, who in 1955 are the same age (seventeen) he is (in 1985). Among other things, he must fend off the sexual advances of his lusty young mother (played by Lea Thompson), who seems to prefer Marty to George (Crispin Glover), his would-be father. In the process, Marty manages to change history so that his parents not only get together but end up happy and successful in the future, when they had originally been downtrodden losers. Much of the plot involves Marty's own efforts to get back to the future (thus the film's title), which he manages to do by conveying the secret of time travel to a 1955 version of Doc Brown, who uses information supplied by his 1985 self to "invent" time travel and thus project Marty back to 1985. Marty, a rock musician wannabe in 1985, also conveys the secret of rock music to Chuck Berry (who has been searching for a "new sound") by playing "Johnny B. Goode" at a high school dance, thus changing the course of American cultural history.

The latter motif is played for amusement, of course, though it does tend to portray rock music as a foreign influence that disrupted the 1950s rather than as an indigenous element of 1950s culture. It also carries the potentially problematic implication that rock music did not evolve from the early blues-based efforts of African-American musicians such as Berry but was in fact invented by a white middle-class teenager. On the other hand, one might also interpret this motif as a comment on the crucial role played by such teenagers as consumers in the evolution of rock music from the margins to the center of American popular culture. In any case, the film does not really address the typical time-travel paradoxes that inhere in the facts that Marty teaches Berry a musical style that he learned from Berry and that he conveys to Doc Brown a technology developed by Doc Brown.

Peggy Sue Got Married is even less interested in the technology of time travel or in time-travel paradoxes. In fact, it suggests (though never unequivocally states) that the sudden leap of protagonist Peggy Sue Kelcher Bodell (Kathleen Turner) from 1985 to 1960 is merely a fantasy brought about by her collapse due to an irregular heartbeat while she is attending her twenty-five-year high school reunion and is thus immersed in memories of the past. Nor is the film really concerned as much with a return to the 1950s as a return to teenagerhood. Nevertheless, Peggy Sue does seemingly travel back, and most of the film details her apparent experiences in 1960, when she is seventeen again but retains all of her memories of the subsequent twenty-five years.

These memories, presumably, will allow her to rectify some of the mistakes of her earlier years, including her early marriage to Charlie

Bodell (Nicolas Cage), which by 1985 has fallen apart. She does, in fact, manage to have a brief fling with Michael Fitzsimmons (Kevin J. O'Connor), the mysterious, hipster poet-type she always wished she had slept with. She also feeds some ideas about coming technologies to high-school science nerd Richard Norvik (Barry Miller), allowing him to go on to become a rich, famous inventor. She does not, however, manage to elude the attentions of Charlie, who charms her by giving up his dreams of being a rock star so that he can settle down in the family business, enabling him to marry and support Peggy Sue. Just as they are having sex for the first time, she awakes in a hospital back in 1985 with Charlie at her side, pledging to work hard to be a good husband if she will take him back.

Peggy Sue Got Married concentrates purely on the protagonist and her personal problems. It tells us essentially nothing about the 1950s as a decade. Nor is the film really nostalgic for that decade. In fact, it ultimately dismisses nostalgia by demonstrating that Peggy Sue's best chance to improve her life is to work on her problems in the present, rather than going back into the past to try to prevent the problems from developing. On the other hand, the film's very existence is conditioned by the prevalence of nostalgia for the fifties in the American culture of the 1970s and 1980s. By the 1990s, however, there were signs that the nostalgic energies of postmodern culture were beginning to slide into the sixties. Indeed, given the generational factor, it was almost inevitable that the 1970s nostalgia for the fifties would soon become a nostalgia for the sixties and even seventies as time went on, though it is also the case that boundaries between these decades began to erode in American cultural memory.

This postmodern collapse of historical distinctions is particularly striking in *Austin Powers, International Man of Mystery* (1997), a work that essentially transports the Cold War espionage drama of the 1960s to the late 1990s, thus producing a film that is nostalgic both for the free sex of the swinging sixties and for the simple black-and-white dichotomies of the Cold War. Music is here relatively secondary, though the film (like its two sequels) does include numerous references to the distinctive rock-music scene of the 1960s. Meanwhile, the conflation of the 1960s and the 1990s is achieved by a sort of reversal of the time-travel premise of films such as *Back to the Future*. Here, rather than having a person from the 1990s travel back to the 1960s, we have precisely the reverse: defeated by his nemesis Austin Powers (Mike Myers) in 1967, archvillain Dr. Evil (also played by Myers) cryogenically freezes himself and blasts off into space, to be later awakened at a time "when free love no longer reigns, and greed and corruption rule again." That time comes thirty years later, when he returns to the world of 1997, ready to work his evil magic once again. This vague bit of social criticism is reinforced by the fact that his lieutenant, Number Two (Robert Wagner), has now made Dr. Evil's former criminal empire into a perfectly respectable multinational conglomerate, suggesting the growing global power of a capitalism that is criminal at its roots. Indeed, Number Two ultimately rebels against Dr. Evil's plans to take over the world, declaring, "You don't realize there *is* no world any more. It's only corporations."

However, this potential critique of capitalism is undermined by the silliness of the entire film, which never takes itself seriously, even as it also pokes gentle fun at the culture of the 1960s, especially James Bond films and 1960s television series such as *The Avengers*, *Secret Agent*, and *The Man from U.N.C.L.E.* This fun centers on the figure of Powers, who has also been cryogenically frozen until the day when he would once again be needed to battle Dr. Evil. Powers and Dr. Evil are thus both walking anachronisms, figures of the 1960s propelled into the 1990s. Powers, a walking collection of clichés of the modish styles of the sixties (as the suave James Bond and secret agent John Drake were not), is particularly striking in this regard. Indeed, his style gradually overwhelms the contemporary style of 1997, and, by the final scenes, the entire film has descended into the style of the 1960s, with Powers's modern partner, Vanessa Kensington (Elizabeth Hurley), donning a tight-fitting leather bodysuit in the image of *The Avengers*'s Emma Peel.

The plot of *Austin Powers* is entirely secondary, of course. Powers and Kensington foil Dr. Evil's plans, driving him back into outer space, but the real point of the film is its sequence of pastiches of 1960s culture and its cavalcade of sight gags, many of them involving breasts or penises. There is little in the film to mark the sixties as a time of political activism and agitation for reform, though there is a suggestion that it might have been a time of freer sexuality and cooler rock music. Ultimately, however, the easy portability of 1960s style into the 1990s suggests a fundamental compatibility between the two decades.

Apparently, by the 1990s, nostalgia isn't what it used to be: 1990s nostalgia for the sixties is especially postmodern in that, unlike most nostalgic visions of the fifties, it is not even based on a fundamental fantasy of difference between the past and present. However, a vague desire for something different remains, even in the postmodern culture of the late twentieth century, which may explain the emergence of a wave of nostalgia for the 1930s, a time that was surely different from the 1980s and 1990s. Given the harsh economic realities of the Depression, the thirties might seem an odd focus for nostalgic visions, though it is also the case that few of the producers or consumers of American culture at the end of the twentieth century could actually remember the Depression. In any case, nostalgic visions of the 1930s have tended to elide the crucial breaking point of October 1929, ignoring historical reality and folding the 1920s and 1930s together as a single interwar period.

Nostalgic films set in the 1930s often tend to ignore the politics of that decade, though it is surely the case that a certain amount of nostalgia for the thirties resides in vague recollections of that decade as a time when political movements of a genuinely radical bent were active in the United States. Unlike the counterculture of the 1960s, these movements, often socialist in nature, sometimes included challenges to the very premises of capitalism. As such, they involved a strong utopian element that envisioned the Depression not only as a disaster but more positively as a harbinger of the fall of capitalism and the rise of better things to come. If, then, the 1950s have functioned (falsely) for some as the decade in which utopia was realized, the 1930s stand out as the decade in which genuine utopia was at least imaginable, if not literally achievable. It is, I think, the viability of utopian ideas in the 1930s that helps to explain the extent to which that seemingly dark decade has become an object of nostalgic representation in recent American film.

Actually, there are a number of reasons why the thirties might function as a focus of nostalgic longing in the postmodern era. For one thing, if the postmodern culture of images and simulacra arises in the 1940s, then one must go back to the 1930s to find a time of presumably more genuine culture. As with the 1950s, the music of the 1930s has also been crucial to these visions—in this case, vintage jazz generally substituting for early rock and roll. In addition, the thirties have functioned in the imagination of many as the true golden age of Hollywood cinema, and those films have predictably been central to nostalgic visions of the decade. Of course, the 1920s and 1930s were also the golden age of organized crime, a fact important not only to the popular memory of the period but to interwar nostalgia as well.

Then again, our collective memory of organized crime in the 1930s is inseparable from the representation of that phenomenon in Hollywood film and, later, on television. Thus, while postmodern gangster films set in the "1930s" may actually extend their historical coverage back into the late 1920s, they are inevitably mediated by the classic gangster movies of the early 1930s, including *Little Caesar* (1931), *Public Enemy* (1931), and *Scarface* (1932). On the other hand, this mediation, by the late twentieth century, had become quite complex. Thus, a film such as Joel and Ethan Coen's *Miller's Crossing* (1990) seems to derive almost all of its characters and plot elements from 1930s gangster films and hard-boiled fiction, but clearly derives much of its visual style and general atmosphere from the later phenomenon of film noir.[9] Similarly, Brian De Palma's *The Untouchables* (1987) produces a vision of early 1930s Chicago via the adaptation of a popular 1950s television series.

Such examples of "crime nostalgia" indicate that music is less central to nostalgic films about the 1930s than to those about the 1950s, probably because the music of the thirties is less clearly remembered and by fewer people. It is also the case that music became a much more important component of American popular culture with the rise of rock music as a huge commercial phenomenon in the 1950s. On the other hand, this same phenomenon has, for some, caused the music of the decades prior to the 1950s to seem more genuine, less commodified, and thus more appropriate as a locus of utopian energies—as in the case of Bogdanovich's nostalgic presentation of the music of Hank Williams Sr. in *The Last Picture Show*.

Woody Allen's *Sweet and Lowdown* (1999), for example, focuses on the jazz music of the 1930s in a highly (postmodern) nostalgic way while relating the career of fictional (and highly uncommercial) jazz guitarist Emmet Ray (Sean Penn). Presented in a mock documentary style, the film effectively achieves the illusion of historical accuracy, an illusion that is furthered by a profusion of period clothing, décor, and automobiles. On the other hand, the film constantly reminds us that little is really known of Ray's life and that much of the information we are being given is the result of rumor or speculation, made even less reliable by Ray's own unpredictable behavior. As we are repeatedly told, where Ray is concerned, "you never know what to believe." Meanwhile, the film is almost entirely disengaged from the actual history of the 1930s. The Depression is mentioned in passing, but does not constitute an important issue in the film, which is concerned entirely with the private experiences of Ray, an artist so self-absorbed that he is almost entirely oblivious to everyone and everything around him. Penn's impressive performance in the lead role is itself highly postmodern, representing a convincing impersonation of an individual who never existed and thus constituting a special form of the postmodern simulacrum.[10]

Of course, the representation of the playing of a great jazz artist is a particularly difficult artistic problem for a postmodern film. As improvisation is the heart of jazz, each performance is an original, with its own distinctive quality that reflects not only the personal style of the artist but also the unique ambience of the moment. Thus, jazz would seem to be the ultimate form of modernist art and a form that is diametrically opposed to postmodern pastiche. To an extent, *Sweet and Lowdown* avoids this problem of capturing the unique style of a jazz artist such as Ray simply because Ray never existed. At the same time, Allen solves the technical problem of representing Ray's playing on film by the fact that Penn, preparing for the role, learned to play guitar well enough that he is able to give an effective imitation of playing, even though the actual playing is done by guitarist Howard Alden, who also gave lessons to Penn.

Once it is recorded, any jazz performance can be recreated endlessly, though jazz here differs substantially from film and the other forms discussed by Walter Benjamin as being central to the character of art in the age of mechanical reproduction. For Benjamin, film inherently lacks the quasi-religious aura of earlier art forms because there is no original, produced by a godlike artist. Instead, a film exists only in a series of mechanically reproduced prints. Here, of course, Benjamin very clearly anticipates the Baudrillardian notion of the postmodern simulacrum, but his analysis would not appear to apply to jazz performances, for which there is, in fact, a unique, if ephemeral, original that differs in fundamental ways from recordings of it because of the physical (or perhaps metaphysical) presence of the creating artist and the ambient environment in which the creation takes place.

Indeed, improvisation is the key to Ray's genius in the film, and ephemerality is crucial to his career. He is presented as a truly gifted artist, second only to Belgian Gypsy Django Reinhardt among the world's jazz guitarists. Again, however, the film chooses not to explore the potential implications of the looming presence of Reinhardt, the first great foreign jazz artist to exert an important influence on American jazz. Instead, Reinhardt functions as a sort of personal bogey of Ray, whose own obsession with Reinhardt is a running gag in the film, which continually plays Ray's various personality quirks mostly for comedy. It treats him quite gently, though, and never suggests that his artistic self-absorption might be politically irresponsible in the context of the Depression. The film thus completely misses (presumably intentionally) the opportunity to comment on the relationship between art and the social world in the charged context of the Depression. Instead, it focuses entirely on the personal world of Ray, even leaving open the question of whether Ray's intense alienation enhances or detracts from the virtuosity of his guitar playing.

Granted, Ray dreams of being a movie star, but he nevertheless has an almost allegorical quality as a kind of living embodiment of the special, uncommercialized innocence of 1930s jazz. It is significant that, according to the film, he flowered briefly in that decade, then disappeared from sight, never to be heard from again. All that remains of him is the small number of recordings that he made during his prime—recordings that, in the film, function as iconic reflections of the now-lost culture of the 1930s, a time when artists such as Ray lived to make beautiful music for its own sake, regardless of the commercial results. The world of jazz in *Sweet and Lowdown* functions as a sort of utopian enclave virtually independent of the social problems of the world at large. Because of his financial irresponsibility, Ray is constantly in debt, and yet his money problems never become important enough to distract him from his art. Indeed, Depression or no Depression, he always seems to be able to get money whenever he really needs it, as in one scene when he literally falls from the sky and lands in the midst of a counterfeiting operation, scaring away the counterfeiters and making off with a large quantity of their product. The substantial racial problems of the 1930s are also nonexistent in Ray's jazz world, where white and black musicians intermingle freely, oblivious to color as long as the sound is right.

This view of jazz is not original to the film but in fact predates the 1930s themselves. Thus, J. A. Rogers, in the essay "Jazz at Home," first published in Alain Locke's *The New Negro* in the mid-1920s, envisions jazz precisely as such a "leveller" that merges black and white cultural forces in a uniquely American democratic mix.[11] In contrast, Robert Altman's rather cynical *Kansas City* (1996), which also focuses on the world of 1930s jazz, would seem to challenge this view of jazz—and most of the other nostalgic reminiscences of *Sweet and Lowdown* as well. Altman's 1934 Kansas City is strictly segregated. Jazz here is a purely black phenomenon, and all of the jazz musicians in the film are black, living and working on the fringes of a thoroughly racist white-dominated society. *Kansas City* also rejects any utopian vision of the New Deal politics of the 1930s, presenting the Democratic Party as a corrupt and ruthless force that uses its power for corrupt purposes and maintains that power through bribery and intimidation of voters. Finally, the film refuses to see the 1930s as a golden age of Hollywood, instead, suggesting that Hollywood exerts a negative influence that exacerbates the problems of the decade.

Kansas City features Harry Belafonte as "Seldom Seen," the proprietor of the Hey-Hey Club, the epicenter of the city's jazz scene. He is also the kingpin of the local black mob, organized crime being as segregated here as all other social activities. In the film, small-time hood Johnny O'Hara (Dermot Mulroney) gets the bright idea of robbing (in blackface) one of Seldom Seen's favorite customers, a high roller who typically loses big in the club's gambling operation. Seldom Seen quickly sees through the ruse and tracks down O'Hara, holding him captive until he decides what to do with him. In the meantime, O'Hara's wife, Blondie (Jennifer Jason Leigh), decides to try to win her husband's freedom by kidnapping Carolyn Stilton (Miranda Richardson), the wife of Henry Stilton (Michael Murphy), a wealthy and powerful advisor to President Franklin Roosevelt. Blondie's reasoning (if you can call it that) is that she will be able to use Mrs. Stilton to force Mr. Stilton to use his connections to win Johnny's freedom.

Within the logic of this film, in which the Democratic Party is itself essentially a version of organized crime, this plan almost seems to make sense, though it is complicated by the fact that the action occurs on Election Day, when all of the party's operatives are busy rigging the election. Ultimately, however, it is not surprising that the plan fails or that both Johnny and Blondie wind up dead. Meanwhile, the film makes it clear that Blondie's conception of such a far-fetched plan has been facilitated by the fact that her imagination has been thoroughly constituted by Hollywood movies, in which such a wacky scheme just might work. She is particularly fascinated by Jean Harlow, whose films she watches over and over in rapt fascination, peroxiding (and nearly destroying) her own hair in an attempt to mimic that of her idol. While holding Mrs. Stilton captive, she even takes her to see *Hold Your Man* (1933), even though Blondie has seen the film many times before.

In *Hold Your Man*, Harlow plays a tough-talking dame of the kind Blondie is trying desperately to be. Unfortunately, Blondie's resultant theatrical manner of speaking sounds more like a travesty of bad Hollywood dialogue than a genuine imitation of Harlow. By extension, one might conclude that Johnny's cockamamie scheme to commit a robbery in blackface was also influenced by his viewing of films, as is his long speech to Seldom Seen in which he argues that it would be bad business for a black gangster, however powerful, to kill a white man. Indeed, one gets the feeling that this speech is precisely the kind that might be expected to work in a Hollywood film, so it comes as something of a shock when we discover that Seldom Seen is unconvinced: he returns Johnny to Blondie, all right, but with a mortal wound in his lower abdomen, perhaps involving his genitals. This shock is then followed by another, as Carolyn Stilton shoots and kills Blondie, who is sobbing over the body of her dead husband.

Among other things, *Kansas City* makes the very Brechtian point that gangsters such as Seldom Seen are simply businessmen following the logic of capitalist competition to its inexorable conclusion. If *Sweet and*

Lowdown wants to depict the 1930s as a more innocent time before rampant commodification had swept up music along with everything else, *Kansas City*, through its treatment of the false dreams purveyed by Hollywood and the complete corruption of the Democratic Party, makes it clear that the decade was already shot through with capitalist rottenness. Indeed, the very corruption of the real world is the very reason why the kind of idealized visions gleaned from the movies can only get one into trouble.

Of course, Altman, in *Buffalo Bill and the Indians* (1976), had already depicted American show business—even in the late nineteenth century—as a contrived and meretricious play for money and fame. *Buffalo Bill and the Indians* does, however, suggest a utopian alternative by opposing, even in the title, the dishonesty and greed of Buffalo Bill to the more genuine and honest culture of the Indians, here represented primarily by the inscrutable and forthright Sitting Bull. *Kansas City*, though more subtly, does pretty much the same thing with jazz, which functions as an island of authenticity amid the counterfeit machinations of the mainstream culture of movies, politics, and business. Thus, the most positive figure in the film, played by Albert J. Burnes, is a teenage boy who dreams of being a sax player and who just happens to be none other than Charlie "Bird" Parker (who was, in fact, a teenager in Kansas City at the time). Altman's loving treatment of jazz in the film can, in fact, be seen by the fact that he also made a companion film devoted strictly to the music and serving as a sort of documentary history of Kansas City jazz in the thirties. *Robert Altman's Jazz '34: Remembrances of Kansas City Swing* (1996) assembles an all-star cast of contemporary jazz artists, who then play their renditions of 1930s Kansas City jazz, attempting to capture the spirit of the time but also acknowledging the irreproducibility of great jazz performances.

The Coen brothers' *O Brother, Where Art Thou?* (2000) also looks nostalgically back on the music of the thirties, but this time seems equally nostalgic about classic Hollywood film. Set in the Depression-era South, this film wistfully views the 1930s as a time when regional differences contributed to a cultural authenticity no longer available in the geographically homogenized environment of late capitalism. But this emphasis on culture points toward the way in which the film's nostalgia for the 1930s is directed not at the historical decade, in which life was fraught with so many difficulties, but at the decade's culture, including early country music and classic Hollywood movies, in which all problems (no matter how extreme or even bizarre) are easily solved.

Despite its overt reliance on earlier films such as Preston Sturges's *Sullivan's Travels* (1941), *O Brother* derives much of its vintage feel from its effective use of traditional gospel and bluegrass music on the sound-track. This music also contributes to the sense that the film represents not the Depression South but pop cultural images of the Depression South. In particular, the music often enters into the film at the diegetic level, where it is heard or performed by various characters, including the three central characters—prison escapees, who, in the course of the film, join forces with the African-American Tommy Johnson (played by blues star Chris Thomas King), clearly based on legendary bluesman Robert Johnson, to form a successful bluegrass group of their own. However, when this music enters the diegetic level, it does so with a slickly produced studio sound that disrupts any potential sense of realistic representation.

One of the most striking examples of this phenomenon occurs in an early scene in which the film's three escapees are camping out in the woods, then hear a revivalist congregation heading down to a nearby river to perform baptism rituals. The congregation is singing the traditional gospel song "Down to the River to Pray" and singing it impossibly well, with a large chorus supporting with perfect, slickly produced pitch and harmony a lead vocal that sounds (for good reason) exactly like the angelic voice of current "newgrass" superstar Alison Krauss. This scene of supposed salvation—dismissed by protagonist Ulysses Everett McGill (George Clooney) as a "ridiculous superstition"—then forms a perfect counterpart to the later scene of temptation when the three escapees encounter three washerwomen sirens, also in a river, singing "Didn't Leave Nobody but the Baby" (a sort of twisted version of an old Negro lullaby, adapted by Gillian Welch and producer T-Bone Burnett), a song that seems designed to mesmerize not only the characters but the audience as well. In this moment of pure cinema, the narrative dissolves, giving way to a frozen moment of beautiful sights and sounds as the enticing sirens move languidly toward their "victims" while singing their enchanting music. That the music is again supplied by Krauss (here joined, in an all-star trio, by Emmylou Harris and Welch) serves as an additional link between this scene of riverside seduction and the earlier baptism scene, among other things reinforcing McGill's perception that the earlier scene was a type of seduction as well.

In *O Brother*, the music often takes precedence over the narrative, and many scenes seem to have been contrived only as a backdrop for the music, thus reversing the usual hierarchy of cinematic procedure. This process greatly contributes to the diminution of plot, which, in this case, is minimal and largely random, despite the central getting-back-home theme. The film thus serves as an important example of the dissolution of narrative in postmodern film. Meanwhile, its special reliance on music to produce this effect is also highly postmodern, contributing to its mediated portrayal of the Depression, which becomes oddly nostalgic, suggesting a past time of precommodified "authentic music" before country went pop.[12] This nostalgic motif, in fact, is announced early on, when the opening titles (and the initial escape from the chain gang) are accompanied by Harry McClintock's hobo anthem "Big Rock Candy Mountain," a utopian fantasy about escape to an ideal land where the policemen all have wooden legs and the bulldogs all have rubber teeth, thus making life easier on those who exist on the margins of the law.

The film calls attention to the mediated nature of this representation of the past through the excessive virtuosity of the film's music, as in the scenes of the baptism and the sirens. Also important in this regard is the scene involving a Klan rally in which the leader sings a stunning rendition of the traditional spiritual "O Death" in the voice of bluegrass legend Ralph Stanley, the "king of mountain soul." Similarly, the three escapees, with no preparation or rehearsal, are able in one scene suddenly to join Tommy Johnson to become a well-coordinated bluegrass group (the Soggy Bottom Boys) and to perform a rousing rendition of "I Am a Man of Constant Sorrow" in which McGill is suddenly able to sing exactly like Dan Tyminski (a member of Krauss's group, Union Station). The patent artificiality of such scenes of performance is almost Brechtian, but is complicated still further by the fact that well-known performers sometimes appear in the film to do their own singing, as when King sings "Hard Time Killing Floor Blues" and the Whites appear to perform "Keep on the Sunny Side." This mix is complicated even more when actor Tim Blake Nelson, playing one of the escapees, does his own singing to lead the Soggy Bottom Boys in a performance of "In the Jailhouse Now," one of the classics of Mississippi's Jimmie Rodgers, the "father of country music."

The ontological confusion of real and fake singers combines with considerable historical ambiguity. Even though O Brother's soundtrack is clearly designed to help create a Depression-era atmosphere, the music, in fact, derives from a wide range of historical periods, here all collapsed into one simulated version of the 1930s. Thus, "I Am a Man of Constant Sorrow," which became something of a hit in its own right, was first published in 1913 and probably dates from even earlier. "Big Rock Candy Mountain" originally derives from the 1910s (but is used here in McClintock's version recorded in 1928). "In the Jailhouse Now" also dates from 1928 (but is used in a new version recorded for the film), while much of the film's bluegrass music comes from recordings in the 1940s and

1950s. The use of modern renditions of older songs complicates this picture further, collapsing historical boundaries, as in the use of Krauss and Welch's new recording of Albert E. Brumley's gospel classic "I'll Fly Away" (again from 1928) to suggest the atmosphere of the 1930s.

The film's official publicity indicates that this historical mishmash is meant to suggest the "timelessness" of this music, which might seem to be verified by the fact that the music was so well received in 2000, when the CD of the soundtrack became a best-seller, eventually winning the Country Music Association's award as the outstanding country music album of the year. Of course, that the film also intends to use this music to suggest the 1930s conflicts with this "timeless" characterization, just as the commercial success of the soundtrack CD complicates the use of this music as an example of precommodified culture. The film, in fact, seems inadvertently to have contributed to the commodification of the very music that it sought to celebrate as untainted, indicating the ability of late consumer capitalism to sweep everything that comes its way— even denunciations of commodification—into its all-consuming maw, excreting the processed results back out as commodities.

O Brother also contributes to the commodification of its music through its refusal to make distinctions among the various kinds of music it uses to evoke the 1930s, treating them all as interchangeable. For example, the film includes two utopian songs of escape, "Big Rock Candy Mountain" and "I'll Fly Away," both used in similar ways to serve as accompaniment to the flight of the three convicts. Yet the first of these arises from the Industrial Workers of the World–inspired leftist politics of McClintock and thus dreams of a material utopia, while the second is a Christian gospel song that envisions a flight from the material cares of the world, thus embodying precisely the kind of escapist quietism mocked in IWW songs such as Joe Hill's classic "The Preacher and the Slave." Indeed, even though a political campaign forms an important part of the action in *O Brother*, the political realities of the Depression are missing almost entirely from this film, a situation that is probably not surprising given the tin ear for leftist politics that the Coens showed in their earlier *Barton Fink* (1991), where they seemed (weirdly) to want to locate responsibility for the rise of fascism in the disengagement of leftist intellectuals from reality.

Herbert Ross's *Pennies from Heaven* (1981) is far more politically astute and even gestures toward potential ways of representing the music of the past that move beyond postmodern nostalgia. The film begins in 1934 and also depends crucially on period music, though this time more mainstream popular music, including the kind that might have been featured in musical films of the period. Written by legendary British television writer Dennis Potter and adapted from Potter's similarly titled 1978 BBC miniseries set in Depression-era London, *Pennies from Heaven* focuses on Arthur Parker (Steve Martin), a Chicago-based sheet-music salesman whose dreams of happiness (inspired primarily by the music he sells) conflict dramatically with the impoverished nature of his real material and emotional life. "I wanna live in a world where the songs come true," laments Parker, but, alas, his is no such world.

Parker makes several attempts in the film to make his dreams come true, but all of his efforts only make things worse. Frustrated by the frigidity of his repressed wife, Joan (Jessica Harper), Parker seeks solace in the arms of schoolteacher Eileen Everson (Bernadette Peters), who winds up pregnant and is driven into a life of prostitution. When Parker finally convinces Joan to let him use the money she inherited from her religious-fanatic father to open his own record store, business is disastrously bad, as one might expect in the midst of the Depression. Business, in fact, is a key topic of this film, and it is of central importance that Parker's engagement with the music he so loves is consistently mediated by the fact that he is an employee of the Culture Industry that produces and distributes this music as a cultural commodity.

Ultimately, Parker runs away with Eileen (now calling herself Lu Lu), only to be tracked down by police, who have wrongly identified him as the brutal murderer of a blind girl he met briefly earlier in the film. He is tried, convicted, and sentenced to be hanged. In what would logically seem to be the film's final scene, he sings a melancholy version of the film's title song as he awaits death on the gallows. Logic does not necessarily apply here, however, and the film suddenly cuts to another scene in which a jubilant Arthur, now inexplicably free, runs to rejoin Lu Lu. "Who ever said you could stop a dream?" he asks her. "We couldn't a gone through all that without a happy ending. Songs ain't like that, are they?" This reunion is followed by an elaborate, upbeat Busby Berkeley–style production number before the film ends with a shot of a rainbow, panning up to a view of a sunny blue sky.

This happy ending is much too patently contrived (especially in relation to the rest of the film) to be taken seriously; it clearly mocks the happy endings of Hollywood movies of the period. On the other hand, it is certainly possible to recuperate it as a mere fantasy on the part of either Parker or Lu Lu, or both. After all, Hollywood films have joined music as the inspiration for Parker's dreams throughout, as is emphasized in one scene in which he and Lu Lu go to see Fred Astaire and Ginger Rogers in *Follow the Fleet* (1936), then enter the film to replace

Fred and Ginger in a song-and-dance number. This kind of frame-breaking is, in fact, central to *Pennies from Heaven*, in which all of the musical numbers (except for Parker's farewell song at the gallows) are lip-synched by the actors, the actual music provided by vintage recordings. The artificiality of this device is sometimes quite startling, especially to those unfamiliar with Potter's extensive use of it in several of his groundbreaking miniseries for the BBC. Thus, early in the film, it comes as a surprise when Parker launches into a performance of "The Clouds Will Soon Roll By" in the ultrafeminine voice of Elsie Carlisle.

These performances, meanwhile, are often accompanied by elaborate production numbers that break the flow of the narrative, as in the spectacular presentation of the title song as lip-synched by the "Accordion Man" (Vernel Bagneris), an itinerate musician and hymn-singer taken in and fed by Arthur (and who later becomes the actual murderer of the blind girl). This number is particularly ironic, as the Accordion Man dances amid a shower of golden coins in front of a large mural that is a collage of classic Walker Evans–style photographic images of Depression-era poverty. Sometimes, however, these musical numbers vaguely contribute to the narrative, as when Christopher Walken (as Tom the Pimp) lures Eileen into prostitution with a rousing tap dance and striptease atop a bar while lip-synching to "Let's Misbehave."

In any case, the musical numbers give insights into the minds of the characters, typically reflecting their inner fantasies but also suggesting the extent to which their fantasy worlds have been colonized—or even produced—by popular culture. Thus, Glen Creeber (discussing the *Pennies from Heaven* miniseries, but in ways that are also relevant to the film) notes the blatant artificiality of the lip-synch device, arguing that the device is "deliberately self-conscious in its appropriation and dissemination of popular music, and seems to address explicitly the growing influence of mass culture on the lives and minds of Potter's characters" (140–41). In this way, for Creeber, the device of intrusive musical numbers "forces the spectator to recognize the forces by which the dominant ideology manipulates Arthur's social reality" (141).

In particular, Creeber compares the intrusiveness of the musical numbers to the use of music as an alienating device in the plays of Bertolt Brecht, a figure with whom Potter is quite frequently compared, especially for his later masterpiece, the 1986 British miniseries *The Singing Detective*—itself adapted to film by Keith Gordon in 2003. Indeed, the contrived happy ending of *Pennies from Heaven* (the miniseries version ends similarly) recalls nothing more than the end of Brecht's *Three-penny Opera* (1929), in which the gangster Macheath is miraculously saved from the gallows, then granted a castle and generous lifetime pension by the newly crowned Queen, simply because "this is an opera" (Creeber, 95). Brecht, however, goes on to make quite clear that this ending does not match reality, in which men must make their own history, rather than wait to have problems solved by "a messenger from the king whenever we want." Potter leaves his ending more vague, even allowing for the positive interpretation that Arthur finds solace in song, allowing him to die happy, winning a last victory over hardship and injustice.

Such a positive spin seems to run counter to the logic of most of the film, in which Arthur's fantasies never seem to do anything but get him into trouble, while destroying the lives of those around him. On the other hand, the very fact that Arthur actually sings on the gallows rather than lip-synching a popular recording does suggest that this final scene differs from the rest of the picture. Then again, Arthur finds considerable solace in song throughout the film, which thereby seems ambivalent in its treatment of popular culture, a characteristic that critics have noted about the miniseries as well. For example, Baxendale and Pawling (discussing the original miniseries), note Potter's generally negative figuration of the impact of American popular culture on Britain, but also suggest that he grants a certain genuine utopian potential to popular music, which encourages audiences to think beyond contemporary reality. In this case, nostalgia "can be a powerful tool" that helps in the recovery of memories of aspects of the past that have been repressed in official histories (179).

In particular, Baxendale and Pawling conclude that the nostalgia in *Pennies from Heaven* contains genuine utopian elements that set it apart from the nostalgia discussed by Jameson in connection with postmodernism.[13] In both the film and the miniseries of *Pennies from Heaven*, there is a clear duality in the treatment of popular music from the 1930s, which enriches the fantasy lives of the characters even as it functions as part of an ideological system that brings the characters nothing but misery in their material lives. Noting Potter's negative view of the dissemination of bourgeois ideology by the commercial music industry of his own day, Steve Brie argues that, in the miniseries, "Potter's defense against the sweeping tide of commercialism was to seek solace in an idealized, pre-rock 'n' roll past," even though Potter himself frequently rejected nostalgia as a form of "cultural philistinism" (207).

In a similar vein, Creeber suggests that Potter's interest in the 1930s might come from the fact that the decade represented a crucial moment in British cultural history, in the midst of a transition from an "amateur and provincial form of musical entertainment to a professional and mass-produced industry" (137). He argues that the particular songs selected often seem to "possess traces of an older and more organic way of life than that represented by the cultural changes sweeping England in the 1930s" (141). Ultimately, then, Creeber sees the lip-synch device as less important for its Brechtian exposure of ideology than for its dramatization of "a time before the cultural Fall of the 1950s and 1960s when mass culture in Britain still apparently seemed to have its roots in an older and more organic working-class tradition" (143).

Of course, this vision of the 1930s as a time of more authentic popular culture in Britain is seriously compromised by the fact that this culture was already, at the time, being heavily influenced by music and film imported from the United States. Indeed, most of the music in *Pennies from Heaven*, even in the British miniseries, is American in origin.[14] This situation, meanwhile, is entirely realistic. As Baxendale and Pawling note, the "hegemony of the American music industry" in Britain was well established by the early 1930s. One could, on the other hand, argue that American culture itself was less commercialized and commodified in the 1930s than in the 1950s and beyond, when music, in particular, experienced a vast jump in profitability due largely to the emergence of rock and roll. In any case, Potter, in keeping with his generally dialectical approach, suggests in much of his work that the populist energies of American rock music might help to revitalize British working-class culture, even as American popular culture in general has historically been one of the most important sources of the destruction of British working-class cultural traditions.

In the case of the American film version of *Pennies from Heaven*, however, the focus is specifically on the U.S. music industry of the 1930s and the way in which, even in the midst of the Depression, this industry, aided by Hollywood, was already beginning to commodify popular music on a large scale. A clear utopian potential still resides in this music, but that potential is the very force that makes it attractive as a commodity, investing it with an almost magical energy of the kind Karl Marx associates with the commodity fetish. This conscription of the utopian potential of popular music by the capitalist Culture Industry is, in fact, one of the major stories of twentieth-century culture. However, the prominence of music in the films discussed in this chapter indicates that, to a certain extent, the story of twentieth-century popular music is in many ways inseparable from that of the film industry.

Postmodern films often rummage not just through the music of the past in search of image fodder but even through the *film* music of the past. For example, Lars von Trier's *Dancer in the Dark* (2000) resembles *Pennies from Heaven* in the way its protagonist, Selma Jezkova (Björk), escapes from the poverty and hardship of her everyday life through a retreat into the world of music. In this case, however, the link to film is much more clear. In particular, most of the music in *Dancer in the Dark* comes from Robert Wise's *The Sound of Music* (1965), the Rodgers and Hammerstein musical that Selma and some of the other locals in *Dancer in the Dark* are preparing to perform until she is forced to withdraw due to her failing eyesight. The actual events of *Dancer in the Dark* are unremittingly bleak. Jezkova has come to the United States seeking a better life, having developed unrealistic fantasies of life in America from watching the movies. Once in the New World, she works a grueling factory job to try to support herself and her young son, only to find that her oncoming blindness is gradually making it impossible for her to work. To make matters worse, her son has the same congenital illness and is fated to go blind as well unless she can save enough money to pay for surgery for him. Working extra shifts and struggling frantically against time, she somehow saves the money, only to have it stolen by her abject policeman landlord, whom she then kills (essentially at his own request) in an effort to retrieve the cash. She is convicted of murder and then hanged (like Arthur Parker) as the film ends—except that Jezkova stays hanged in a brutally naturalistic scene that contrasts starkly with the ending of *Pennies from Heaven*.

These events make it clear that, on the surface at least, *Dancer in the Dark* could not be more different from the blissfully optimistic film that serves as its most important filmic referent. Indeed, partly because of this difference, the dialogic encounter between *Dancer in the Dark* and *The Sound of Music* is far richer than that which one might normally associate with postmodern pastiche. In particular, the brutally tragic texture of *Dancer in the Dark* radically calls into question the seemingly sweet and optimistic nature of the Wise original, calling attention to aspects of the earlier film (in particular the looming Nazi threat that is about to engulf the Austrian setting of the story) that have otherwise been ignored by many viewers in favor of the film's emphasis on the inspirational power of love and music. On the other hand, the reverse is also true: this dialogue with *The Sound of Music* adds an oddly positive energy to *Dancer in the Dark*. Thus, the solace Jezkova derives from music (and film) provides a certain utopian element, enhanced by the fact that the protagonist is a far more admirable and virtuous figure than is the highly problematic Arthur Parker.

Dancer in the Dark illustrates that a certain potential for productive dialogue with previous texts continues to exist in the postmodern era. In that sense, it provides a reminder that Jameson's vision of postmodern pastiche is only a general description of a postmodern textual characteristic, one that some texts might display to a larger extent than others. Still, the reliance of *Dancer in the Dark* on *The Sound of Music* demonstrates the persistent postmodern tendency for films to draw upon earlier films (rather than reality) as *materia poetica*, however extensive (or not) the rewriting of those earlier texts by the postmodern ones. I discuss the use of film itself as a source of film material in the next chapter, through the optic of Jameson's theorization of postmodern pastiche.

Chapter 3

LIKE SOMETHING FROM A MOVIE

FILM AS THE OBJECT OF REPRESENTATION IN POSTMODERN POPULAR FILM

Quentin Tarantino's *Pulp Fiction* (1994) was overtly (and extremely successfully) marketed as a film about film, and as a film made by a film buff for film buffs. Indeed, *Pulp Fiction* openly presents itself as a cinematic spectacle, a collection of references to earlier movies, and as such is a perfect illustration of the phenomenon of pastiche in postmodern film. Tarantino, of course, is well known as a movie buff, a former video-store clerk living out his wildest dreams by making it big in Hollywood. As Amanda Lipman notes in an early review, *Pulp Fiction* functions as a sort of "rag-bag of film references," including references to earlier projects in which Tarantino himself had been involved, such as his own *Reservoir Dogs* (1992) and *True Romance* (1993, directed by Tony Scott, but scripted by Tarantino). Indeed, Lipman points out that even the casting of the film seems to be a form of pastiche in which numerous actors (including John Travolta) seem to be "playing warped versions of characters for which they are known" (51). Such references can be taken merely as signs of Tarantino's famed coolness, as in-jokes to help audience members feel cool themselves. On the other hand, Peter Chumo argues that *Pulp Fiction* engages in a productive dialogue with its filmic sources, helping Tarantino to "breathe new life into the old forms he loves" (26). As Chumo sees it, "Tarantino's use of movie references goes beyond a simple postmodern recycling of old movie bits and generic plot lines to a thoughtful look at how such relics of the filmic past can come alive in the present" (17).

Whether one sees Tarantino's use of images and motifs from previous films as superficial play or as a meditation on time and history may be largely a matter of interpretation, though it is certainly the case that there is very little in the actual content of *Pulp Fiction* that would support the latter view. It may well be, for example, that the mysterious glow inside the briefcase held by Jules Winnfield (Samuel L. Jackson) at the end of the film can be taken as a reference to Robert Aldrich's *Kiss Me Deadly* (1955), but there is little in this fact to suggest a new reading of *Kiss Me Deadly* that would not have otherwise been available. Similarly, Winnfield's final desire to leave crime in favor of religion hardly presents the kind of alternative that might function as an effective utopian gesture. Meanwhile, the way *Pulp Fiction*'s allusions to films (and other cultural artifacts) slip and slide around in time suggests not a renewal of the past so much as a refusal to recognize historical sequence or to historicize its various references.

The tendency of postmodern films to represent not reality but preexisting representations of reality may be, to a certain extent, merely an extension of a trend that has been present in the movie industry virtually from the beginning. Indeed, the increasing tendency in the second half of the twentieth century for films to base themselves on other films can be at least partly attributed to the simple fact that, as time passes, there are more and more films available to draw upon. On the other hand, the particularly self-conscious and ahistorical way in which many recent filmmakers have drawn upon previous movies or other cultural artifacts seems to represent a genuinely new phenomenon, one that can be usefully described in terms of Fredric Jameson's discussion of the importance of pastiche in postmodern culture.

Jameson sees rummaging through the styles of the past for usable images as a central strategy of all postmodernist art, but he suggests the "nostalgia film" as a particularly telling example of the postmodernist fascination with the past. Jameson is thinking of overtly nostalgic representations of the past in films such as *American Graffiti* (1973), as well as the retooling of past genres in works such as the neo-noir films *The Long Goodbye* (1973), *Chinatown* (1974), and *Body Heat* (1981). Of course, the film noir is a particularly effective source of pastiche because it is so highly stylized. One might, for example, now add to this list such neo-noir films as Curtis Hanson's *L.A. Confidential* (1997) and Brian De Palma's *The Black Dahlia* (2006), both based on novels by James Ellroy, a master of the noir style. However, this practice of generic pastiche is part of a much broader postmodern phenomenon in which films increasingly take both their style and their subject matter from other cultural artifacts, rather than from anything in material reality. The most obvious aspect of this phenomenon is the increasing tendency of films, in a variety of ways, to take other motion pictures as their objects of representation.

The noir tradition is central to the background of *Pulp Fiction*—and perhaps even more to that of Tarantino's first film, *Reservoir Dogs*. It is by now a cliché to note that Tarantino burst upon the scene with the screening of *Reservoir Dogs* at the 1992 Sundance Film Festival, an event that left many in the audience agog and amazed that they had seen something genuinely new and different, something they had never seen before. But this description is not really accurate. Even the nonlinear plot structure, an early version of the hyperlink structure that would categorize Tarantino's later films, was not all that new, being basically an extension of the time-honored flashback technique. What the first audiences of *Reservoir Dogs* experienced was not the shock of the new, as in the old avant-garde, but the shock of being bombarded with more recycled materials than they had ever before seen assembled in one place. Tarantino's subsequent films (most notably *Pulp Fiction*) would continue and extend this phenomenon, establishing a distinctive and instantly recognizable style, yet one that is achieved primarily through the assemblage of preexisting cultural materials. Moreover, the films achieve their consistent and recognizable style primarily through the almost compulsive repetition of certain trademark motifs, including graphic violence, hyperlink plot structure, and heavy (generally nostalgic) use of references to popular culture.

Even the distinctive title of *Reservoir Dogs* is assembled from previously existing materials, in this case through a combination of Louis Malle's touching *Au revoir, les enfants* (1987) and Sam Peckinpah's ultraviolent *Straw Dogs* (1971), a combination that already indicates the crucial role played in Tarantino's films by both New Wave French cinema and violent American cinema. The remainder of the picture is then chock full of specific references to and stylistic echoes of other films, including the opening title sequence in which the black-suited "dogs" walk together in slow motion in an obvious imitation of the conclusion of the original *Ocean's Eleven* (1960). This scene thus refers to one of the best-known heist films in American cinema history—and one that is particularly noted for being "cool," the single adjective that would come to be used most often in describing Tarantino's film. *Reservoir Dogs* echoes any number of other heist films as well, especially noir films about failed heists such as John Huston's *The Asphalt Jungle* (1950) and Stanley Kubrick's *The Killing* (1956). It also shows the international range of Tarantino's influences, being reminiscent of French heist films, especially Jean-Pierre Melville's *Bob le flambeur* (1955) and Jules Dassin's *Du refifi chez les hommes* (1955), and having echoes of John Woo's violent Hong Kong crime films, such as *Ying hung boon sik* ("A Better Tomorrow," 1986).

Reservoir Dogs ultimately goes beyond even such predecessors as Peckinpah and Woo in the levels of its graphic and bloody violence, a tendency that would itself become a trademark of Tarantino's films. Yet this violence, in all of Tarantino's films, is balanced by segments of cool, snappy dialogue, generally about nothing more than the trivialities of everyday existence. Popular culture is a favorite topic of Tarantino's dialogues, as in the opening sequence of *Reservoir Dogs* in which Tarantino himself (as the doomed Mr. Brown) leads the gang in a discussion of possible interpretations of Madonna's early hit song "Like a Virgin." In a later conversation, the gang debates whether or not the 1970s television series *Get Christie Love* starred Pam Grier in the title role. It didn't: she instead played the title role in the 1974 film *Foxy Brown*, as the undercover cop Mr. Orange (Tim Roth) points out, noting that *Get Christie Love* "was like a Pam Grier TV show without Pam Grier." Meanwhile, the very reference to Grier foreshadows Tarantino's later casting of her in the title role in *Jackie Brown* (1997). Such nostalgic, intertextual casting is typical of Tarantino, who seems especially to enjoy bringing back nearly forgotten actors who had risen to fame in the 1970s, that central time focus of Tarantino nostalgia. The resurrection of Travolta in *Pulp Fiction* is the most prominent example of this kind of casting, but *Jackie Brown* also features Robert Forster (a staple of 1970s cop shows, such as the anthology *Police Story*) in a key role, while the role of Bill in the *Kill Bill* films (2003, 2004) is played by David Carradine, still best known for his starring role in the television series *Kung Fu*, which ran on ABC from 1972 to 1975. Carradine also appeared in Martin Scorsese's *Mean Streets* (1973), completing Tarantino's perfect record of casting at least one actor from that film in all of his own, at least through the *Kill Bill* sequence.

Reservoir Dogs is sprinkled with other allusions to popular culture as well. For example, Mr. Orange seems to be a fan of Marvel comics. He has a poster of the Silver Surfer on the wall of his apartment, and he describes Joe Cabot (Lawrence Tierney), the gang's burly leader, as looking exactly like the Thing from the Fantastic Four. Meanwhile, the opening discussion of Madonna in *Reservoir Dogs* points to Tarantino's effective use of popular music in all of his soundtracks, another signature characteristic of his style. This music again often comes from the

1970s, as in the use of the 1970 hit "Little Green Bag" by the George Baker Selection as the opening title music. Throughout, the soundtrack of *Reservoir Dogs* consists primarily of diegetic broadcasts of a radio program entitled "K-Billy's Super Sounds of the '70s," which features a deadpan disc jockey (played by comedian Steven Wright) spinning classic hits from the seventies by such artists as Stealers Wheel, Joe Tex, and Blue Swede. This music is quite popular with the jewel thieves who are the major characters in the film, especially the highly professional Mr. Pink (Steve Buscemi) and the sadistic Mr. Blonde (Michael Madsen), who dances gleefully as Stealers Wheel's "Stuck in the Middle with You" (a hit from 1973) plays on the radio during his brutal torture and mutilation of a captured policeman.

Tarantino's self-conscious resurrection of earlier film forms reaches a new high in the *Kill Bill* films, which depend so extensively on a pastiche of Hong Kong martial arts pictures, as well as other sources. Self-consciousness is, indeed, the key here. The two *Kill Bill* films are sometimes accused of being about nothing but the glorification of violence, and they are certainly violent, featuring such items as beheadings and amputations that result in geysers of movie blood. But it is most definitely *movie* blood, released by *movie* violence. These films are not about violence, but about movies; they are really about their own making—and the making of films in general. As Roger Ebert put it in a review of *Kill Bill: Vol. 1*, "The movie is all storytelling and no story."

But this kind of reflexive self-consciousness, often associated with the strategies of high modernist art, is here pure pop culture. Among other things, Tarantino returns in these films to a more self-consciously borrowed style, announcing that he is perfectly comfortable with cadging his styles from someone else. Indeed, the *Kill Bill* films are largely lessons in how to borrow styles gracefully. *Vol. 1* (2003) draws in a very obvious ways on Asian martial arts films, while *Vol. 2* (2004) adds important elements modeled on the Spaghetti Western; they thus take central inspiration from distinctive pop-cultural film phenomena that have long been among Tarantino's favorites. Both of these cinematic models are also notably violent, so perhaps it is no surprise that, in *Kill Bill* (especially *Vol. 1*), Tarantino's films reach a level of violence that goes beyond even the already notorious violence of his earlier ones. The narratives of both parts of *Kill Bill* are relatively straightforward, telling single stories (rather than the interwoven stories of the hyperlink style), although the stories are still related in a nonlinear fashion that requires audiences to reassemble the different segments into a coherent whole. In short, the films retain all of Tarantino's trademarks, employed with a new confidence that these trademarks are enough to make a good movie and that Tarantino need not worry about adding new ingredients. His particular form of filmmaking reaches its zenith in these pictures, and if *Pulp Fiction* remains the best film by Tarantino, the *Kill Bill* films are clearly the films that best represent Tarantino's special traits as a filmmaker.

Kill Bill: Vol. 1 signals early on that it is meant as a lighthearted romp, rooted in popular culture and not meant to be taken too seriously, however dark its material. It begins with an overtly retro series of opening titles that announce the beginning of "Our Feature Presentation," thus creating nostalgic echoes of bygone days at the movie theater. But the nostalgia here is of a particularly hip, cool, and up-to-date kind that is never in danger of appearing old-fashioned or sentimental. The opening also features an entirely appropriate (given the revenge theme of the film) epigraph: "Revenge is a dish best served cold." This bit of proverbial wisdom appears in many different Earth cultures but that is here given a pop cultural spin by being identified as an "old Klingon proverb"—as it had been in *Star Trek II: The Wrath of Khan* (1982).

Kill Bill: Vol. 1 draws upon numerous pop cultural sources. For example, it again shows the influence of film noir and the French New Wave that is typical of Tarantino's work. The film is also openly cartoonish at numerous points, a strategy it can get away with by announcing that it *knows* it is cartoonish: it even includes one literally animated segment done in Japanese animé style (and that was, in fact, created by Japanese animators). But its most obvious borrowings are from Asian martial arts films, including the casting of Japanese legend Sonny Chiba as Hattori Hanzo, the sword maker who crafts the weapon used by the Bride, the film's unnamed protagonist (played by Uma Thurman), to defeat Tokyo gangland leader O-Ren Ishii (Lucy Liu) and her large array of trained assassins. Chiba, whose films (especially the "Streetfighter" series from the 1970s) have long been acknowledged as crucial influences on Tarantino, had been a key figure (along with Bruce Lee) in the 1970s explosion in martial arts movies, so Tarantino's casting once again nostalgically looks back to his favorite decade. Meanwhile, the final fight between the Bride and O-Ren and her gang occupies about one-third of the film in an extended pastiche sequence that reenacts almost every conceivable element of the Asian martial arts films of the 1970s—with the addition of a cool Japanese girl band that just happens to be on the scene to provide musical accompaniment.

Tarantino was widely criticized for breaking up *Kill Bill* into two "volumes" just to make more money, and it is certainly the case that

Vol. 2 directly continues the narrative of *Vol. 1*, if "continues" is an appropriate word in a narrative that is nonlinear throughout. *Vol. 2* includes less trademark Tarantino over-the-top violence and more trademark Tarantino witty dialogue, but it is still all Tarantino through and through. Which is to say it is all borrowed from somewhere else, though here the sources are somewhat different than in *Vol. 1*, leading to the production of a decidedly different film, with different moods and different styles. *Vol. 2* is, for example, less cartoonish and includes no animated segments, though we do discover that Bill is a fan of superhero comic books, especially *Superman* (which marks his taste in such matters as a bit old-fashioned and square).

In *Kill Bill: Vol. 2*, the Bride's name (spoken several times in *Vol. 1*, but always bleeped out) is revealed to be Beatrix Kiddo. Having begun her program of revenge in *Vol. 1* by killing off the first two members of the Deadly Viper Assassination Squad, of which she had formerly been a member, Kiddo proceeds in *Vol. 2*, quietly and grimly in the mode of Clint Eastwood's nameless gunslinger, to kill off the remaining two Vipers (though, strictly speaking, one actually kills the other, and the remaining one is not unequivocally dead at the end). These two, incidentally, are played, respectively, by Tarantino favorite Michael Madsen and by Daryl Hannah, whose casting represents another Tarantino blast from the past. Kiddo then, after a brief interlude in which it appears that she might show mercy after all, finally kills Bill himself.

All of this is predictable, despite the considerable difficulties (such as being buried alive) encountered by Kiddo in besting these formidable foes, but predictability here is a virtue, not a flaw, part of the fun of the film. The *Kill Bill* films announce early on what kind of films they are going to be, thus creating certain specific audience expectations. They then proceed to fulfill those expectations, teasing audiences with the occasional hint of a possible surprise, but always ultimately delivering just what audiences want and expect. This is, of course, the Hollywood formula to perfection, and it is a formula that Tarantino employs like a master in these films, while keeping the formula fresh, partly because of his female protagonist and partly because he so lovingly and playfully employs the formula, treating it with respect without taking it too seriously. As usual with Tarantino, the hip soundtrack helps greatly here, combining with Tarantino's numerous winks at the audience (and at his own style) to help the films achieve his usual coolness and to create a sense that these pictures are somehow transgressive and subversive of bourgeois virtue. The films are thus guilty pleasures that audiences can enjoy, not despite but *because* they feel like they are being slightly bad to appreciate such fare. In this, the films are also paradigms of post-modernist culture and of the strategies of late capitalism as a whole, which deftly maintains the loyalty of its subjects largely by allowing them to feel that they are able to get away with being a little bit disloyal any time they want.

In *Kill Bill: Vol. 2*, Tarantino even supplies audiences with additional comfort by supplying a sentimental happy ending. Having completed the campaign of revenge that has been her sole purpose in life, Kiddo is not (in the mode of *Memento*'s Leonard Shelby) left empty and point-less. Instead, she is reunited with the now four-year-old daughter she thought had been killed in her womb when she herself was wounded and left for dead years earlier by Bill and the Deadly Vipers. The baby, as it turns out, had been snatched from her wound as she lay near death, then given a loving upbringing by Bill himself (who is, after all, the girl's father). All of this, of course, is pure Hollywood cliché, but then both of the *Kill Bill* films are largely collections of clichés borrowed from the movies, heaped knowingly and lovingly one upon another with joyous ebullience. This is postmodern pastiche with a vengeance, unapologetic about its origins in previous works of popular culture and unashamed that it has nothing new to say.

One might compare the end of *Kill Bill: Vol. 2* with the ostenta-tiously artificial happy ending of Oliver Stone's *Natural Born Killers* (1994), which is in fact based on a story by Tarantino. Here, however, the comfortable settlement of Mickey and Mallory into the banalities of everyday bourgeois existence has a powerful satirical bite, not only sug-gesting the violence that underlies orderly bourgeois existence but at the same time deriding Hollywood's preference for comfortably happy, even if silly, endings. *Kill Bill* makes no such statements with its ending (other than one last acknowledgment, even celebration, of its own lack of origi-nality), just as it fails to critique the penchant for violence in American society. But neither does *Kill Bill* celebrate the violence of American life: it merely declares that violence irrelevant to its project, which is to rep-resent popular culture itself, without an exploration of the roots of that culture.

Kill Bill is not about reality; it is about movies. The same might be said of numerous works by other prominent postmodern filmmakers. For example, if Tarantino has built his career on channeling the generic tradi-tions of film noir and martial arts movies, Robert Altman has built his important and distinguished career as a film director largely on the basis of revisiting established genres from a slightly skewed perspective. Thus, Altman "does" (or perhaps "redoes") the war movie in *M*A*S*H* (1970), revisits the Western in *McCabe and Mrs. Miller* (1971), and engages the hard-boiled detective story/film noir in *The Long Goodbye* (1973). Additional Altman films are built from preexisting materials of other kinds, as in his use of the country music industry in *Nashville* (1975), his engagement with the general American show-business ethos in *Buffalo Bill and the Indians* (1976), his related look at the fashion industry in *Prêt-à-Porter* (1994), or his satirical critique (and yet endorsement) of the movie industry in *The Player* (1992). Finally, other Altman films are direct adaptations of specific well-known earlier works from other media, such as *Popeye* (1980) and *The Prairie Home Companion* (2006).

Joel and Ethan Coen, though in a quirkier fashion, have pursued a career arc that is in many ways similar to that of Altman. They began with *Blood Simple* (1984), a relatively straightforward neo-noir film with just a few extra offbeat touches. Other noir-influenced Coen brothers films include the gangster drama *Miller's Crossing* (1990) and *Fargo* (1996), probably their most respected film to date. *O Brother, Where Art Thou?* (2000) builds on a number of predecessor traditions, while *Intolerable Cruelty* (2003) is a screwball comedy and *The Ladykillers* (2004) is a remake.

Meanwhile, in *The Man Who Wasn't There* (2001), the Coens take the practice of generic pastiche to a new high. Here, they literally attempt to recreate, from beginning to end, the classic film noir—in terms of both style and content. Set in 1948, this black-and-white picture looks very much like a film noir from that period. Music again plays a key role here, especially in the way romantic music suggests a past time of emotional fullness no longer available to the characters in the story. For example, one of the key moments in the film occurs when the narrator and protagonist, Ed Crane (Billy Bob Thornton), suddenly hears romantic piano music that contrasts dramatically with the emotional poverty of his own life. That life, however, is not entirely without incident. He hears the music as he is emerging from a crucial conversation in which Big Dave Brewster (James Gandolfini) has confessed that he is being blackmailed because of his involvement in an affair with a married woman, whom he claims Crane does not know. This conversation has a special charge, partly because of its atmosphere: it occurs in the midst of the annual Christmas party at Nirdlinger's Department Store, which Big Dave manages and which Dave's wife, the former Ann Nirdlinger (Katherine Borowitz), owns. But Crane's talk with Brewster has special significance to Crane primarily because he himself is the blackmailer, and he knows perfectly well that the woman with whom Big Dave is having an affair is Crane's own wife, Doris (Frances

McDormand), who works for Nirdlinger's as a bookkeeper. However, it is also the case that, given Crane's radical alienation from all of those around him, Brewster is perfectly correct in stating that Crane does not know the woman in question.

Crane, as the title indicates, is a hollow man, a walking embodiment of the postmodern waning of affect (displaced back into the 1940s), so estranged from the world around him and so little a part of that world that he is, in a very real (emotional) sense, simply not there. Later in the film, on trial for a murder he didn't commit (after escaping prosecution for the eventual killing of Brewster, which he *did* commit, albeit in self-defense), Crane muses that the only thing he is really guilty of is "living in a world that had no place for me." He is thus a paradigm of the alienation of which American society was beginning to become increasingly aware in 1948, the year in which the action of *The Man Who Wasn't There* takes place. Indeed, as I have explained in *Monsters, Mushroom Clouds, and the Cold War*, the phenomena of alienation (in the class Marxist sense) and routinization (in the sense indicated by Max Weber in his vision of the magicless, routinized, rationalized world of modern capitalism) are perhaps the two central concepts required to understand American society and culture during the entire period of the long 1950s (1946–1964). Crane, even though his lack of affect seems typical of a later period, is in this sense a character straight out of the pulp novels and films noirs of the long 1950s. Not only is he radically alienated, but his life is a routinized stream of mind-numbing repetition, symbolized in his work as a barber, repeatedly cutting the same hair in the same styles, so that it can grow back only to be cut again. In this sense, the striped barber pole outside the shop becomes a key image in the film; ever-moving and seeming to strive to climb upward, the pole, like Crane, never gets anywhere. As Crane himself later describes his work in the barbershop, which has been mortgaged to pay Doris's legal fees after she has been charged with Brewster's murder, "We were trying to stay afloat, make the payments, tread the water. Day by day, day by day."

Much of *The Man Who Wasn't There* revolves around the story of Crane's attempts to escape the stifling routine of his barber job. Unfortunately, Crane does not have a great deal of imagination, and the world around him offers few opportunities for adventure and romance. Most of the plot is actuated by his vision of getting out of the haircutting business and into the emerging field of dry cleaning, hardly the most romantic of endeavors. He then blackmails Brewster to get money to invest in the dry-cleaning business, beginning a series of calamities in Crane's life and ultimately leading to his execution for a murder he did not commit.

However, the idyllic music that Crane hears after his conversation with Big Dave at the Christmas party seems for once to offer a hint of something genuinely different, something pure and grand, that might hold the key to overcoming his alienation and routinization. When he follows the sound of this music to its source, he discovers that it is being played by Rachel "Birdy" Abundas (a then-unknown Scarlett Johansson), a local teenager with whose father, local lawyer Walter Abundas (Richard Jenkins), Crane is vaguely acquainted. Appropriately enough, given Crane's pathetic predicament, the music being played is the slow second movement of Beethoven's Piano Sonata No. 8 ("Pathétique"). However, the uncultured Crane does not recognize the music and instead asks Birdy if she "made it up." "Oh no," she replies. "No, that was written by Ludwig van Beethoven." "Well, it was quite something," says Crane. "Yes," says Birdy, "he wrote some beautiful piano sonatas."

Those sonatas, in fact, form the heart of the soundtrack of *The Man Who Wasn't There*, which also includes passages from Sonatas 14 ("Moonlight"), 15 ("Pastorale"), 23 ("Appassionata"), 25, and 30. These sonatas carry much the same utopian resonance that Caryl Flinn notes in relation to the classical music in the scores of Hollywood films of the 1940s. However, in this case the allusion to Beethoven is mediated through the more direct allusion to late-1940s cinema, just as the nostalgia of the Coen brothers' film seems to be directed more at that cinema than at the classical music of the nineteenth century. Still, the sonatas play a major thematic role in the film and do not serve merely to contribute to the evocation of the look and feel of a 1940s film. The "Pathétique" is especially important, functioning throughout the film as Birdy's personal specialty and Crane's personal favorite, perhaps because its melancholy mood matches his own. However, the sonata also suggests depths of emotional experience of which Crane himself is entirely incapable, thus highlighting his emotional impoverishment.

As the film progresses and Crane's troubles mount (he kills Big Dave in a scuffle, then Doris is charged with the crime and commits suicide in jail), he becomes more and more obsessed with Birdy and her music. He finds, in listening to her play, "some kind of escape, some kind of peace." This music-based longing for escape precisely echoes the utopian use of classical music in 1940s Hollywood films, though in Crane's case it also serves as a sort of sublimation for his obvious sexual attraction to the young girl. The complete intermixture, in Crane's mind, of Beethoven's music and the girl Birdy is strongly emphasized as he approaches her from behind as she sits at the piano, her silhouette, lit from the front, looking decidedly dreamlike.

Then again, as Flinn notes, musical utopias in film noir are quite commonly associated with women, such films tending "to associate femininity with lost, musical moments" (117). For Crane, both Birdy and her music become emblems of what is missing from his current life. After Doris's death, he dreams of giving up his job as a barber in order to manage Birdy's professional career on the concert stage, thereby helping her and at the same time gaining the opportunity, as he puts it, to "be with her. Enough to keep myself feeling okay. Why couldn't that work?"

Why it couldn't work is pretty obvious (even if he could be content with a purely professional relationship, no one could possibly be more ill-suited to a career in music management than Crane, who knows nothing about either music or management), and this plan seems decidedly unpromising from the outset. It seems even more doomed retrospectively when we learn at the end of the film that all of the action is being narrated in flashback by Crane as he awaits execution in the state pen. This predoomed quality of Crane's utopian dreams is typical of the film noir: one here thinks of predecessors such as Rudolph Maté's *D.O.A.* (1950), which begins with the protagonist's announcement that he has been murdered, then proceeds to tell the story of the killing in flashback.

Birdy, as the pubescent object of Crane's middle-aged desire, is the direct successor to James M. Cain's Lola Nirdlinger, the young stepdaughter of Phyllis Nirdlinger in James M. Cain's novel *Double Indemnity* (1936). In the book, protagonist-narrator Walter Huff begins an abortive courtship with Lola, seeking something pure and unsoiled amid the tawdriness of his life, which includes an earlier and decidedly soiled affair with Phyllis, in which he helped her to murder her husband, Lola's father, in the hopes of collecting his life insurance. Indeed, Huff is an empty man very much like Crane, and the links between *The Man Who Wasn't There* and *Double Indemnity* are numerous. The Coens' prominent use of the name Nirdlinger is clearly meant to signal this connection to Cain's novel, though the more obvious connection, in terms of both theme and style, is to Billy Wilder's 1944 cinematic version of *Double Indemnity*. In the film, however, Huff's name is changed to Neff, and the Nirdlinger family name is changed to Dietrichson, so that the Coens' use of the Nirdlinger name clearly indicates the novel, rather than the film. In addition, *The Man Who Wasn't There* also includes a coroner named Diedricksen, thus acknowledging the name change.

That the Coens would refer to *Double Indemnity*, perhaps the single most representative work of the film noir genre, is no accident: *The Man Who Wasn't There* goes out of its way to indicate its participation in that genre, which has heavily informed the work of the Coen brothers ever since *Blood Simple*. If anything, Wilder's film is even darker and more cynical than Cain's novel; however, the film, taking full advantage of its medium, is also much campier and more theatrical. Thematically, the Coens' film, emotionally flat and dead, is almost totally lacking in this theatrical energy, making it the darkest of the three. On the other hand, the Coens' picture is a stylistic tour de force, and the obvious anachronism of its style contains campy resonances of its own.

Of course, Wilder's film version of *Double Indemnity*, like film noir in general, is already stylistically over-the-top, already tending toward the postmodern. Crane is even more postmodern than Huff/Neff and is even further gone toward total loss of cognitive mapping and complete subjective dissolution, his thorough lack of genuine identity signaled by the impoverished nature of his language relative to the snappy dialogue that is so central to the film version of *Double Indemnity*. Walter and Phyllis may speak in clichés, but their dialogue contains a zany energy, while the dialogue (and narration) of Crane is almost totally bereft of such energy, just as the film itself is almost entirely lacking in the sexual charge that crackles through the scenes of *Double Indemnity*. More than anything else, the laconic Crane is a quiet man who speaks as little as possible. When he does speak, he sounds tired: tired of his marriage, tired of his job, tired of his life—to the point that he genuinely seems to welcome the death by electrocution that awaits him at the film's end after he has been convicted of the murder of the traveling dry-cleaning entrepreneur with whom he had hoped to do business and who had actually been killed by Big Dave, who thought him the blackmailer.

All of this confusion and misrecognition resonates thematically with Crane's own sense of being lost in a world he cannot understand. In Birdy, however, he sees a potential anchor, a possible fixed point in the turning world. It is also clear that, whether he admits it to himself or not, Crane sees in Birdy a potential restoration of his lost sexual energy, the correspondence in their avian names indicating (to viewers, though probably not to Crane) what he sees as a possibly fateful match. The problem, however, is that Birdy, far from being the gifted artist he takes her for, is a rather ordinary teenager who would rather be a veterinarian than a concert pianist. In this sense, she is highly reminiscent of Vladimir Nabokov's Lolita (another character from the era of film noir), just as Crane's attempts to explain his desire for the teenage girl in terms of a respect for art resemble Humbert Humbert's attempts to explain his craving for nymphets in purely aesthetic terms in *Lolita*. Of course, Humbert is himself an aesthete who can draw on the entire tradition of

Western art and literature in an attempt to substantiate his spurious claim. Crane, on the other hand, is a working-class stiff who knows nothing about art or music and does not realize that Birdy's playing of the "Pathétique" sonata is uninspired, just as he seems entirely unaware that the slow movement of this sonata is unusually easy to play by the standards of the classical canon.

When Crane takes Birdy to San Francisco to audition for a prestigious piano teacher, Jacques Carcanogues (Adam Alexi-Malle), he is informed that her playing, while technically accurate, is totally lacking in passion or genuine talent. Her playing, in short, lacks emotional energy, in keeping with the theme of waning affect that runs through this film like a musical leitmotif. "Nice girl," explains the flamboyantly pretentious teacher. "However, stinks." Driving back to their Northern California home, Birdy assures Crane that she really doesn't care and she greatly appreciates his efforts to help her—so much so that she dives headfirst into his lap in an attempt to "make him happy." As she fumbles at his fly with the intent of performing fellatio, Crane is completely flustered. In contrast to the snappy erotic comebacks of his predecessor Walter Neff, he is able merely to utter, "Heavens to Betsy, Birdy," before running off the road and crashing the car.

The zany cinematography of the car crash scene is pure Coen brothers and represents one of the few cases in which the film breaks with its film noir predecessors in terms of style. The car is shown flying through the air in slow motion, followed by a blackout and a whimsical shot of a shiny rolling dislodged hubcap (reminiscent of the enigmatic hat that blows across the landscape of the Coens' *Miller's Crossing*) that eventually metamorphoses into a flying saucer and zips away into the distance. Flying saucers (and visual echoes of them, such as round light fixtures and lamps) constitute an important part of the background world of the film, as do references to the notorious Roswell UFO incident, a key marker of the year 1948 in the mythology of American popular culture. Indeed, similar circular images circulate throughout *The Man Who Wasn't There* in what might be taken as signs of something whole, complete, and perfect that contrast with the obvious imperfection of Ed Crane's life. As Flinn notes in relation to the use of similar sequences of round images in *Detour*, such images might also, from a Freudian perspective, be taken as signs of the feminine (123). It is certainly the case, in *The Man Who Wasn't There*, that women form an important part of the film's pattern of failed utopian images, Doris standing in for a past that is lost and irretrievable, Birdy functioning as an emblem of a future that can never be.

In any case, amid the rampant routinization of everyday life as presented in the film, the flying saucers of *The Man Who Wasn't There* seem to offer at least some hope that there really is something more than the dreary routine of going to work and paying bills, a phenomenon that also partly explains the fascination with science-fiction films (and UFOs) in the long 1950s. This motif might also be taken as a typical example of Coen-brothers quirkiness, though it should be noted that such science-fictional hints of something outside the ordinary sometimes occur even in the original films noirs of the period, as in the drug-induced hallucinations of *Murder, My Sweet* (1944) or the (apparently nuclear) explosion that helps *Kiss Me Deadly* (1955) to end with a definite bang.

Still, no matter how authentically *The Man Who Wasn't There* may reproduce the style and content of the films noirs of the long 1950s, it is surely the case that this style has a different meaning in a movie released in 2001 than it might have had in one released in 1948. For the most part, *The Man Who Wasn't There* looks and feels very much like a film noir from the forties. But its self-conscious pastiche of 1940s film noir style inevitably introduces postmodern effects that would not be present in an actual picture from the 1940s. The Coens may have produced a near-perfect imitation of a 1940s film, but it is an imitation nevertheless—and one that openly acknowledges its own secondary and mediated status.

The gestures toward science fiction in *The Man Who Wasn't There* indicate the importance of particularly well-defined popular genres such as science fiction and horror (in addition to film noir) as models for postmodern film. For example, Canadian director David Cronenberg began his career in the tradition of the horror film, moving eventually into science fiction and film noir as well. As William Beard puts it, Cronenberg's cinema "is an outstanding example of a body of work, signed by a single person, that manifests an incredibly tight and consistent group of subjects, themes, and attitudes as well as an identifiable style—in other words, all the essential requirements for status as authorial cinema" (ix). However, much of what is distinctive about Cronenberg's work does not involve breaking new ground so much as reworking old generic ground in interesting ways.

Cronenberg's first commercial film, *Shivers* (1975), already contains many of the characteristics that would come to be associated with his unique style. In a rather classic horror-film mode, *Shivers* involves the inhabitants of a luxury high-rise apartment building (Starliner Towers), who find their building invaded by weird parasites produced as a result of the experiments of Dr. Emil Hobbes (Fred Doederlein), a mad scientist who lives in their midst. Here the similarities to the relatively demure traditional horror films up to that time end. For one thing, the parasites turn those they infest into ravening sex maniacs, and the film features numerous graphic scenes of rape and nudity as those who are infected sexually assault the uninfected, in the process transferring the parasite to their victims. To this extent, the picture is a fairly transparent allegory about venereal disease, and indeed another scientist in the film, Dr. Rollo Linski (Joe Silver), at one point describes the parasites as a "combination aphrodisiac and venereal disease."

However, *Shivers* goes well beyond this simple allegorical interpretation. For one thing, the parasites are produced out of Hobbes's neo-Freudian belief that civilization had made human beings unhappy and unhealthy by distancing them from their natural animalistic inclinations and that a truly better world could be achieved by stripping away inhibitions and allowing individuals to act on their natural erotic impulses. In this way, the film interrogates many of the assumptions of the sexual liberation movement of the 1960s, while also engaging an intellectual tradition that goes back not only to Freud but to nineteenth-century degeneration theory.

Furthermore, in its depiction of the assault of the parasites on the human body, *Shivers* goes beyond anything seen in commercial cinema to that time. The mob of infected maniacs is in many ways reminiscent of the cannibalistic zombies of George Romero's cult classic *Night of the Living Dead* (1968), but Cronenberg's film is far more graphic. Particularly shocking is a bloody scene (clearly anticipating the notorious "chest-bursting" scene of 1979's *Alien*) in which one host, Nicholas Tudor (Allan Kolman), has several of the parasites burst through his abdomen. One of these then leaps onto the face of Linski, who has come to the high-rise to try to fight the infestation. As it lands on Linksi, it apparently secretes a sort of acid that begins to burn its way through the skin. When Linski attempts to fight off the parasite, he is attacked and beaten to a bloody pulp by Tudor. Ultimately, the parasites win out, and the inhabitants of the high-rise issue forth into the countryside to spread the contagion as the film comes to an ominous end.

As Cronenberg's *Rabid* (1977) opens, Dr. Dan Keloid (Howard Ryshpan), the head of Keloid Clinic, discusses with his wife, Dr. Roxanne Keloid (Patricia Gage), and their business partner, Murray Cypher (Joe Silver), the possibility of turning their clinic into the flagship of a chain of franchised plastic surgery clinics. Roxanne and Cypher are enthusiastic about the idea, but Dan is reticent, noting that he has no desire to become the Colonel Sanders of plastic surgery. Then, a motorcycle crash near the clinic sends Rose (former porn star Marilyn Chambers) into emergency surgery, where Dan, lacking the facilities he needs for such an operation, decides to gamble on an experimental procedure to repair her injuries. As a result of this surgery, Rose's tissue begins to evolve in weird directions. In particular, she develops a strange, vulva-like wound under her arm from which a tentacle-like appendage emerges and injects those who come near her (Dan Keloid himself will eventually be one of the victims) with a contagion that turns them into crazed, drooling vampire-zombies, attacking anyone who comes near them. Their saliva contains the contagion, and anyone bitten by them in turn becomes a vampire-zombie.

The authorities react quickly, dispatching expert teams to kill the zombies and destroy their bodies. Nevertheless, the contagion seems to be spreading. Rose is essentially a carrier only; she remains unaffected by the contagion. However, she is eventually killed by one of the zombies, and the film ends as her body is picked up by one of the government disposal teams, though it is unclear whether they will be able to hold the contagion in check.

Rabid is in many ways a fairly conventional vampire/zombie film, though the wound and tentacle under Rose's arm, composed of tissue that has evolved from her own but that is now alien to her, prefigures the sort of images of the mutability and permeability of the human body that will mark Cronenberg's work throughout his career. Meanwhile, the fact that Rose's problems begin with a traffic accident also anticipates one of Cronenberg's major fascinations: the way our technology often causes violent damage to the physical body. Vehicle crashes are, after all, a prime example of technology gone out of control, with often dire consequences for humanity.

The Brood (1979) deals with the attempts of psychiatrist Hal Raglan (Oliver Reed) to develop a new form of therapy known as psychoplasmics. Unfortunately, the therapy (through some unstated mechanism) seems to have a tendency to cause cancer in many of his patients. Meanwhile, the effect on star patient Nola Carveth (Samantha Eggar) is even more bizarre. Somehow, the therapy has caused her to produce a brood of deformed offspring who respond to her moods. In particular, they have a proclivity for brutal, murderous attacks on anyone toward whom she feels anger. After a number of such murders are followed by the kidnapping of Nola's "normal" daughter Candice (Cindy Hinds), Nola's husband, Frank Carveth (Art Hindle) finally tracks the brood back to their hideout in Raglan's compound. While Raglan attempts to free Candice from the brood upstairs, Frank tries to calm Nola downstairs (and thus render the brood passive) by proclaiming his ongoing love for her. In the film's key moment, the beautiful Nola opens her robe to reveal her now grotesque body, deformed by numerous huge tumors, including an external flesh sack in which she produces her mutant children. Realizing that Frank finds her body repellant, Nola grows angry, causing the brood to kill Raglan. Candice escapes after Frank kills Nola, causing the brood to die as well. The film ends, however, with a suggestion that Candice might have been infected with the same affliction that made her mother a monster.

In *Scanners* (1981), Cronenberg moves into science fiction, as the unscrupulous ConSec Corporation attempts to develop mutant telepaths (the "scanners" of the title) for use as weapons. "Psychopharmacist" Dr. Paul Ruth (Patrick McGoohan), who accidentally created the first scanners as the side effect of an experimental drug, Ephemerol, that he developed as a tranquilizer for pregnant women, now works for the corporation, but finds that his efforts are being opposed by an underground organization of the scanners themselves, led by Darryl Revok (Michael Ironside), who turns out to be Ruth's own mutant son. The corporation, meanwhile, employs scanner Cameron Vale (Stephen Lack) in opposition to Revok. In the resulting battle, Ruth is killed, and ConSec's entire computer system is destroyed in an effort to stop Vale, who is using his psychic powers to hack into the system. In a final confrontation between Revok and Vale, Revok reveals that Vale is his brother, but Vale still refuses to cooperate with him. In a titanic duel of psychic powers, Vale's body is dramatically destroyed then burned, but his mind ends up in possession of Revok's body, making Vale the victor after all—though we are left to wonder about the eventual fate of the scanners in general. Numerous women seem to be pregnant with scanner babies, and there are hints that the scanners may eventually dominate the world.

In *Videodrome* (1983; discussed in the next chapter as an example of postmodern films addressing the phenomenon of television), Cronenberg combines horror and science fiction in a typically postmodern mode of genre mixing, much as Ridley Scott's classic *Blade Runner* (1982) combines science fiction and film noir.

In *The Dead Zone* (1983, released only a few months after *Videodrome*), Cronenberg returns to straight horror, but in somewhat more mainstream style—and begins to demonstrate his skills as an adaptor of novels to film. In this case, the source is a novel by horror master Stephen King. Here, protagonist Johnny Smith (Christopher Walken) is badly hurt in an automobile accident early in the film, but otherwise there is relatively little emphasis on the kind of damage (or modifications) to the human body that are perhaps the most memorable images from Cronenberg's early works. Instead, the modification here is psychic: awaking from a five-year coma after the accident, Smith finds that he has somehow gained psychic powers that enable him to have visions of the possible futures of people with whom he comes into contact. He eventually realizes, however, that he can also use the knowledge gained from these visions to take action to change the future. Thus, when he shakes hands with sleazy senatorial candidate Greg Stillson (Martin Sheen), he has a vision that shows Stillson one day ascending to the presidency and then initiating a nuclear holocaust. Determined to prevent this future from occurring, Smith attempts to assassinate Stillson. He fails (and is himself killed in the process), but Stillson's cowardly reaction to the attempt (he grabs and holds up a baby to shield himself from the bullets) ruins his political career and achieves the desired effect after all. *The Dead Zone* is one of Cronenberg's most commercial efforts, and it is perhaps not surprising that the same material later became the basis for a successful television series (with which Cronenberg was not involved).

With *The Fly* (1986), Cronenberg remade a classic 1950s B-movie science-fiction/horror flick. However, this film's graphic depiction of the technology-induced transformation (and ultimate destruction) of the body and mind of scientist Seth Brundle (Jeff Goldblum) is vintage Cronenberg.

In a similar way, *Dead Ringers* (1988) is loosely based on preexisting material, in this case the novel *Twins* (1977) by Bari Wood and Jack Geasland, which was itself based on the true story of twin gynecologists Stewart and Cyril Marcus. Once again, however, Cronenberg puts his distinctive stamp on the film, though this time relying more on general creepiness than graphic visuals, and more on psychological than physical disturbance and destruction. The Marcus twins here become Elliott and Beverly Mantle (both disturbingly portrayed by Jeremy Irons), and the film becomes largely a psychological exploration of their status as a single mind somehow split between two individual bodies, with the tragic result that both twins are doomed to incomplete and unfulfilling lives.

Dead Ringers marked the emergence of Cronenberg as a far more serious filmmaker than many had earlier given him credit for being. In *Naked Lunch* (1991), he further established his status as a cult director when he took on the formidable task of adapting William S. Burroughs's classic 1959 novel of the same title, a surreal fantasy generally regarded as impossible to dramatize on the screen. Indeed, Cronenberg does not so much adapt the novel to film as attempt to convey on screen some of the basic atmosphere of the original. The result is less than satisfying, especially as an adaptation, but it is certainly interesting to watch, providing an ideal vehicle for some of Cronenberg's trademark images of bodily destruction, a motif that would reach its cinematic zenith in *Crash* (1996), probably Cronenberg's most notorious film.

Crash again centrally relies on dialogue with earlier films, in this case with the whole history of violence in the cinema. In a film based on J. G. Ballard's 1973 novel of the same title, Cronenberg's characters literally become sexually fascinated with the destruction of their own bodies in automobile accidents. The sexually charged violence of *Crash* also drew an NC-17 rating and made it one of the most controversial movies of the 1990s. Actually, this film contains relatively little violence and depicts less actual destruction of the human body than most Cronenberg films. What was contentious was the inclusion of highly graphic sex scenes and its attempt to relate the erotic energies of those scenes to the rush derived from the violence of car crashes. The picture was eventually released in a watered-down R-rated version (which eliminated the most graphic sex scenes from the original cut), although even this version seemed depraved to many critics and viewers, who saw it as a voyeuristic look at a group of sick weirdos who get their sexual kicks from car crashes. That description is not entirely inaccurate, but it entirely fails to comprehend the film's core premise: The characters who seem so sexually aroused by cars in general and even by the destruction of the human body in car crashes are not aberrant perverts—they are the personification of a very mainstream fascination with technology, regardless of the violence that technology might do to the human body.

The most sinister character in *Crash* is Vaughan (Elias Koteas), a former traffic systems analyst who has now become a sort of performance artist of car crashes. As he puts it, the primary fascination of his project is "the reshaping of the human body by modern technology," though he later admits that this is a "crude science fiction concept" that he uses to put a more acceptable veneer on the sexual nature of his fascination. Nevertheless, his stated focus is very much that of Cronenberg's films, so that *Crash* could be taken as a sort of ironic interrogation of Cronenberg's own oeuvre. Meanwhile, the film's central figure is James Ballard (James Spader), a TV producer, so that television is also implicated in the film's exploration of our culture's mutually implicated fascination with sex, violence, and technology.

Crash, however, explores this fascination in an oddly oblique way, by stipulating a sexual fetish so weird that no one in the audience is likely to share or even to understand it. It is probably the strangeness of this fetish to most viewers that makes the film seem so perverse (or just plain boring) to many of them, though this strangeness also potentially produces a cognitive distance that invites viewers to think about the workings of fetishism and fascination in general, rather than becoming emotionally involved in the lives of the characters. Still, this very estrangement from reality makes the film a sort of postmodern simulacrum: a representation of something of which there is no original in reality.

Otherwise, this highly controversial picture is actually not all that unusual: numerous films focus on sexual passion and have equally graphic sex scenes, but in them the sexual passion is ignited by something more conventional (and socially acceptable), such as the physical attractiveness of the partners, especially the female ones. Cronenberg does not entirely dispense with such conventional motifs (Deborah Kara Unger looks exquisite in one of the principal erotic roles), but *Crash* largely depends on a sort of "invented" passion that will appear natural to almost no one. *Crash* potentially assesses the central emphasis on sex and violence in the movie industry as a whole by making it appear contrived and artificial. In the same way, the film may comment on the way in which our growing reliance on technology is making *every* aspect of life more artificial, though it is unlikely that the film would cause many viewers to rethink their attitudes toward technology in any serious way.

Cronenberg further explores the deterioration of reality as a result of our reliance on technology in *eXistenZ* (1999), one of several reality-bending science-fiction films that appeared around the end of the 1990s, spurred by popular interest in the growth of technologies for the generation of virtual reality. Other such films include Robert Longo's *Johnny Mnemonic* (1995), Kathryn Bigelow's *Strange Days* (1995), Brett Leonard's *Virtuosity* (1995), Alex Proyas's *Dark City* (1998), Josef Rusnak's *The Thirteenth Floor* (1999), and Andy and Larry Wachowski's *The Matrix* (1999) and its sequels. *EXistenZ* is clearly a science-fiction film, though its particular visuals, more than any of these other films, are reminiscent of the horror film, reflecting Cronenberg's roots in that genre.

Cronenberg's play with the horror film is especially striking, but even an "art film" director like David Lynch (in addition to his extensive engagement with the tradition of film noir) has made significant use of this presumably lowly genre in his work. For example, Lynch began his career in feature films with the decidedly strange *Eraserhead* (1977), a film that is difficult to categorize but is clearly related to the horror genre. A nightmarish surreal fantasy that has become a cult classic despite (or perhaps because of) the fact that it breaks all the rules of Hollywood cinema, *Eraserhead* is nearly uninterpretable in terms of normal categories of plot and character, relying instead on its striking black-and-white images to produce emotional effects.

Set in a blighted and decaying urban industrial environment, *Eraserhead* can be read as science fiction, especially as dystopian fiction. The film has a protagonist, in the person of Henry Spencer (Jack Nance, who would remain a regular in Lynch's films until his own death in 1996), a sort of Everyman who encounters a sequence of nightmares of modern life, ranging from the banal dinner with the girlfriend's parents to the birth and death of his grotesquely mutated baby to actual nightmares involving a singing and dancing girl who lives in the radiator of his seedy apartment. But the actual nightmares of his sleeping hours and the nightmarish texture of his waking life are really all of a piece, constructed of the same surreal dreamlike imagery in an attempt (apparently) to make a statement about the dehumanizing nature of modern life.

Eraserhead may be as close as Lynch ever comes to producing a unique individual statement on film, though even it derives its style from mixing horror and science fiction with preexisting avant-garde models. Further, its statement about modern urban life is not exactly original, either, even if the images with which it conveys this message are decidedly outside the ordinary. Interestingly, this, Lynch's strangest film, was followed by what is probably his most conventional, *The Elephant Man* (1980).

The *Elephant Man*, also shot in black-and-white, occasionally drifts into visuals that are reminiscent of *Eraserhead*, as in the surreal opening sequence or the long dream sequence midway through the film, but these visuals are mere punctuations (or perhaps distractions) within what is otherwise a reasonably straightforward account of the life of Joseph Merrick (John Hurt in an Oscar-nominated performance), a hideously deformed young man who actually lived in Victorian England from 1862 to 1890. Merrick, however, is identified in the film as "John Merrick," as he had been in early biographies. Otherwise, the film is relatively true to the historical record, although in this case historical truth is a sort of horror story. Most of the plot deals with Merrick's rise to public prominence (he becomes a favorite of Queen Victoria herself) as the result of his befriending by prominent physician Dr. Frederick Treves (Anthony Hopkins). While the real Treves discovered Merrick at a train station, in the film Treves first meets Merrick when the latter is a featured exhibit in a carnival freak show, emphasizing the horror elements of the story.

Merrick's story makes for some compelling human drama, and Lynch does an effective job of creating sympathy for his plight in relatively conventional Hollywood fashion. Presumably, the inserted moments of surreal strangeness are intended to suggest something of what it must have felt like to be Merrick or how Merrick might have appeared to his contemporaries. Some of the images involving large-scale steam-powered Victorian machinery look back to *Eraserhead* and can be taken to locate the beginnings of the urban blight of that film in the industrial revolution of the nineteenth century. Nevertheless, these rather modern scenes seem largely gratuitous and anachronistically out of place in what generally seems to be an attempt to evoke the authentic historical look and feel of Victorian London.

Ultimately, then, the actual point being made by *The Elephant Man* is no more precise (or original) than that made by the ostensibly much more obscure *Eraserhead*. Both films suggest that modern society is filled with horrors and that it is up to each individual to try to find moments of grace amid it all.

Similarly, *Dune* (1984), Lynch's adaptation of Frank Herbert's classic science-fiction novel, is a fairly ordinary genre film, energized with some trademark Lynch visuals. The look of this picture is probably the least distinctive of all of Lynch's films, perhaps because of its science-fictional setting on the planet Arrakis, but also because it was limited by a low budget that made it impossible for Lynch to achieve all of the effects he desired; Lynch himself has expressed displeasure with the final product. Fans of Herbert's novel have also generally panned Lynch's cinematic version, but the film is actually not nearly as bad as its reputation, even if, once again, it seems more interested in style than substance, while in this case failing to achieve the artistic effects that Lynch had hoped for.

Much of the work of Tim Burton also represents a particularly interesting example of postmodern engagement with the horror genre, though he has generally treated the genre more playfully than Cronenberg or Lynch—and in ways that have proved popular with broader audiences. Burton began his career as an animator for the Disney studios, producing such short films as *Vincent* (1982) and *Frankenweenie* (1984). The first of these was an animated short about a little boy who is obsessed with the ghoulish world of Vincent Price movies. In the film, the boy's morbid fascination with death eventually leads him simply to collapse and die, at least in his own mind. Predictably, Burton encountered considerable resistance concerning this film from Disney, which wanted to supply a happy ending. Equally predictably, Burton's career with Disney was short-lived. *Frankenweenie* was not even released by the studio in the United States and became available to the public in its full version only as an extra feature in the DVD release of *The*

Nightmare before Christmas (1993), an animated film produced, though not directed, by Burton—and one that shares much in macabre spirit with the later animated feature *The Corpse Bride* (2005), which Burton did co-direct.

Frankenweenie retells the Frankenstein story (especially as refracted through the 1931 James Whale film version of the Frankenstein story) in the setting of modern suburban America, with the monster replaced by a household dog, Sparky. When the dog is hit and killed by a car, its owner, schoolboy Victor Frankenstein (Barret Oliver), is plunged into despair. Using information gleaned from his school science class, young Victor brings the dog back to life, but its subsequent strange appearance (it has been roughly stitched back together and has a bolt in its neck) causes the neighbors to hate and fear it, eventually leading them to become a mob in the mold of the villagers of the original *Frankenstein* film, then to drive the dog to a second death. In the process, however, Sparky saves the life of Victor, leading the neighbors to realize that they have misjudged the animal. They then circle him with their automobiles and jump-start him back to life by wiring their car batteries to the bolt in his neck.

This time Burton does supply a happy ending, but a rather contrived one that cannot obscure the darkness of the film and its commentary on the hate and fear of the Other in suburban America. It was clear from the film that Burton's imagination was not well in tune with that of the Disney company. On the other hand, *Frankenweenie* drew the attention of Paul Reubens, who was looking for a director for a feature film based on his Pee-wee Herman character. *Pee-wee's Big Adventure* (1985) then launched Burton's career as a director of feature films, many of which are closely related to the horror genre. Perhaps the best example of this phenomenon is *Beetlejuice* (1988), which, like *Pee-wee's Big Adventure*, is essentially a live-action cartoon, though here the afterlife setting and supernatural theme allow Burton to suspend the laws of physics almost entirely, producing effects that are limited only by his imagination and available resources, both financial and technological.

Again, the plot of the film is rudimentary, and the movie is really a sequence of images rather than events. A happy couple, Adam and Barbara Maitland (Alec Baldwin and Geena Davis) are killed in an auto accident and find that, by the rules of the afterlife, they are required to remain in their former house for a period of 125 years before moving on. That, in itself, does not seem so bad, until the house is bought by the horrid Dietzes, Charles and Delia (Jeffrey Jones and Catherine O'Hara), who move into it, along with their brooding, black-clad daughter, Lydia (Winona Ryder). In response, the Maitlands attempt to drive the Dietzes away by haunting the house, aided (or perhaps hampered) by the antics of Betelgeuse (Michael Keaton), a professional bio-exorcist who specializes in getting rid of living humans who are causing problems for the dead. After a series of comic fiascos, Betelgeuse is eventually sent back to the afterlife where he belongs, while the Maitlands and Dietzes agree to coinhabit the house in peace.

However, the real story of *Beetlejuice* is not the plot, but the sequence of superb sight gags that help it to turn the horror/ghost story genre into an opportunity for high visual comedy, highlighted by the over-the-top performance of Keaton as the sex-obsessed title character, whose outrageous antics match his preposterous appearance. The opening sequence of the film, for example, is a long overhead tracking shot of a small New England town, apparently shot from a helicopter, which allows the shot to travel the full length of the town, ending with a view of an isolated house on a hill overlooking the town. But then this house (along with the entire town that has been shown in the opening sequence) turns out merely to have been a scale model built by one of the characters in the film. We are thus warned at the outset to expect the illusions of movie magic, and we will not be disappointed.

If *Beetlejuice* turns the horror story into comedy, it also subverts the boundaries of genre in that, again like *Pee-wee's Big Adventure*, it has the outward appearance of a children's film, but actually contains a great deal of adult material. For example, many of the jokes in *Beetlejuice* involve allusions to other films, such as *Night of the Living Dead* (1968), *Dirty Harry* (1971), and *The Exorcist* (1973), that many children would probably not recognize. Betelgeuse himself is practically a character from pornography; he spends much of his time in the film inhabiting Dante's Inferno, a supernatural whorehouse, meanwhile fondling Barbara at every opportunity and planning to force the pubescent Lydia to marry him so that he can have free access to her tender young body.

In addition, the basic subject matter of the film tends to undermine its status as a light comedy for children. Indeed, there is a darkly pessimistic undertone to the film's representation of the afterlife, which turns out to involve not an escape from life's troubles and worries but, if anything, an intensification of them. For one thing, ghosts in the afterworld still bear the marks of the wounds or ailments that sent them there, apparently doomed to bear these marks for eternity. For another, the afterworld itself is a bureaucratic tangle of waiting rooms, offices, and endless paperwork. Thus, death brings no respite from the routinization that penetrates everyday life under late capitalism, and, in *Beetlejuice*, the postmodern inability to imagine a better utopian future is extended to the ultimate, beyond the historical world to an afterlife of eternal, regimented tedium.

The surprising commercial success of both *Pee-wee's Big Adventure* and *Beetlejuice* led Warner Bros. to entrust Burton with the reins of *Batman* (1989), their big-budget adaptation of the classic comic book. In turn, Burton produced another commercial success, though one that involved a very different vision of the Caped Crusader than audiences might have expected, especially after the casting of Keaton in the title role. Burton interprets the comic book through the lens of film noir and through the "Dark Knight" of Frank Miller's graphic novels, producing a dark, dystopian Gotham City (which might here have been called Gothic City), pictured through spectacular visuals as a hotbed of sin and crime, a sort of big-city version of the dystopian Pottersville of Frank Capra's *It's a Wonderful Life* (1946). This dark city also clearly echoes the urban vision of Ridley Scott's *Blade Runner* (1982), a film whose visual style has made it a central example of the postmodern science-fiction genre. Meanwhile, after his performance in *Beetlejuice*, one might have expected Keaton to present a campy, over-the-top Batman, perhaps somewhat in the mold of the popular television series that ran from 1966 to 1968. Instead, Keaton produces a dark, brooding, Byronic Batman who is very much at home in the film's hellish Gotham City. Keaton's version of millionaire Bruce Wayne, Batman's alter ego, is much kinder and gentler, however, and Burton clearly seeks to present the Wayne/Batman dichotomy as a case of postmodern split personality.

With Keaton playing it essentially straight, the film derives most of its campy and comic elements from Jack Nicholson's bravura turn as the literally cartoonish Joker, a mad criminal genius with a personal grudge against Batman. Wayne, it turns out, has a grudge against the Joker as well, after he discovers that the Joker (then a young thug by the name of Jack Napier) murdered both of the elder Waynes in Bruce's childhood, helping to produce the dark strain in the boy's personality that would eventually become Batman. Most of the film's plot derives from the fact that the Joker initiates a reign of terror in the city, hoping thereby to establish himself as the head of all of the city's criminal operations, while killing the hated Batman in the process. All ends well, however. After a series of spectacular battles punctuated by superb special effects, Batman kills the Joker in a climactic duel, then recedes into the background, assuring the authorities that he will reappear if another crisis occurs. Wayne even gets the girl, in the person of beautiful photographer Vicki Vale (Kim Basinger), who loves him despite (or perhaps because of) his complexity and his dark side.

Batman thus turns out, at the level of plot, to be far less dark than its look would seem to imply. The sequel, *Batman Returns* (1992), is genuinely much darker, however, and Batman's split personality is emphasized even more, partly because he now acquires a love interest, Catwoman (Michelle Pfeiffer), who has a similar dark side. As Batman tells her in one scene, "We're the same. Split right down the center." In fact, like their principal antagonist, the grotesque Penguin (Danny DeVito), they are freaks, outsiders who can function within polite society only if they suppress an important element of their personalities.

This depiction of Batman as a troubled outcast contributes to the film's overall darkness, which triggered considerable initial criticism from adults who feared that it would traumatize small children. However, despite the ominous plot, the true darkness of the film again comes from its images, not its events. Here, though, the images—of the city, Batman, Catwoman, and the Penguin—are bleaker than ever. Film noir is again an important referent, in relation both to the shadowy, urban setting and the dark, divided protagonist. There are also a variety of other intertextual connections as well, including a number of Biblical echoes. For example, the young Penguin, monstrously deformed at his birth, is placed in his basket, Moses-like, in a small "river" (actually a drainage ditch). Then, 33 years later, à la Christ, he emerges from obscurity to pursue his mission.

Such Biblical allusions are potentially effective both because they are easily recognized by Christian audiences and because they carry significant symbolic resonance. One might, then, expect the Biblical echoes in *Batman Returns* to serve a symbolic function that adds meaning to the narrative, somewhat along the lines of the young couple representing Joseph and Mary in Ingmar Bergman's *The Seventh Seal* (1957). However, Burton's allusions are merely static and participate in no such large symbolic structures. Indeed, as a whole, the allusions in *Batman Returns* do not cohere into any sort of final meaning, but are simply there, piecemeal, operating like the images of the film to create isolated and fragmentary effects—or to provide pleasure to audiences who can congratulate themselves on catching the allusion.

Another particularly interesting instance of Burton's reliance on images rather than narrative can be seen in *Sleepy Hollow* (1999), his adaptation of Washington Irving's classic horror tale "The Legend of Sleepy Hollow." Here, Burton continues his project of updating earlier works and genres, this time (as with his adaptations of the Frankenstein story) reaching back to the early nineteenth century for source material. However, the film is only very loosely based on Irving's story, which is essentially a comic character study of protagonist Ichabod Crane, a gaunt and somewhat ridiculous New England schoolmaster. In the story, the ambitious and venal Crane contracts a fascination for local heiress Katrina Van Tassel, largely because of her family's wealth. He is then scared away by Katrina's other beau, Brom Van Brunt, who poses as the Headless Horseman, a fearsome figure of local legend, frightening Crane so badly that he flees the area never to return. This disappearance triggers rumors that he has, in fact, been carried off by the supernatural Horseman, but the story itself clearly treats this superstition with amusement, making clear Van Brunt's ruse and poking gentle fun at Crane's gullibility in falling for it.

Being a character study, "The Legend of Sleepy Hollow" is decidedly short on action, though it does contain two striking horror-genre images: the scarecrow-like figure of Crane, and the imposing figure of the Headless Horseman, who, despite the fact that he is a mere legend, managed to tap into the popular imagination and become an icon of American popular culture. Burton begins with these two images and produces a number of others, creating a supernatural tale in which the Headless Horsemen is real and is terrorizing Sleepy Hollow with a series of murders. In a typical case of postmodern genre bending, Burton also enriches the narrative by making it a sort of detective story. His Ichabod Crane (Burton favorite Johnny Depp) is a young detective from New York, sent to Sleepy Hollow to investigate the killings there. Crane, a devotee of new, scientific methods of investigation, is decidedly ahead of his time, though. By setting the action in 1799, Burton suggests a world that is itself on the cusp of a new, more enlightened century.[1]

This vague hint at sweeping historical change seems somewhat out of step with the typical ahistoricity of postmodernist culture. However, this nod at temporal specificity is largely illusory and is undermined by the film itself. If Crane's faith in science contrasts with the religiosity and superstition of most of the inhabitants of Sleepy Hollow, it is also the case that the real existence of the supernatural Horseman tends to undermine his scientific vision, suggesting that there are more things in Heaven and Earth than are dreamt of in his modern philosophy.

In any case, Burton's extremely loose adaptation of the Irving tale represents an especially good example of his particular postmodern vision of the process. Any adaptation, of course, selects the important elements of the original and then reemphasizes them. Traditionally, film versions of novels or stories have concentrated on plot and character in this regard, but Burton (in keeping with his usual emphasis) largely ignores these in favor of images. Thus, the most memorable images of the original story (the twisted and misshapen tree, the flying pumpkin, and—most of all—the figure of the Headless Horseman himself) are all there, even if the plot and characters have been substantially reformulated.

Burton, in fact, has cheerfully plundered the entire archive of cinematic history in constructing his films. In Burton's works, image truly is everything, creating a special kind of postmodern fragmentation. Burton does not foreground the fragmentation, stylistically and thematically, in the manner of Mike Figgis's *Timecode* or Christopher Nolan's *Memento* (both 2000). Instead, he employs relatively conventional editing and tells relatively straightforward, continuous stories, except that his films place little real emphasis on narrative and rely far more than do most Hollywood films on the visual flair of their director, a former Disney animator with a decidedly un-Disneylike gothic streak. As a rule, Burton's films use plot merely as a device to add a certain amount of motivation and coherence to what is otherwise primarily a sequence of striking visual images, almost in the mode of a slide show—or a comic book.

In some cases, the plots and themes of Burton's films seem downright silly; at other times they are vague and, at best, unmemorable. What is almost always memorable about Burton's films is their creation of striking images with a distinctive "look," whether it be in the infantilized commodity world of *Pee-wee's Big Adventure* (1985), the comic afterworld of *Beetlejuice*, the modern fairy-tale world of *Edward Scissorhands* (1990), the ominous, dystopian urban space of *Batman* and *Batman Returns*, or the simian-ruled alternative world of his remake of *Planet of the Apes* (2001). In his construction of films as streams of images, Burton resembles a number of other postmodern directors, although it should be emphasized that his image streams have little of the avant-garde feel of the films of say, Peter Greenaway, which hark back to the surrealist image collections of Luis Buñuel, while Burton's images remain in the realm of popular culture. Thus, the comparison between the painterly images of Greenaway and the cartoonish images of Burton again illustrates the dual heritage of postmodernism in the avant-garde and popular culture.

Pee-wee's Big Adventure, Burton's first feature film, directly addresses the Hollywood movie industry. Here, Burton already displays many of the characteristics that would mark his later work, even though this film was largely conceived by writers Phil Hartman and Paul Reubens based on their own (somewhat risqué) stage show, in which Reubens played the title character and Hartman played a variety of other characters. The character of Pee-wee Herman, himself a quintessential postmodern figure, thus owes essentially nothing to Burton. For one thing, he is a walking embodiment of postmodern boundary-crossing, an androgynous man-child who spans the oppositions between child and adult and male and female, just as the film itself clearly attempts to appeal to both adult and child audiences.[2] Pee-wee is also postmodern in the extent to which he is pure surface image with no depth, enacting Jameson's notion of the scattering of the subject in a postmodern era. The character of Pee-wee represents an interesting case of the postmodern simulacrum. In the film, Reubens does not *portray* Pee-wee so much as he *is* Pee-wee in an autobiographical role. Thus, in the cast credits, Reubens is not listed. Instead, the fictional character Pee-wee Herman is listed as playing himself.

All of these characteristics of the title character can be attributed to Hartman and (especially) Reubens, but the flow of the film is typical Burton. There is a rudimentary, quasi-mythic plot, in which Pee-wee embarks on a cross-country quest to recover his stolen bicycle. But this plot (or, rather, pastiche of a plot) is merely a loose framework that provides a vague connection among what are really just a series of skits and sight gags. Probably the most memorable of all of these is the opening scene in Pee-wee's home, a child's dream world richly adorned with toys, pets, contraptions, and other fantasy objects, described by Ken Hanke as "the most fantastic and pointlessly joyous excess imaginable" (58). The most important of all of these possessions is his one-of-a-kind custom bicycle, which has attained the status for Pee-wee of a commodity fetish. Thus, when it is stolen, he can neither live without it nor simply replace it. Instead, he must seek it out at all costs, leading to a sequence of comic misadventures.

Ultimately, and almost inevitably, the search leads Pee-wee to Hollywood, where he discovers that his beloved bicycle is being used in a film being made by Warner Bros., the studio that produced *Pee-wee's Big Adventure*. Where else would the ultimate commodity wind up but as a centerpiece in the ultimate form of commodified culture? Disguised as a nun, Pee-wee infiltrates the set and makes off with the bike, leading to a spirited chase around the Warner Bros. lot that allows Pee-wee to move, in rapid succession, from one set to another, passing through a beach movie, a children's Christmas movie, a Japanese monster movie, a hairband rock video, a Tarzan movie, and a western. This sequence thus essentially mimics the experience of television channel surfing. The chase dramatizes postmodern generic pluralism, ending in a gesture of postmodern intertextuality when Pee-wee escapes the lot by launching his bike into the air, riding across the sky in a send-up of the famous scene in which a bicycle takes flight in *E.T. the Extra-Terrestrial* (1982).

Impressed by Pee-wee's heroism, Warner Bros. decides to make a film about his adventures. Vaguely echoing such self-referential films as

8½ (1963), this is essentially a remake of the picture we've just seen, although, Hollywood being Hollywood, they grossly distort the "facts" in their remake, casting James Brolin as a dashing, James Bond–style Pee-wee glamorously battling ninjas and Soviet spies. Of course, these distortions are entirely ironic, as they do not really deviate from facts, but from fiction. The Brolin film is itself a simulacrum, a copy of a copy. Moreover, though ostensibly based on the events we've just seen in *Pee-wee's Big Adventure*, it is itself embedded within that movie, leading to a spiraling confusion of ontological levels, like mirrors in mirrors—as evidenced by Pee-wee himself making a cameo appearance in the film-within-a-film, thus becoming Reubens playing Pee-wee playing Pee-wee playing a bellhop.

The lighthearted satire of Hollywood in *Pee-wee's Big Adventure* lacks the artistic self-consciousness of Federico Fellini's *8½* or the satirical punch of Altman's *The Player*, but then *Pee-wee* is mostly an all-in-fun exercise in postmodern play. Thus, Pee-wee's immersion in commodities is hardly effective as a critique of modern consumer capitalism, even if it might be possible to tease such an appraisal out of the film with sufficient critical effort. For example, Pee-wee's total alienation (he is, we are repeatedly reminded, however comically, a loner and a rebel), combined with his utter lack of psychological depth, might be taken to suggest the destruction of the stable bourgeois subject in the consumerist environment of late capitalism. Neither male nor female, neither child nor adult, Pee-wee lacks any real identity at all. He is, in fact, merely a walking collection of quotations, speaking in scripted routines ("I know you are, but what am I?") and identifying himself only through the commodities he owns. Thus, his terror at the loss of his prize possession, the bicycle, might be attributed to the fact that, without the bicycle, Pee-wee doesn't know who he is.

Granted, the makers of *Pee-wee's Big Adventure* do not seem to intend this sort of interpretation, and Pee-wee, despite his distress, goes through the film in a rather good mood, accompanied by his trademark giggle. He is, after all, a comic character. However, lacking any real emotional depth, he can change moods suddenly and dramatically. For example, there is a point soon after the theft of his bike when he descends into despair and bitterness, snarling and hissing at everyone around him amid a dark mise-en-scène that seems largely remembered from film noir. In one scene, he walks through dark city streets, his shadow flaring up ominously on the buildings around him. Approached by a gang of street punks, he turns on them a visage so filled with hatred and angst that they run away in terror. This scene is not serious, of course; it is a mere set piece, a play-within-a-play. Pee-wee's dark side soon disappears, never to return in the film, and the obvious inauthenticity of this "evil" Pee-wee suggests the inauthenticity of his identity as a whole.

Pee-wee's identity is all style and no substance, making him the perfect character for Burton's all-image style—and also a particularly direct forerunner of Burton's version of Willy Wonka in *Charlie and the Chocolate Factory* (2005). Pee-wee is also very much a forerunner of Burton's version of the title character in *Ed Wood* (1994), the Burton film that is most directly about filmmaking. *Ed Wood*, however, displays a typical postmodern disregard for high/low distinctions by focusing on the career not of one of Hollywood's greats but of the filmmaker widely regarded as the worst of all time. *Ed Wood*, which traces Wood's career from the making of *Glen or Glenda* (1953) to the premiere of *Plan 9 from Outer Space* (1959) can also be seen as another example of postmodern nostalgia for the 1950s, though it includes virtually nothing in the way of historical context, concentrating its nostalgia entirely on Wood and his films, as if longing for a simpler time when it was still possible to make and even distribute such god-awful films.

As an expression of nostalgia for the 1950s, *Ed Wood* is a companion piece to Burton's later *Mars Attacks!* (1996), which similarly draws on nostalgia for the notorious science-fiction films of the 1950s, in this case Martian-invasion films such as *The War of the Worlds* (1953) and *Invaders from Mars* (1953). There is also an element of postmodern pastiche in *Ed Wood*, as Burton, one of Hollywood's virtuoso image makers, ironically seeks to create a simulation of the careless, low-budget style of Wood. Thus, the film opens with a cheesy sequence in which one of the characters introduces the film from a coffin in a haunted house in the midst of a lightning storm, followed by opening credits printed on gravestones in a fake-looking graveyard, and ending with incredible hokey-looking flying saucers bobbing about on the screen. This sequence, described by Hanke as "a kind of compendium of Ed Wood's films" (171), sets up the illusion that the picture is shot in Wood's own signature style. It is, however, only an illusion, created partly by the subject matter and largely by the fact that the film was shot in black-and-white (a decision that Burton rightly saw as crucial to the movie but that caused him to have to switch studios for its production when Universal balked at the idea of producing a black-and-white film).

This simulation of Wood's style is also aided by the fact that much of the film shows Wood at work on his own cheap sets and thus features a mise-en-scène that, though mediated, recalls the typical Wood film. The hokey feel of *Ed Wood* is further enhanced by the acting, for example, the over-the-top performance by Bill Murray as Wood associate and would-be transsexual Bunny Breckenridge. Especially important in this sense is Depp's outrageous turn as Wood himself, supposedly derived, on Burton's advice, from studying Mickey Rooney's manic performances in the old Andy Hardy films (Hanke, 162).[3] Depp's performance here is essentially the opposite of his later turn as Willy Wonka, yet both performances deftly suggest a postmodern lack of authentic subjective depth. Depp's portrayal of Wood also well conveys Wood's zany optimism and enthusiasm, while at the same time imparting a campy feel to *Ed Wood* that suggests the campy reception of Wood's films, especially *Plan 9 from Outer Space*, which have become cult classics.

The irony, of course, is that Wood apparently did not intend for his work to be campy but was actually trying to make good films. His one claim to success in this regard involved the fact that he was able to convince an aging and dilapidated Bela Lugosi (played brilliantly here by Martin Landau) to appear in his films. Landau's performance, which won him a Best Supporting Actor Oscar, is the only one in *Ed Wood* that might be regarded as conventionally "good" acting, as if to emphasize that Lugosi was the one authentic element in Wood's otherwise awful career. Meanwhile, Lugosi is treated in the film as a pathetic figure, a shadow of his former self, living in a virtual museum of his earlier pictures and immersed, in the 1950s, in nostalgia for the 1930s, when his career was at its peak.

The touching portrayal of the relationship between Wood and Lugosi obviously echoes Burton's own relationship with his childhood hero, 1950s-vintage horror star Vincent Price, who had appeared in *Edward Scissorhands* and who, in fact, was the focus of Wood's first film as a young animator for Disney, *Vincent*. Burton also treats Wood gently and almost lovingly. Rather than mock the legendarily bad director (which would be all too easy), he presents Wood much as he apparently saw himself, as a sort of misunderstood artist with a genius of his own, somewhat in the mode of Orson Welles. Among other things, Burton gives *Plan 9* an entirely fictional, but triumphant, premiere at the prestigious Pantages Theater, then allows Wood to ride off into the sunset on a high note, leaving out the years of alcoholic decline that followed the real-world failure of *Plan 9*—though it must be said that Wood remained indomitable, directing several more tawdry (and often pornographic) films after *Plan 9* and writing many others. But then *Ed Wood* is not particularly concerned with historical accuracy, seeking instead simply to convey the flavor of Wood's films and filmmaking process.

The science-fiction tradition is also crucial to Burton's "reimagining" of the 1968 sci-fi classic *Planet of the Apes* (which had been directed by Franklin Schaffner and was itself based on a novel by Pierre Boulle, making Burton's film an adaptation of an adaptation, a copy of a copy). Here, Burton maintains the central idea of an astronaut who lands on a planet ruled by apes, complete with the requisite images of apes in various forms of human garb, but otherwise dispenses with most of the original plot. For one thing, astronaut Leo Davidson (Mark Wahlberg) lands alone on the planet, while Schaffner's George Taylor (Charlton Heston) had been accompanied by three other astronauts. For another, Wahlberg's acting style is extremely subdued compared to the consistent overacting of the histrionic Heston, though for once Heston's style might here be justified: who wouldn't react strongly when placed in such a situation?

Davidson wouldn't, as it turns out, and he calmly makes his way through the film as if faced with a minor difficulty, like fixing a flat, though part of his calm might arise from the fact that the humans on the planet seem almost like regular everyday folks and thus can provide him with considerable support, while the humans in the original had degenerated into a state of near-bestiality. Such modifications make the Burton film seem emotionally absent, though it is no doubt also flattened because it is a remake and audiences thus know perfectly well that Davidson is going to end up on a planet ruled by apes. Burton also updates the nature of the film as a cautionary tale about the dangers of scientific research. The Cold War original is an anti–nuclear war story, the inversion of ruling species having been enabled on Earth because human civilization was destroyed in a nuclear holocaust. In the new version, genetic research is the culprit, the ascent of the apes having been triggered by the arrival on the planet of genetically modified super-apes from Earth.

Burton's cautionary tale is far less viscerally powerful than Schaffner's, partly because the technological threat it warns of seems less imminent and partly because his planet of the apes may not even be Earth. Meanwhile, Burton's film is quite self-conscious of its secondary status as a sort of reflection of Schaffner's film. For example, one of its best (and most postmodern) moments occurs in a scene in which Heston appears as a wise, aged ape who warns against the dangers of allowing humans to rebuild their once-mighty civilization. Heston's character then adduces an ancient, rusty gun as the epitome of the destructiveness of human civilization, a moment that is genuinely weird, both because it reverses Heston's earlier casting as a human opponent of the apes and because it seems to reverse the position of Heston, a well-known pro-gun advocate, on gun control.

As the film ends, Davidson attempts to return to Earth, landing in front of what appears to be the Lincoln Memorial, which thus plays the role played by the Statue of Liberty in the original. To his surprise, he discovers that the statue in the monument is not of Lincoln but of General Thane (Tim Roth), who had been Davidson's principal antagonist during his stay on the planet of the apes. Then, ape police arrive as well, making it clear that, if this is Earth, then Earth, too, is now ruled by apes. One possible explanation is that, as in the original film, Davidson was on Earth all along, but the ending is left intentionally vague. As a result, the visceral shock of the original ending is replaced by mere postmodern puzzlement.

The most extreme example of a postmodern remake is probably Gus Van Sant's 1998 reshooting of Alfred Hitchcock's *Psycho* (1960) with exactly the same script, virtually the same camera setups and mise-en-scène, and the same musical score. The only major deviations are the decision to shoot the new *Psycho* in color and the necessity of using a different cast of actors, with Vince Vaughan and Anne Heche replacing Anthony Perkins and Janet Leigh in the key roles of Norman Bates and Marion Crane. The results were mixed, to say the least, but Van Sant's version nevertheless represents a fascinating experiment in postmodern pastiche: the 1998 *Psycho* is essentially devoid of any commentary on Hitchcock, merely reproducing Hitchcock's film in an absolutely neutral way.

At the same time, the initial impact on audiences of Van Sant's *Psycho* differed dramatically from that produced by Hitchcock's. Van Sant's film has the flavor of a laboratory experiment and is emotionally quite flat, while Hitchcock's was widely regarded as one of the most shocking and emotionally powerful films ever to have appeared in mainstream American cinema. No doubt part of this difference is simply due to the audience awareness that Van Sant was reproducing Hitchcock, making his *Psycho* a sort of postmodern simulation of a film rather than a film proper and giving it an almost campy aspect. And one could, of course, argue that, even using Hitchcock's script and camera placements, Van Sant simply lacks the master's flair. Similarly, one could suggest that, atmospherically, the original black-and-white presentation was more effective than the color one, or that the acting in the original (the power of Perkins's performance, in particular, is by now legendary) was simply better and more evocative than the acting in the remake.

But surely Van Sant's film would have differed from Hitchcock's even if he had shot in black-and-white, even if he could somehow have reproduced the original performances exactly: audiences would still inevitably have read his film through the prism of Hitchcock's, forcing a different reception than the original film received. Indeed, even if, somehow, Van Sant could have found audiences that were entirely unaware of Hitchcock's original, it clearly means something different to make precisely this film in 1998 than it did in 1960, just as the *Don Quixote* produced by Jorge Luis Borges's Pierre Menard differs from that produced by Cervantes in the early seventeenth century, even though the two texts are identical word for word. For one thing, audiences in 1998 had seen lots of slasher films, virtually all of them far gorier than *Psycho*. For another, they had seen lots of movies that derived their material from earlier ones, especially from the works of recognized masters such as Hitchcock, as in most of the early films of Brian De Palma.

De Palma's filmic dialogue with Hitchcock represents one of the best-known examples of intertextuality in postmodern cinema, though it should also be noted that De Palma films such as *Carrie* (1976) and *The Fury* (1978) draw more upon the horror-film tradition in general. De Palma, in fact, has often been seen as a paradigm of the postmodern in general, as when John Belton calls him the "most 'postmodern'" of the filmmakers of the film-school generation (358) or when Jameson calls his films the "American equivalents" of French postmodernist works such as Jean-Jacques Beineix's *Diva* (1981). Indeed, if Van Sant's remake of *Psycho* is the ultimate example of postmodernist pastiche, then De Palma's own recycling of images and motifs from Hitchcock demonstrates, perhaps more than any other single phenomenon, the way in which the object of representation in the artifacts of postmodern culture is often not reality but other cultural artifacts. De Palma's career also nicely illustrates the lack of any real boundary between the popular and the postmodern in contemporary American culture. While his earlier films are self-consciously postmodern, especially in their pastiche of Hitchcock, many of his later ones are much more purely commercial efforts (though not necessarily successful ones).

The single characteristic of De Palma's filmmaking that is best known and most commented upon by critics is his pastiche of Hitchcock in films such as *Sisters* (1973), *Obsession* (1976), *Dressed to Kill* (1980), *Body Double* (1984), and *Raising Cain* (1992), all of which function fairly well as thrillers in their own right, but none of which can be properly understood without understanding the great extent to which they draw their thematic material (and even specific camera shots) from classic Hitchcock films, especially *Vertigo* (1958), *Rear Window* (1954), and *Psycho*. Indeed, De Palma's pastiches of Hitchcock serve almost as a postmodern genre, or at least a postmodern phenomenon, in their own right.

After beginning his career with a series of anarchic comedies, De Palma began to find his characteristic style with *Sisters*, which is overtly derived from *Psycho*, with a few touches of *Rear Window* thrown in for good measure. For example, the theme of voyeurism is introduced in the very first scene, in which Phillip Woode (Lisle Wilson) looks on in the dressing room of a bathhouse as a young blind woman comes in and begins to undress, unaware of his presence. Then, in a typical post-modernist move, the frame is broken to reveal that this scene is actually part of a television game show, modeled on *Candid Camera*, in which contestants try to guess what course of action will be taken by unknowing participants such as Woode when they are placed in unusual situations in front of hidden cameras.

The woman, meanwhile, is not really blind but is simply an actress, Danielle Breton (Margot Kidder), hired by the show. Woode, as it turns out, takes the honorable course, leaving the room discreetly before Danielle can completely disrobe. Then, the two meet as they appear together live on the show. Her prize for participation in the show (ominously, at least in retrospect) is a set of cutlery, while his is dinner for two at the African Room, which he takes as a racist gesture (he is African American). But he makes the most of it and invites Danielle to accompany him there, initiating a sequence of events that takes the two back to her Staten Island apartment, where they make love that night and where, the next morning, she (or someone who looks like her) murders him with a piece of the prize cutlery as he invites her to cut her birthday cake. Thus, Woode, who appears to be the protagonist of the film, is removed early on, in a mode reminiscent of the early exit of Marion Crane in *Psycho*, though in a murder scene that features much more blood and graphic violence than in the Hitchcock film.

In a motif that again recalls *Rear Window*, neighbor Grace Collier (Jennifer Salt), a newspaper reporter, witnesses Woode's murder from her apartment across the street. She frantically calls the police, who come to the scene, but investigate rather unenthusiastically, apparently because of their animosity toward Collier, who has recently written an exposé of police brutality in the area. By the time they reach the apartment, Danielle, with the help of her ex-husband, Emil Breton (William Finley), has cleaned up the mess, hiding the body by folding it inside a sleeper sofa. In a moment vaguely reminiscent of Hitchcock's *Rope* (1948), in which a body is hidden inside a chest during a dinner party, the body remains in the sofa while the police and Collier mill about the apartment.

After the police find no evidence of a murder, Collier decides to pursue the investigation on her own, aided by a somewhat comical private detective, Joseph Larch (Charles Durning). This investigation, which again clearly recalls *Psycho*, reveals that Danielle had been one of a pair of Siamese twins and that she and her sister, Dominique, had been surgically separated only a year before, so that Danielle would be able to pursue a normal marriage with Breton, a doctor at the clinic where the twins grew up. Dominique died on the operating table, but (in a postmodern literalization of the motif of split personality) the experience of the separation has left Danielle with a psychological imbalance that causes her to take on the murderous personality of Dominique whenever she becomes sexually aroused. "Dominique" then assaults Danielle's partners, her preferred mode being a knife to the genitals, thus reversing the usual De Palma motif in which women are the targets of such violence, while at the same time almost daring critics to interpret the motif as evidence that the violence against women in De Palma's subsequent films emanates from castration anxiety.

Many of the details of Danielle's malady are left slightly vague because most of the explanation of these details occurs in a final dream sequence in which a sedated Danielle remembers her background. The explanation thus avoids the heavy-handedness of the ending of *Psycho,* in which a psychiatrist delivers an unnecessarily lengthy discourse on the illness of Norman Bates. The plot is still wrapped up fairly neatly, though: not only does the audience understand what has happened, but the police finally figure it out as well, rescuing Collier and taking Danielle away for incarceration. The only one left hanging is Larch, who, in a final comic example of voyeurism, remains suspended high on a utility pole in rural Quebec, maintaining his surveillance on the crucial sleeper sofa, which has been moved there in an effort to get rid of the body.

This final humorous touch is indicative of the way De Palma tends to provide relatively comforting endings to his Hitchcock pastiches, backing away from the disturbing content that constitutes the bulk of the films. Such touches also add an element of irreverence to De Palma's treatment of Hitchcock, raising the question of whether De Palma's pastiches look back to a golden age when giants such as Hitchcock walked the Earth, or whether he is simply suggesting that Hitchcock wasn't all that gigantic to begin with.

Such questions especially arise when, as in the case of *Obsession*, he rewrites Hitchcock extensively. Here, he converts the heart-rending conclusion of *Vertigo* into a happy father-and-daughter reunion. However, it should be pointed out that *Obsession* was originally conceived not by De Palma, but by screenwriter Paul Schrader, who envisioned the film as a combination of *Vertigo*, with its theme of the simulated restoration of a lost love, and Yasujiro Oku's *An Autumn Afternoon* (1962), with its focus on father-daughter relationships. Still, in the hands of De Palma (and, for that matter, in the eyes of viewers, most of whom did not know the Oku film), the Hitchcock model became predominant.

Obsession is overtly Hitchcockian from the very beginning, including opening titles and credits reminiscent of the distinctive titles that open most of Hitchcock's films. Like *Sisters*, it is also accompanied by the highly atmospheric music of Bernard Herrmann, who had supplied the music for any number of Hitchcock films, including the crucial trio of *Vertigo*, *North by Northwest*, and *Psycho*.

Obsession begins in 1959, as New Orleans businessman Michael Courtland (Cliff Robertson) celebrates his tenth anniversary of delirious marital bliss with wife Elizabeth (Geneviève Bujold). This bliss comes to an abrupt end later that night, when both Elizabeth and their young daughter, Amy, are kidnapped. Later, both are apparently killed in a botched rescue attempt after Courtland, on the advice of the police, fails to pay their ransom. He thus blames himself for their deaths, much as Scottie Ferguson feels responsible for the (apparent) death of Madeleine Elster in *Vertigo*. Devastated by the experience, Courtland returns to his business, working with partner Robert La Salle (John Lithgow), but confines his emotional life to frequent visits to the shrine (a scale model of the Florence church in which he and Elizabeth first met) he has erected in a memorial park to his wife and daughter—located on a highly valuable piece of property on which he therefore refuses to allow development, much to the frustration of La Salle.

Fifteen years later, Courtland returns to Florence on a business trip with La Salle. There, he visits the church where he had originally met Elizabeth, only to discover Sandra Portinari (Bujold again), a young Italian woman who seems to be an absolute double for the woman he had met more than twenty-five years earlier. From there, the plot rolls rather inevitably forward. Courtland immediately falls in love with Sandra, although (like Ferguson remaking the rediscovered "Madeleine") he first teaches her to be even more like Elizabeth, including teaching her Elizabeth's "Bryn Mawr" walk. Soon, he convinces Sandra to return to New Orleans with him, where they are to be married. (They do not, however, have premarital sex, because she is a devout Catholic.) Then she, too, is kidnapped, and the ransom is again botched. This time, however, we learn that La Salle, playing the Gavin Elster role, has pocketed the ransom money and that he, in fact, had been behind the original kidnapping as well.

Even more importantly, we learn that Amy had not been killed in the original kidnapping, just as the woman Ferguson had thought to be

Madeleine was not dead. Instead, the girl had been spirited away to Florence by La Salle, there to be reared by friends of his. Blaming Courtland for the death of her mother, Amy has been working in league with La Salle in an attempt to wreak revenge by destroying Courtland. La Salle's own motivations are purely materialistic—he is plotting to gain control of the memorial park so that he can develop the land. In the end, Courtland discovers the plot, kills La Salle, and tracks down Amy, who in the meantime has attempted suicide in a fit of remorse. Then, in a final scene virtually lifted from *The Searchers* (1956), Courtland approaches Amy, seemingly about to kill her, but then takes her up in a loving fatherly embrace, accompanied by a 360-degree circular tracking shot like the one that shows us the reunion of Ferguson and the remade Madeleine in *Vertigo*.

If *Obsession* is in many ways a pastiche of *Vertigo*, *Dressed to Kill* draws on *Psycho* in much the same way. Here, the film begins with an intense focus on the life, dreams, and problems of frustrated housewife Kate Miller (Angie Dickinson), establishing an identification between the audience and this character similar to the one Hitchcock engineers between his audience and Marion Crane in *Psycho*. Then, less than a third of the way into the film, Kate is shockingly and brutally murdered— slashed to death by a male psycho dressed as a woman. The killer, as it turns out, is Dr. Robert Elliott (Michael Caine), Kate's psychiatrist, a character whose troubled sexual identity leads his/her feminine side murderously to emerge whenever the masculine side feels sexually attracted to a woman. Elliott will then eventually be tracked down by prostitute Liz Blake (Nancy Allen) and high school science nerd Peter Miller (Keith Gordon), Kate's son—just as Norman Bates is exposed by Sam Loomis and Lila Crane, Marion's sister. His malady is then explained to us in detail by another psychiatrist, à la the oft-criticized final explanation scene of *Psycho*.

The obvious similarity here to the basic scenario of *Psycho* is no accident, of course, though in some ways what is most interesting about *Dressed to Kill* is the way it deviates from and goes beyond *Psycho*. Unlike Van Sant in his literal but unexciting remake, De Palma seems to know that, to achieve an emotional impact in the postmodern era, he needs to go well beyond Hitchcock in a number of ways, especially in a much more overt and graphic representation of the hints of violence and sexuality that constantly inhabit the margins of Hitchcock's film but are not directly represented on screen. Thus, Kate is murdered fully clad in an elevator, rather than naked in a shower, but we see a much more graphic representation of the attack, including realistic looking shots of a straight razor slicing into Kate's flesh. There are also copious amounts of blood, though the visceral impact of the latter is, to an extent, muted by the fact that the blood looks patently artificial. Thus, the final shot of Kate's blood-smeared face looks as if the tracks of blood have been painted on.

Meanwhile, there are in fact shower scenes, including one especially erotic sequence at the beginning of the film in which Kate (in a dream as it turns out) soaps herself in the shower in a masturbatory fashion while her husband shaves at the sink with a straight razor, foreshadowing the later razor attack. This scene includes surprisingly candid (for the time) shots of Kate (via a body double) lovingly fondling her genitals, thus inviting the audience to act as voyeurs. This invitation is rudely interrupted when Kate is sexually assaulted in the shower by a strange man, leading her to awake to find her husband laboring away atop her in what she will later describe to Elliott as one of his inattentive "wham-bam-thank-you-ma'am" specials.

Such graphic representations of sex and violence, quite typical of American films in the last decades of the twentieth century, have been widely decried by conservative groups as not just a sign but also a cause of declining moral standards and of a loss of traditional values in American culture during that period. Such charges are, of course, clearly silly, not to mention profoundly un-American. After all, the notions of moral standards and traditional values are themselves directly opposed to what has been the central informing value of American society from the very beginning—a profound commitment to constant innovation and to the situational ethics this innovation requires. Moreover, it should be obvious that basic changes in attitudes toward sexuality, violence, and other emotionally charged experiences must already have been in place in order to make it possible to make and release a film such as *Dressed to Kill*, given the multiple layers and kinds of censorship through which American films must pass ever to reach the screen.

Indeed, the postmodern waning of affect in American life advanced dramatically between 1960 and 1980. On initial release, the much less graphic *Pyscho* was far more shocking and powerful than *Dressed to Kill*, but not because Hitchcock was somehow that much more masterful at evoking emotion than De Palma was and certainly not because subtlety and innuendo are inherently more evocative than direct representation. After all, Van Sant's remake of *Psycho* goes for the same subtlety as Hitchcock's original but also remains emotionally flat. The greater impact of *Psycho* derives from the simple fact that audiences in 1960 were much more susceptible to shock than were audiences in 1980. This waning of affect is no doubt furthered by exposure to gradually increasing levels of graphic imagery in film (and even, to an extent, television), a road along which *Psycho* is clearly one of the most important milestones. But the real culprit is surely not Hollywood but late capitalism itself, which creates an increasingly radical alienation from genuine emotional experience, thus producing a diminution of affect that makes graphic representations thinkable, while at the same time producing a lingering desire to feel *something* that makes such representations desirable.

De Palma's extension of Hitchcock into the realm of more and more extreme images peaks with *Body Double*, a film in which De Palma almost seems intentionally to defy his critics. Having developed a critical reputation for ripping off Hitchcock and portraying misogynistic scenes of violence against women, De Palma responded with his most overt (though campy) imitations of Hitchcock and his most graphic and abject violence against women, including the brutal murder of a dazzling beauty via a giant and preposterously phallic electric drill. *Body Double*, with its excesses that spill over into parody and its complex of self-conscious gestures toward a variety of film genres, is also De Palma's most representative work, at least when viewed within the context of postmodernism.

In *Body Double* Hitchcockian motifs and shots are mixed with elements of graphic slasher movies, schlocky horror films, and hard-core pornography to produce a mixture of *Vertigo* and *Rear Window* that constantly verges on flagrant self-parody, yet somehow manages to be a fairly effective thriller nevertheless. In addition to its excessively broad nods to Hitchcock, *Body Double* also openly engages the genre of the horror film, acknowledging De Palma's participation in that genre. Further, *Body Double* introduces a dialogue with the genre of pornographic films, almost as if in defiance of critics who have seen something pornographic in De Palma's apparent fascination with the violent penetration of female bodies. Finally, *Body Double* is a movie about both the art and the business of filmmaking, placing it in communion with the tradition of films about Hollywood.

The engagement of *Body Double* with the horror film is obvious from the very beginning, when the opening credits are displayed in dripping red letters apparently painted in blood, in the manner of horror film cliché. These titles then lead into an opening scene that features a vampire awakening in his coffin. Unfortunately, this vampire has claustrophobia (his version of Scottie Ferguson's vertigo or L. B. Jefferies's broken leg in *Rear Window*), causing him to freak out in the confines of his coffin. The vampire is, we quickly learn, an actor, Jake Scully (Craig Wasson), and his claustrophobia causes an interruption in what turns out to be the filming of a scene in *Vampire's Kiss*, the picture in which Scully is currently performing.

This opening scene from the film-within-a-film thus involves not only a mixture of genres but also a confusion of ontological levels, a confusion that will turn out to be central to the entire picture, in which the distinction between appearance and reality is virtually impossible to maintain. It also recalls the openings of *Sisters* and *Blow Out* (1981) and points toward the way in which the repetition of certain distinctive images and motifs in De Palma's films eventually begins to make them pastiches not just of Hitchcock but of each other as well. Indeed, much of the near-campiness of *Body Double* can be attributed to the fact that, in this film, De Palma is not just doing Hitchcock but doing De Palma *doing* Hitchcock. Thus, when Scully later, peeping-Tom-like, observes a murder, the obvious Hitchcockian referent is *Rear Window*, but the scene also derives from *Blow Out* and (especially) *Sisters*, particularly as it involves a swirling confusion of mixed-up identities.

In addition to its gestures toward a variety of film genres and its obvious relationship to the canon of Hitchcock and the earlier works of De Palma himself, *Body Double* is chock full of apparent allusions to other films. What is striking about these, however, is that they are almost entirely superficial and even gratuitous. Recognizing the allusions adds relatively little to our understanding of this film, and their inclusion accomplishes little more than a vague suggestion of the way in which our consciousnesses are pervaded by films and other cultural artifacts, so that allusion to such artifacts is entirely natural.

Thus, as Susan Dworkin notes in her interesting book-length account of the making of *Body Double*, Scully, in the film, has developed a *Vertigo*-like sexual fascination with beautiful Gloria Revelle (Deborah Shelton) after repeatedly watching her perform an erotic striptease and masturbation routine via his telescopic surveillance of her apartment. *Body Double* thus literalizes the voyeurism that is merely hinted at in *Rear Window*, just as De Palma often directly represents Hitchcock's hints at sexuality and violence. In *Body Double*, this same surveillance then reveals Gloria's assault (leading to her grotesque murder with the large electric drill) at the hands of a mysterious "Indian," who has apparently been stalking her. Soon, however, we learn that Gloria has been killed all right, but that the woman performing the routine that originally attracted Scully's attention was not Gloria at all, but porn actress Holly Body—based to an extent on adult film star Annette Haven, but played by Melanie Griffith, whose casting inevitably alludes, however vaguely, to the casting of her mother, Tippi Hedren, in *The Birds* (1963) and *Marnie* (1964). Holly, meanwhile, had been hired by Scully's acquaintance Sam (Gregg Henry) to impersonate Gloria, much in the manner that body doubles are frequently hired to stand in for actors in movies, especially in nude scenes.

Scully then makes the acquaintance of Holly by taking a part in one of her films, thus giving the audience a sort of inside view of the adult film industry, a motif that had appeared in De Palma's work as early as *Hi, Mom!* (1970), in which the protagonist, Jon Rubin (Robert De Niro) is an aspiring pornographer. *Hi, Mom!* also satirizes the intellectual pretentiousness of socially relevant documentaries as shown on public television, here figured as "National Intellectual Television." The resulting dialogue between pornography and such documentaries prefigures the mixture of cultural referents in *Body Double*, while also identifying both pornography and documentary filmmaking as aspects of the fascination with voyeurism that De Palma's films consistently identify as a central element of American culture. In the case of *Hi, Mom!*, Rubin's desire for attention and publicity also suggests the flip side of this voyeurism—the craving of Americans to be seen and noticed, as if somehow to validate their flagging identities via their fifteen minutes of fame.[4]

As an actor, Jake Scully in *Body Double* also desires to be seen, even as he acts as the film's principal voyeur. He manages to strike up a relationship with Holly, thus restoring his lost object of desire, much as Scottie Ferguson gets a second chance in *Vertigo*. Meanwhile, we, along with Scully, discover that the Indian was actually Sam in disguise and that Scully had been set up all along to witness the murder (attributing it to an Indian), thus leaving Sam in the clear. Sam then nearly kills Gloria, thereby threatening to reenact Ferguson's double loss in *Vertigo*, while Scully, again like Ferguson, is hampered in his attempts to save her by his claustrophobia. In this case, however, Holly is saved nevertheless— through the unlikely expedient of having Sam's own dog accidentally knock him into the swirling water coming from a reservoir, presumably drowning him, just as he is about to bury both Holly and Scully alive.

This sudden rescue may be reminiscent of the end of *North by Northwest*, but it is also again indicative of De Palma's tendency to tack relatively happy, or at least recuperative, endings onto his Hitchcock pastiches, as when Courtland and his daughter are reunited at the end of *Obsession* or when the apparent murder of Liz Blake at the end of *Dressed to Kill* turns out merely to be a nightmare, from which she then awakes. This expedient, which also occurs at the end of *Carrie*, is perhaps one of the easiest ways suddenly to reverse an apparently tragic ending, which turns out not "really" to have happened at all. However, the patent artificiality of this dream technique (which foreshadows the famous retrospective conversion of an entire season of the television series *Dallas* into a dream) also reflexively calls attention to the fact that the films are fictions, that nothing "really" happens in them, and that De Palma can make them end any way he chooses. Thus, the sudden shift from the fiction of the dream to the "truth" of "reality" ultimately represents a postmodern dismantling of the distinction between fiction and reality, because here the waking reality is just as fictional as the dream.

Indeed, *Body Double* is shot through with all sorts of reminders of its own artificiality, including the title metaphor, which is reiterated in one final scene in which Scully goes back to work on *Vampire's Kiss*, working with an actress's body double with whom he shoots a scene in which he bites the neck of a naked woman in a shower. Thus, Hitchcock's famous shower scene appears in De Palma once again, though this time the obvious sexual innuendo associated with the vampire attack is less reminiscent of *Psycho* than of *Dressed to Kill*, with a side glance at the shower scene in the slasher movie from *Blow Out*.

One might have expected that *Body Double*, with its self-conscious repetition of déjà vu all over again, would have taken De Palma's pastiches of Hitchcock as far as they could go, thus bringing the cycle to its end. However, the later *Raising Cain* retreats back to pre–*Body Double* De Palma, doing Hitchcock somewhat in the mode of *Dressed to Kill*. On the other hand, all the disguises and mistaken identities of *Body Double* call attention to the artificiality and instability of all identities in the postmodern era, a motif on which *Raising Cain* builds quite directly. In this case, the identity in question is that of child psychologist Carter Nix (John Lithgow), who had been converted, in childhood, into a multiple personality, thanks to the mad-scientist experiments of his father, also played by Lithgow. As a child turned psycho through the actions of a parent, Nix thus follows directly in the footsteps of Norman Bates, but also of Danielle Breton. And an even more direct predecessor of Nix is De Palma's own Robert Elliott, another psychological professional who is also a psycho.

In *Raising Cain*, the elder Dr. Nix reappears, enlisting the aid of his son (or at least of some of the manifestations of his son's personality) to kidnap neighborhood children (including Carter's own daughter) to use as subjects in his ghoulish experiments. In the process, Carter also goes on a murder spree that includes the apparent killing of his wife, Jenny

(Lolita Davidovich). After that (as if the links to *Psycho* weren't clear enough), Carter puts Jenny in her car and pushes it into a marsh, where it begins to sink, then pauses tantalizingly before going under. As usual, however, De Palma doesn't just do Hitchcock, but outdoes him: in this case, Jenny regains consciousness in the pause and frantically attempts to escape from the car before going under with it. This motif adds a little action and suspense to the moment, but it also deprives the scene from *Psycho* of its most delicious irony: the fact that audience members almost inevitably find themselves identifying with Norman as he watches the car, rooting along with him for it to submerge.

Thus, once again, De Palma goes well beyond Hitchcock in the frank and graphic representation of violence, but falls far short of Hitchcock in emotional impact. The additional suspense introduced in this scene is also indicative of the way in which *Raising Cain* is the most postmodern of De Palma's films in terms of narrative structure. Here, De Palma eschews continuity and logical flow almost entirely, constructing the narrative instead via a fragmented sequence of moments of high suspense. He then winds it all up with still another happy ending, in which Jenny, rather improbably, turns out to have escaped after all, then joins with the police in foiling Dr. Nix's evil schemes and rescuing the children. In the process, the whole situation is made clear, producing the kind of epistemological closure that is typical of De Palma's pastiches of Hitchcock, though here the resolution of the plot seems even more forced and artificial than usual. Meanwhile, the fact that the Hitchcock references in *Raising Cain* are by now also references to earlier De Palma films is made even more obvious by the casting of Lithgow, who also functions as the principal villain in *Obsession* and *Blow Out*.

The latter film, incidentally, demonstrates that De Palma's practice of postmodern pastiche goes well beyond his use of Hitchcock. *Blow Out* is not overtly based on anything in Hitchcock, but is instead a variation on Michelangelo Antonioni's *Blowup* (1966), inflected through Francis Ford Coppola's *The Conversation* (1974), itself partly inspired by Antonioni's film. *Blow Out* is a film that is quite literally *about* image-making in film, even as it carries out that practice in its own construction, not only drawing on specific sources but also employing De Palma's full bag of cinematic tricks, such as split-screen and slow-motion effects. From its very title onward, *Blow Out* asks us to recall Antonioni's *Blowup* (and thus asks us also to consider *Blow Out* in relation to European art cinema, which *Blowup* did much to popularize in the Anglophone world). *Blow Out*'s relationship to *The Conversation* is obvious as well, but neither *Blowup* nor *The Conversation* is really modified by its contact with *Blow*

Out, perhaps because both are largely modernist films centering on the subjectivities of their protagonists, while *Blow Out* is a postmodernist film focusing on the image itself.

Jameson calls *Blow Out* "perhaps the most revealing specimen" of American postmodernist film, due to its focus on "the primacy of the image itself, the commitment to the consumption of images and to the world's transformation into visual commodities" (*Signatures*, 60). Indeed, *Blow Out* presents a world of filmic images from its very opening scene, which is not a scene from *Blow Out* proper, but from a low-budget slasher flick for which protagonist Jack Terry (John Travolta) is providing the sound effects. In fact, it is not quite a scene from the slasher film, either, but a *representation*, within *Blow Out*, of the slasher film scene, which itself is pure cliché, featuring the invasion of a girls' dorm by a mysterious, knife-wielding killer, who makes his way through the dorm, culminating in the obligatory murderous attack on a naked girl in the shower.

This scene calls attention to the formulaic nature of such pictures, which is further emphasized when the scene is interrupted to show Terry and the film's director viewing the slasher scene in a screening room. Terry and the director, we learn, have worked together on five movies in the past two years, all essentially identical. At the same time, the presence of this shower scene in a film by De Palma inevitably reminds us that Hitchcock's *Psycho* was the progenitor of all such scenes and, for that matter, all such slasher movies—a fact that in itself virtually destroys any lasting illusion that there might continue to be, in American film of the late twentieth century, a clear distinction between high art and low, epitomized, respectively, by Hitchcock and cheap slasher films. Of course, De Palma epitomizes this phenomenon in that most of his films collapse the boundary between high art and cheap exploitation.

The director of the slasher film featured in *Blow Out*, meanwhile, is having problems because the actress playing the victim in the shower scene (who was hired for her body, not her acting skills) produces a particularly weak and unconvincing scream, leading the director to order Terry to find a better scream to dub into the scene. For that matter, the director himself is tired of Terry's use of the same worn-out sound effects over and over in all their movies, and so orders him to find some fresh material for background noises such as wind blowing through trees. This injunction activates the entire plot, in which Terry goes out into the countryside to record some natural sounds and inadvertently records the assassination of a presidential candidate. He then spends the remainder of the film, aided by semi-prostitute Sally (Nancy Allen), trying to convince the authorities that the death, which has been ruled an accident, was really an assassination.

At this stage, the plot of *Blow Out* follows quite closely that of *Blowup*, in which a photographer, Thomas (played by David Hemmings), goes to a park to get some shots of trees and grass, only to obtain inadvertently possible photographic evidence of a murder. However, while *Blowup* features a number of scenes of Thomas using his professional skills to process the evidence, the film is not really about the production of images at all. Instead, it is a modernist study of the alienation of the photographer, who, as the film opens, is devoid of any real human connections (especially with the fashion models who constantly make themselves sexually available to him, but toward whom he shows nothing but misogynistic contempt). The plot then allows him to experience a few moments of enthusiasm as he uses his professional skills in an attempt to do good by producing blown-up photographs that reveal evidence of the murder. He thus acts out a fantasy of nonalienated labor, working to produce a valuable tangible effect rather than simply to make money, only to sink back into his emotional lethargy in the end, having accomplished nothing. Meanwhile, we the audience are never granted the solution to the mystery that the detective-story form of the plot has teased us into expecting. The emptiness of the plot resolution thus mimes the psychic emptiness of the central character, asking the audience to feel some of what he feels, or, more properly, doesn't feel.

In this sense, *Blow Out* is far less radical than *Blowup*, because here we know for sure that a murder took place, and we even know who did it—the sinister Burke (played by De Palma favorite John Lithgow). De Palma adds a surveillance motif picked up from *The Conversation* (Terry was formerly an electronic eavesdropping expert involved in an investigation of police corruption) and tosses in his own contemporary plot touches with the motif of assassination and political conspiracy and even vague references to Chappaquiddick, but the plot of *Blow Out* is virtually beside the point. The same might be said for both *Blowup* and *The Conversation*, both of which are really character studies of their intensely alienated protagonists. In *Blow Out*, however, character, too, is almost irrelevant. Terry has some of the tormented past of *The Conversation*'s Harry Caul (both have inadvertently caused the deaths of others through their surveillance activities), but he is much flatter and more superficial. He is, in fact, just one element in the sequence of images that makes up the film. *Blow Out* is, first and foremost, about images and the conversion of reality into images (rather than the representation of reality *through* images), a fact that becomes most clear in the final scene, in which Terry, having recorded Sally's death screams as she is killed by Burke, dubs that recording into the shower scene of the slasher film, making even something as intense as bloody murder a mere source of images.

The echo of *Psycho* in the shower scene in the embedded film within *Blow Out* demonstrates the way in which even De Palma films that are not overtly constructed with Hitchcock's films as models include plot motifs and (especially) cinematography that is highly reminiscent of those used by him. Hitchcock, of course, is the perfect resource for this exercise in postmodern pastiche. For one thing, his films already bridge the gap between modernist high culture and popular low culture, making them to an extent postmodern in their own right; there is probably no other filmmaker who can match the combination of artistic reputation and widespread familiarity that marks Hitchcock's major films. These works contain numerous moments of virtuosity that invite imitation, and, unlike most "art films," they are well enough known that audiences will be able to recognize what is being imitated.

Among other things, De Palma's frequent inclusion of direct references to filmmaking in his movies is also a form of pastiche of Hitchcock, whose frequent references to voyeurism have often been seen as comments on the task of the filmmaker and the activities of movie audiences. Meanwhile, De Palma's more open references to filmmaking make his pictures even more self-referential and postmodern, linking them to an important family of films that employ the technique of postmodern pastiche by taking moviemaking and the movie industry as their central subjects.

The great forerunner of all such postmodern films is Fellini's *8½*, in which the protagonist, Guido Anselmi (Marcello Mastroianni), is an aging filmmaker who struggles to make a movie. However, caught in the midst of a personal spiritual crisis, Anselmi has completely lost any overall vision of what he is trying to accomplish in the film. Desperate, he brings in an intellectual critic (played by Jean Rougeul) as a consultant on the project. The critic, whose view of Anselmi's work has often been quite unfavorable in the past, reads the script and declares it a confused mess. Lacking any unifying thesis, the film, according to the critic, is merely a "series of gratuitous episodes, perhaps amusing for their ambiguous realism." Unfortunately, at least for the critic, this realism is itself a problem, leaving Anselmi with a conception that "doesn't even have the merits of an avant-garde film, but it has all the shortcomings."

Of course, in a bit of ironic self-reference, the film that the critic is describing (and that Anselmi is trying to make) is essentially *8½* itself, which is indeed a fragmented series of episodes, made all the more confusing because of the radical intermixture of material from different ontological levels, including the fictional film Anselmi is making and Anselmi's "real" life, as well as Anselmi's dreams, memories, and fantasies. In this sense, 8½, like other self-referential postmodern films (*Timecode*'s satirizing of its own potential pretentiousness immediately comes to mind), can be described as a pastiche of itself, echoing Jameson's characterization of postmodern culture as nostalgic for the present. That Anselmi's film is blatantly autobiographical, while Anselmi is patently based on Fellini himself, adds an extra dimension to this ontological confusion. Ultimately, however, 8½ makes a virtue of the confusion, using it as the stuff of art and producing one of the most respected films in cinema history. As such, it seems to endorse Walter Benjamin's vision of fragmentation as a positive virtue of film as a medium, though it should also be said that Fellini's notoriously apolitical stance hardly seems designed to pursue the politicization of art espoused by Benjamin.

As a landmark film about filmmaking, Fellini's 8½ has exercised a hefty influence on subsequent directors, most notably in Woody Allen's *Stardust Memories* (1980), essentially a reinscription of 8½, but with Allen's biography substituted for Fellini's as a central source of material. Allen's film, though it has its serious moments, is also considerably more comical than Fellini's and, in general, feels like a much less self-serious work of art. Indeed, especially given Fellini's *auteurist* reputation, one is tempted to read the movement from 8½ to *Stardust Memories* as a transition from modernism to postmodernism. On the other hand, 8½, with its self-referentiality, its ultimate acceptance of the impossibility of producing well-made artworks, and its celebration of fragmentation, can itself be taken as a key marker of the growth of a postmodern sensibility in film.

Nevertheless, Allen's film is certainly more thoroughly postmodernist than Fellini's, even if Allen maintains a certain modernist desire to be a serious artist, producing serious films in the manner of Fellini or even Bergman. Thus, the central running joke of *Stardust Memories* is the continuing complaint by critics and fans alike that protagonist Sandy Bates (Allen) has gotten too serious and no longer seems able to make funny movies. Meanwhile, Allen's own "serious" films, while heavily reliant on predecessors such as Fellini and Bergman, tend to be constructed much less overtly of materials derived from the tradition of cinema itself, suggesting that Allen regards such films about film as examples of postmodern play.

Perhaps the most obvious example of such play occurs in *The Purple Rose of Cairo* (1985), which avoids nostalgia about its historical setting in the Depression decade of the 1930s only to replace this nostalgia with nostalgia for the escapist films of the 1930s, which, according to the logic of the film, offered an immersion in fiction and concomitant relief from reality that may no longer be available in movies of the 1980s. The film's protagonist, Cecilia (Mia Farrow), suffers greatly in the real world of Depression-era New Jersey, where she works slavishly as a waitress then takes in laundry after work, only to have her income squandered by her abusive wastrel of a husband, Monk (Danny Aiello). Her only solace is the motion pictures she sees in the Jewel Theater, films that take her mind off her troubles, if only for a while.

One day, Cecilia is attending a film called *The Purple Rose of Cairo* for the fifth time, when one of the characters suddenly notices her and then steps off the screen and into the theater so that he can meet this woman, who seems so devoted to his film. The character, Tom Baxter (Jeff Daniels), soon falls in love with Cecilia and attempts to convince her to return with him to live in the idyllic world of film. Accustomed to the brutish Monk, Cecilia is nearly swept off her feet by the dashing Baxter, even if she is a bit bothered by the fact that he is only a fictional character. Then, afraid that the scandal of Baxter's appearance in the real world might ruin his career, Gil Shepherd (also Daniels), the actor who plays Baxter, comes to New Jersey to try to deal with the situation. He, too, begins to court Cecilia, eventually winning her away from Baxter on the basis of the fact that he is preferable because he is at least real. The dejected Baxter then reenters the film, after which the projector is hurriedly cut off and all prints of the film are destroyed. Cecilia then prepares to leave the abusive Monk for an adventurous new life with Shepherd, only to discover that the actor, having safely removed Baxter from the real world, has now skipped town, returning to Hollywood. Crushed and all alone in the difficult world of the 1930s, Cecilia seeks refuge in her favorite movie theater, which is now showing Fred Astaire and Ginger Rogers in *Top Hat* (1935). Despite her troubles, Cecilia becomes absorbed in the film, and, as Allen's movie ends, a smile slowly steals across her face, suggesting that her immersion in film might have a positive value, even though this immersion seems mainly to have made her life worse. Indeed, Allen seems to see 1930s films as especially restorative. One might compare here the scene in *Hannah and Her Sisters* (1986) in which television producer Mickey Saxe (Allen) weathers a moment of existential crisis by becoming absorbed in a screening of the Marx Brothers' *Duck Soup* (1933).

By treating Baxter's crossing of ontological barriers literally, somewhat in the mode of magical realism, *Purple Rose* is much more postmodern than, say, Buster Keaton's *Sherlock, Jr.* (1924), in which

Keaton's character steps from the world of reality into the world of film, but only in his dreams. Still, Allen's movie in no way confuses fiction with reality and therefore retains strong residual realist elements. In fact, it makes clear that the world depicted in Hollywood film is vastly different from the real world. However, it suggests that the film world is in many ways preferable and that the existence of this superior imaginary world can actually bring needed solace to those in the real world. The cinematic world itself functions as a very weak utopian image (because it can never be reached in reality), but the medium of film is declared to serve a useful utopian function by making it easier for audiences to deal with reality. Then again, escapism is also problematic as a form of utopianism: by making present-day reality more bearable, it might also discourage audiences from mounting genuinely political action to change that reality.

The world of Hollywood film is also prettier than the real world of the 1930s in Allen's *Zelig* (1983), a mock documentary detailing the life of human chameleon Leonard Zelig (played by Allen), who can expertly (though unconsciously) mimic the appearance and mannerisms of those around him. Praising most of the film for the way it "recreates the look of old documentaries" with its grainy black-and-white stock and flickering images, Foster Hirsch complains that the inserted scenes from a fictional 1935 Hollywood film about Zelig's life "look too smooth and modern" (226). But that is precisely the point: reality looks rough and worn, the world of film looks glossy and beautiful.

This visual suggestion of the superiority of classic film fiction to Depression reality is just as nostalgic as the depiction, in *Purple Rose*, of the solace offered by Hollywood films during the 1930s. On the other hand, here Allen depicts the individuals involved in the movie *business* as unscrupulous, selfish weasels; the media as a whole are depicted in much the same way in *Zelig*. This depiction of a disjunction between film art and the film and media business is not surprising in the work of Allen, a director who has resolutely (and successfully) remained an outsider to the Hollywood film industry throughout his long and prolific career.

Another recent film exploring both the film industry and the instability of postmodern identity is *Being John Malkovich* (1999), scripted by Charlie Kaufman, one of the few screenwriters to have gained widespread recognition as a sort of film auteur, a designation usually reserved for directors. Kaufman had a number of credits as a writer for television beginning in 1990, but he burst upon the scene as a writer of feature films with *Being John Malkovich*, widely acknowledged as one of the most original films of the 1990s. This was also the first feature for director Spike Jonze, known at the time as a director of music videos. However, it makes little use of MTV-style quick-cut editing, even if it also blatantly ignores most of the rules of Hollywood filmmaking.

Declaredly off the beaten Hollywood path from its very first scene—a puppet ballet performed by puppeteer Craig Schwartz (John Cusack)—*Being John Malkovich* zanily careens from one improbable moment to the next. In the film, the puppet business (here representing "genuine" art) being slow, Schwartz is forced to seek work for his nimble fingers as a file clerk for the Lester Corporation, whose bizarre low-ceilinged offices are located between the seventh and eighth floors of a Manhattan office building. There, Schwartz discovers a strange portal that allows anyone passing through it to experience life for fifteen minutes from the point of view of actor John Malkovich (played by himself), before being dumped back out as one's original self on the side of the New Jersey Turnpike outside the city.

This bizarre premise would seem to break all the rules of Hollywood cinema and would thus appear to escape the postmodernist tendency toward pastiche, despite its central reliance on the figure of Malkovich. But this reliance is actually only one of many ways in which this film is very much about the Hollywood movie industry (with attendant metaphorical resonances about directors as puppeteers and actors as momentarily inhabiting someone else's identity). Indeed, while critics gushed about the unending creativity of this film, the fact is that it resorts to a number of the staples of Hollywood in order to bring its unusual story to anything like a coherent end. Thus, bizarre premise notwithstanding, the film ultimately involves romantic triangles, chases, gunplay, and battles for power of a kind easily recognizable to contemporary movie audiences.

In short, the very inventiveness of *Being John Malkovich* seems to demonstrate the inescapability of Hollywood formulas. After all, if even this film ultimately has to resort to tried and true techniques (however ironically), what film could possibly avoid them? Kaufman's immediate follow-up to *Being John Malkovich* was the relatively obscure (but again highly inventive) *Human Nature* (2001), directed by French music video director Michel Gondry. However, it was with *Adaptation* (2002), once again directed by Jonze, that Kaufman moved to true auteur status. Taking the self-referentiality of postmodern film to a new level, this picture is, in essence, a pastiche not of previous films, but of itself, although it also makes clear reference to the convoluted storytelling that made Kaufman a rising Hollywood star in *Being John Malkovich*. In *Adaptation*, Kaufman makes himself (or a version of himself) the central character (played by Nicholas Cage). Having already written *Being John Malkovich*, Kaufman is engaged to write the screen adaptation of Susan Orlean's nonfiction book, *The Orchid Thief*. Orlean (played by Meryl Streep) is a real writer, and *The Orchid Thief* is a real book, though in this film the boundary between fiction and reality is a tenuous one, and Orlean appears here as a highly fictionalized character, as does Kaufman. Meanwhile, though *Adaptation* does dramatize considerable material from Orlean's book, it is first and foremost the story of a struggling screenwriter who tries to write an adaptation but writes a script about a struggling screenwriter who tries to write an adaptation but writes a script about a struggling screenwriter, and so on, ad infinitum.

In addition to this self-referential feature, *Adaptation* is also very much a story about the Hollywood film industry. Kaufman's difficulties in writing the script within the film arise largely from the fact that he wants to produce something genuinely original, while the demands of the industry require something formulaic. The film also takes a few satirical shots at the whole how-to-be-a-screenwriter industry in its portrayal of real-world screenwriting guru Robert McKee (played by Brian Cox), whose advice Kaufman regards as nonsense. Yet Kaufman's fictional identical twin brother Donald, portrayed as a no-talent jerk, produces and sells (for big money) a screenplay using McKee's advice. The real punch line, however, occurs, when *Adaptation* itself descends into formula, resorting to a variety of Hollywood clichés in order to bring its narrative to an action-packed end, including chases, car crashes, and gunplay. There's no escaping Hollywood formulas, the film once again seems to say: the best one can hope for is to reproduce these formulas with an ironic self-consciousness.

Though Kaufman is famed for his creativity and inventiveness, *Adaptation* is in fact only an especially prominent case of the spate of movies about the motion picture industry that began to appear in the 1990s. These include such films as George Huang's Hollywood satire *Swimming with Sharks* (1994); Tom DiCillo's *Living in Oblivion* (1995), which explores the difficulties of low-budget indie filmmaking; and David Mamet's *State and Main* (2000), which looks at the comic impact of the arrival of a Hollywood film crew on a typical American small town. Such films are typically quite cynical about the industry and its effect on American society, but in ways that seem designed to make this cynicism seem hip. John Waters's *Cecil B. Demented* (2000), for example, hardly even bothers to comment on mainstream Hollywood films but simply takes it for granted that these films are little more than insipid, commercialized pabulum designed for mindless consumption by infantile audiences. Starting from this premise, Waters then turns his satirical focus not on the products of Hollywood studios but on the outlaw underground cinema of which he himself is one of the better-known practitioners. In the film, a group of young guerrilla filmmakers, led by the title character (Stephen Dorff), conceive a plan to kidnap Hollywood star (Melanie Griffith) and force her to play the lead in their own reality-based underground film. The resulting mayhem is good fun, but most of the amusement is at the expense of the guerrillas, rather than the system they are seeking to subvert, thus making them highly ineffective as a utopian alternative.

One of the most prominent films about Hollywood from the 1990s is *Barton Fink* (1991), in which Joel and Ethan Coen demonstrate that they are clearly far more interested in the world of film than the world at large. Meanwhile, true to the spirit of Preston Sturges's 1941 classic *Sullivan's Travels* (which lurks in the background of much of the work of the Coen brothers), *Barton Fink* scoffs at the idea of socially engaged cinema. Its title character (played by John Turturro) is a leftist dramatist from New York who is lured to Hollywood by the promise of bigger audiences (and bigger paychecks). Based perhaps most obviously on Cliff Odets, Fink also recalls a long Hollywood legacy of leftist screen-writers, a legacy that would ultimately draw the fire of the House Un-American Activities Committee (HUAC), resulting in an extensive blacklist of writers, actors, and directors with suspect political ideas.

The Coens, however, are not interested in examining the McCarthy-ist purge of Hollywood, setting their film in the pre-McCarthy year of 1941 (the same year in which *Sullivan's Travels* is set). Nor are they particularly interested in criticizing the studio system, even though they portray Hollywood as a sort of Hell, vaguely invoking literary precedents such as Dante and Goethe to suggest (if only jokingly) that Fink, by coming to California, has sold his soul to the Devil. They also introduce a devilish insurance salesman, Charlie Meadows (John Goodman), who torments Fink because of his obliviousness to the common people about whom he claims to care so passionately. When asked by Fink why he has singled him out, Meadows simply says, "Because you don't listen." Thus, while *Barton Fink* includes the requisite sleazy studio execs and boot-licking toadies, its principal censure is aimed at Fink himself, who is portrayed as an effete intellectual completely cut off from the lives of the common people for whom he professes to serve as an advocate in his writing. Indeed, although they do not suggest a preferable alternative within the film, the Coens clearly indicate that the kind of socially engaged cinema Fink hopes to create is pretentious and silly.

For their own part, the Coens make no attempt at sympathetic representation of the lives of the poor. Most of the characters of *Barton Fink* are film industry types. The major working stiffs of the film are two anti-Semitic policemen, who are somewhat less than thrilled that a pointy-headed Jewish intellectual like Fink sympathizes with their working-class condition, and Meadows, who is not only Satanic, or at least Mephisthophelean, but also a crazed killer (aka "Madman" Mundt) who likes to decapitate his victims. Further, Meadows/Mundt seems vaguely (but only vaguely) associated with the rise of fascism in Europe: in his madman persona, he has a German surname, and at one point he says "Heil Hitler" as he kills one of his victims. The latter scene, however, is complicated by the fact that he seems to speak the line with disdain, while his victim, police detective Deutsch, also has a German name and vaguely fascistic, or at least anti-Semitic, tendencies. In any case, Fink's failure to "listen" seems intended to tell us that leftist intellectuals like him were too busy pursuing their own selfish interests to effectively oppose the rise of fascism, a point that is historically entirely inaccurate: American (and British) writers in the late 1930s put their own proletarian agendas completely aside in order to participate in a Popular Front alliance against fascism. They then strove mightily to sound a call of warning about the evils of fascism, but were ignored by the British and American governments and general populations.

That the Coens would choose to level a charge of irresponsibility against the only group in America that actively sought to oppose the rise of fascism is itself highly irresponsible and shows a complete ignorance of (or perhaps lack of interest in) historical reality. Such ignorance and apathy, of course, are typical of postmodern film, which views the past not as the prehistory of the present but as a warehouse of images to be raided for material. Of course, *Barton Fink* makes no claim to be realistic or historically accurate, representing 1941 Hollywood as a collection of art deco images derived not from reality but from films, magazine covers, and other visual art of the period.

Barton Fink ends with a final enigmatic comment on representation and the relationship between art and reality in general. Throughout the film, Fink has been fascinated by a postcard-like painting of a woman sitting on the beach that hangs over the rickety table on which he types in his dilapidated hotel room. In the film's final scene, he himself walks on the beach, then encounters a woman who looks exactly like the one in the painting, then eerily strikes a pose precisely like that in the painting as well. The film ends here, without comment, leaving Fink (and audiences) to meditate on the implications of this scene, which I take as a suggestion that it would be genuinely weird were art to reflect reality in such an accurate and direct manner. Furthermore, the very fact that this scene seems to demand allegorical or symbolic interpretation suggests that such ostensibly transparent representation would only trigger additional waves of meaning that would themselves create a gap in the representation, making it finally impossible for art to reflect reality directly and without mediation.

Barton Fink, like *Sullivan's Travels,* ultimately endorses the work of the Hollywood dream factory. Indeed, given the congruence between these two films, it should be no surprise that the Coens would place one of their later films even more directly into dialogue with Sturges's film. Though set in the American South in the Depression years of the 1930s, the Coens' *O Brother, Where Art Thou?* (2000) claims, in its opening titles, to be based on Homer's *Odyssey.* This attribution alerts audiences to be on the lookout for references to Homer (of which there are many in the film), but it also playfully invites audiences to mull over (but not too seriously) the implications of the intertextual dialogue between the film and the epic poem. Among other things, one immediately thinks of James Joyce's use of the *Odyssey* in his *Ulysses,* and the Coens almost suggest this comparison by naming their protagonist Ulysses, rather than Odysseus, and then even giving him an Irish surname. Moreover, the Coens' Ulysses Everett McGill (George Clooney) is, like Joyce's Leopold Bloom, decidedly unheroic, a far cry from Homer's Odysseus. McGill is also, like Bloom, a know-it-all who constantly discourses on any and all topics, often to the annoyance of those around him, while both McGill and Bloom return home to discover that their wives have not been quite so faithful as Odysseus's patient Penelope had been.

Of course, Joyce's book is based far less on Homer than its title (and much critical commentary) would suggest, but this fact in itself serves, in some ways, to increase the ironic energy that Joyce is able to generate through the seemingly incongruous juxtaposition between the epic world of ancient Greece and the prosaic world of colonial Dublin. Among other things, this juxtaposition initiates a subversive challenge to the authority of the epic and to the authority of the literary past as a whole, as Joyce refuses to acknowledge that Homer is more important than any number of other sources that he draws upon, including pop cultural ones.[5]

O Brother is similarly based only in the loosest sense on the *Odyssey,* but lacks this aspect of genuine dialogic engagement in its juxtaposition of ancient Greece with the Depression South. Most viewers of the film, I suspect, decline the invitation to think about Homer and ignore the reference to the *Odyssey* altogether—or simply treat it as a joke. *O Brother* does not engage Homer in dialogue but merely alludes to him, much in the way that postmodern buildings allude to various architectural styles from the past. My invocation of postmodernism here is, in fact, important, because it indicates a crucial difference between Joyce's modernist novel and the Coens' postmodernist film, the former engaging in a serious dialogue with Homer, the latter simply pointing toward Homer while engaging him only in an entirely superficial way.

O Brother actually derives far more directly from the classic Hollywood motion pictures of the 1930s and early 1940s than from the *Odyssey*. The most overt of these filmic sources is *Sullivan's Travels*, in which the socially engaged film that the title character (played by Joel McCrea) initially hopes to make is entitled *O Brother, Where Art Thou?* Sullivan's subsequent research leads him to change his mind, concluding that the poor are better served by escapist comedies that can help them, if only for a few moments, forget the hardships of their impoverished lives. The Coen brothers' version of *O Brother* is, in fact, just such a wacky farce, though it is set during the Depression and deals with the lives of downtrodden characters, including a trio of escapees from a Southern chain gang. Moreover, while Joyce's intertextual shenanigans in *Ulysses* are set against the backdrop of a vividly realistic portrayal of 1904 Dublin, the comic resolution of all of the hardships suffered by the central characters in *O Brother* is mirrored by the very postmodern way in which the film represents the Depression era not as a time of genuine material hardship but as a collection of images remembered from film and other kinds of popular culture (especially music), with Homer tossed anachronistically into the intertextual mix.

In addition to its allusions to specific films such as *Sullivan's Travels*, *O Brother* is a virtual catalog of pastiches of classic Hollywood film genres, continuing the tendency of the Coens to evoke a variety of generic precedents (especially film noir) in all of their pictures. Take a social problem drama such as *I Am a Fugitive from a Chain Gang* (1932), toss in liberal doses of the anarchic comedy of the Marx Brothers, the musical production numbers of Busby Berkeley, road films, and screwball comedies, then add just a touch of the magic of *The Wizard of Oz* (1939), and one would get something of the texture of *O Brother*. In this sense, *It Happened One Night* (1934) becomes an especially important (and complex) intertextual referent. For one thing, *It Happened One Night* already combines the screwball comedy, road movie, and social problem genres. For another, it stars Clark Gable, of whom George Clooney, playing the lead role of McGill in *O Brother*, does a virtual running pastiche through the entire film. Finally, *It Happened One Night* was directed by Frank Capra, a favorite director of Sturges's Sullivan, who admires the social relevance of Capra's films.

Perhaps the most important work in initiating the new wave of films about the film industry in the 1990s was Altman's *The Player*, which uses a detective story format to lampoon the shallowness, venality, and inauthenticity of the values that drive the Hollywood movie industry. In so doing, Altman clearly seeks to use Hollywood as a metaphor for American society as a whole, though the film is less successful in this sense than Altman's earlier use of the country music industry in *Nashville*. *The Player* is notable for its numerous Hollywood inside jokes and cameo appearances by prominent Hollywood stars, both of which lend an air of authenticity to the satire, which is strong but not bitter. This lampoon of the industry is, in fact, infused with a clear affection for film, from the elaborate opening allusion to the extended cuts in Hitchcock's *Rope* (1948) and the famous crane shot at the beginning of *Touch of Evil* (1958), to the movie posters that constantly pop up in the film, to the tendency of most of the principals to speak largely in terms of film allusions.

These allusions tend to focus on the films of the 1950s and late 1940s, including *Sunset Boulevard*, and there is a vague hint throughout the film of nostalgia for the golden age of Hollywood. Thus, there are vague hints in this lampoon of the contemporary motion picture industry that things were better in the old days, when giants such as Welles and Hitchcock walked the Earth. However, such nostalgic hints are not really an important part of the film. Indeed, many of the posters, in particular, refer to somewhat questionable products of Hollywood's classic period, reminding us that the old-style studio system (of which neither Hitchcock nor Welles was representative) turned out some real clunkers.

There are also numerous suggestions that part of the trouble with Hollywood is its inability to break free of the past. Consequently, most of the characters who are involved in making new films tend to approach "innovation" in terms of the kind of "recombinant thinking" that Todd Gitlin sees as central to television programming—and indeed to capitalism as a whole—in which economic efficiency requires a combination of constant innovation and a basic stability (77). Thus, new films are constantly being pitched as (sometimes highly unlikely) combinations of old ones, as when one is described as "*Out of Africa* meets *Pretty Woman*" and another as "*Ghost* meets *Manchurian Candidate*." Sequels are also crucial to the films being developed within *The Player*, as when Buck Henry (in one of the film's numerous cameos) appears to pitch a sequel to *The Graduate*, which he originally scripted, or when studio executive Griffin Mill (Tim Robbins) envisions the making of a more commercial American version of Vittorio De Sica's 1948 Italian neorealist classic *The Bicycle Thief*.

This suggestion of the constant recycling of older materials resonates in an obvious way with Jameson's notion of the importance of pastiche in postmodern culture. *The Player* is relentless in its almost Flaubertian dissection of Hollywood corruption, decadence, and anti-aesthetic commercialism. Yet Altman's film is somewhat good-humored in its satire, treating these aspects of the industry as given (and almost natural), rather than railing against them. The film's villain goes unpunished and even triumphs, emerging as the head of a major studio, but this motif is treated as comic. Further, the film itself incorporates most of the formulas and stereotypes that it criticizes, as if to acknowledge that such elements have become inescapable. *The Player*, famous for the many cameo appearances by Hollywood luminaries, clearly functions as an insider's critique of Hollywood rather than a thoroughgoing rejection of a Hollywood system to which it offers no alternatives.

The Player depicts Mill as an ambitious but insecure studio executive who spends half his time hearing pitches from would-be screenwriters for potential films and the other half in political maneuvering to try to undermine those whom he identifies as his competition. Tops on this list is up-and-coming whiz kid Larry Levy (Peter Gallagher), rumored to be on his way to supplanting Mill as the studio's second-in-command. Much of the plot, meanwhile, is actuated by the anonymous threatening notes that Mill has been receiving for months. Given his style of operation and the nature of his business, in which virtually all pitches have to be turned down, Mill has lots of enemies. He concludes (wrongly, it turns out) that the notes are being sent by screenwriter David Kahane (Vincent D'Onofrio), whom Mill had treated particularly rudely after a recent pitch.

Mill tracks down Kahane—at a showing of *The Bicycle Thief*, here humorously acknowledged as a key example of genuine cinematic art, as opposed to the commodified productions of Hollywood. (When *The Bicycle Thief* comes up in a discussion at the studio, Levy dismisses it as "an art movie. It doesn't count. We're talking about movie movies.") Mill tries to make a deal with the writer, but they end up fighting in a darkened parking lot. Kahane is killed; Mill takes his wallet to make it look like a robbery, then flees the scene. Much of the rest of the film involves the attempts of the Pasadena police, led by detectives Susan Avery (Whoopi Goldberg) and Paul DeLongpre (Lyle Lovett), to solve the killing, while Mill spends much of his time trying to avoid implication in the crime. In the meantime, however, he calls attention to himself by beginning an affair with artist June Gudmundsdottir (Greta Scacchi), a sexy (but somewhat icy) mystery woman who causes Mill to abandon his long-time girlfriend, story editor Bonnie Sherow (Cynthia Stevenson), the only wholesome and virtuous film-industry employee in the entire picture.

In the end, Mill does successfully avoid prosecution. Moreover, in a parody of the required Hollywood happy endings that are satirized throughout the film, he becomes the head of the studio, marries June, and lives happily in a luxurious fairy-tale home. Bonnie, meanwhile, is fired from the studio after she vehemently protests its perversion (due to poor test-audience results with the original) of a dark, existential drama (entitled *Habeas Corpus*) into a stereotypical bit of optimistic fluff, complete with big-name stars (Bruce Willis and Julia Roberts, who appear in *The Player* as themselves). Bonnie is left weeping on the steps of the studio offices, while Mill happily drives his Rolls-Royce home to his ideal home and ideal wife. In Hollywood, virtue is not rewarded; it is, in fact, a definite liability.

The film ends with a paradigmatic postmodern turn. On his way home, Mill receives a call on his car phone from the sender of the earlier threatening messages, offering him a script for a film, called *The Player*, about an ambitious Hollywood executive who kills a screenwriter he thinks has been threatening him, then gets away with it. Mill agrees that it sounds like a good idea for a movie, especially if it can have a happy ending. Then, Mill arrives at his idyllic home and is greeted by a now-pregnant June, who asks him what took him so long. "Traffic was a bitch," he says, which is also the closing line spoken by Willis to Roberts in the commercialized version of *Habeas Corpus*.

Such self-referential turns provide an element of fun, contributing to the ongoing joke that *The Player* is essentially identical to the commodified films it ostensibly criticizes. This overt declaration that *The Player* has no alternatives to offer would seem to be an ultimate surrender of utopian vision. However, the particularly self-parodic way in which *The Player* collapses in on itself does potentially comment on the Hollywood film industry in ways that go beyond the mere blank quotation envisioned by Jameson as typical of postmodern culture. Indeed, Cynthia Baron argues that *The Player* employs parody, rather than pastiche, because "it presents us with a critical distance between itself and the tradition of Classical Hollywood Cinema" (29). In fact, she sees the film as producing an alienation effect along the lines of the epic theater of Bertolt Brecht that asks audiences to stand back and consider their typical reactions to Hollywood films in a critical way. In addition, Baron sees a utopian dimension in *The Player*'s use of so many cameos by big stars, whose very appearance in such small parts suggests their willingness to work together and to forgo their egos in the interest of participating in the making of a quality picture.

At the same time, the good-humored way in which *The Player* critiques the corruption, venality, and lack of creativity in the film industry suggests a very postmodern skepticism about the effectiveness of any such critiques. The film seems to assume that, given the general political atmosphere in Hollywood and in the United States as a whole, there is little chance that any such critique might actually lead to genuine reform. In this sense, the film looks back to the assassination scene at the end of Altman's *Nashville*, in which even the most traumatic of events seems to have little effect on the spectators at the concert at which the assassination occurs. Indeed, the concert continues almost uninterrupted, even after the shooting of one of its headline performers on stage.

Nashville's use of the country music industry as a source of material also illustrates the way in which postmodern pastiche in film goes beyond the borrowing of motifs from previous movies and includes borrowings from other forms as well. Television is particularly prominent as a source of material for postmodern films, as in the influence of MTV music videos on the editing style of current films. Pastiche of material from television and other sources in recent popular movies is discussed in the next chapter.

Chapter 4

As Seen on TV

Television and Postmodern Film

The 2001 film *Josie and the Pussycats*, based on a classic comic book that had also become a popular television cartoon series, illustrates well the tendency of postmodernist films to derive their content from media rather than reality. The title characters are a three-girl rock band, so that the movie relies for its material heavily on the entire culture of rock music, in addition to the original comic book and cartoon. In many ways, in fact, the most important source of the film is the cable music channel MTV, so often cited as the epitome of postmodernism in American television.[1] Not only does the film look essentially like a string of music videos, but it overtly even acknowledges its source with frequent references to MTV. The principal subject matter of the film—the commodification of culture (and everything else) in contemporary America—is also directly related to MTV. If conservative critics have accused the network of promoting immorality and the destruction of traditional American values, leftist critics have been equally concerned about the network's complicity in the production of a generation of mindless, programmed consumers.

Actually, while *Josie and Pussycats* is nominally critical of the commodification of culture as represented by MTV, it serves largely as a running commercial for the network and was in fact heavily promoted on MTV when it was showing in theaters. The film also epitomizes the central strategy of the network of answering critics by pretending to agree with them, but doing so in a ridiculous way that presumably makes the critics look ridiculous as well. One might cite here the notorious MTV animated program *Beavis and Butt-head*, in which the two adolescent protagonists have been rendered mindless, amoral, and destructive by watching too much MTV. Of course, the inanity of such programming was intended precisely to suggest the silliness of charges that MTV was ruining the minds of America's young people, while at the same time congratulating America's youth on being far smarter than Beavis and Butt-head (and thus giving them additional gratification from watching the show).

Josie and the Pussycats similarly takes on charges of the complicity of contemporary popular culture, including MTV, with late capitalist consumerism by presenting a dystopian America in which commodification has been pushed to an extreme, preposterous, and comical level. As the film begins, we see adoring fans practically swooning at the sight of Du Jour, a manufactured boy band whose very name suggests that their fame is likely to be fleeting. After all, their success comes not from their talent but from the marketing efforts of their record company, Mega Records, a fact that is emphasized when they board their private tour plane, which is wallpapered in logos for the Target department store chain and stocked wall-to-wall with product placements for various consumer goods. The joke here is that the film itself openly joins in the marketing mentality of Mega Records.

The depiction of Du Jour obviously comments on the megasuccess of boy bands such as 'N Sync and the Backstreet Boys. However, their story takes a melodramatically ominous turn when the band members discover that Mega Records has placed a secret track on their latest recording that consists of subliminal messages urging young Americans to get to their malls and spend their money on all the latest trends and fads. When the band members protest, their manager, Wyatt Frame (Alan Cumming), crashes their tour plane, presumably killing them off. Indeed, we later learn that the conspiracy goes well beyond Du Jour and that all of the numerous deaths of rock stars in plane crashes and by drug overdoses in the past have been similarly engineered by record companies in the service of this same diabolical project—which turns out, at root, to be administered by the U.S. government as a way of promoting consumption and thus stimulating the economy.

With Du Jour gone, Mega Records has to seek a new band to convey their message. Almost any band will do, of course, so Frame grabs the first band he runs across, which turns out to be Josie and the Pussycats, a struggling local group in Riverdale, Illinois. He quickly signs the girls to a recording contract, then whisks them off on their own tour plane (similarly filled with logos and product placements) to an ultracommercialized, neon-lit New York City, all the buildings of which have now been decorated with advertisements. Meanwhile, we witness a meeting between Fiona (Parker Posey), the head of Mega Records, and her government sponsors. In the meeting, she explains exactly how the company goes about planting its subliminal messages in popular music recordings, thus creating trends, fads, and fashions. "We turn your world into one giant TV commercial," she tells them.

The band quickly records an album, which Mega Records electronically enhances to meet their calculated requirements for marketability. Of course, given that the record company is also in charge of manipulating the tastes of young audiences, the album is a huge success and the Pussycats become immediate stars. They even appear on MTV's popular *Total Request Live* (*TRL*), hosted by Carson Daly (played by himself), which allows a number of in-jokes based on the fact that the film's young audience would recognize Daly as the then-boyfriend of actress Tara Reid, who plays Melody, the band's ditzy drummer. As it turns out, Daly and MTV are key players in the conspiracy to control America's youth via popular music, but of course the plot collapses in the end and the Pussycats triumph, becoming stars even without subliminal enhancements.

In the final scenes, *Josie and the Pussycats* backs away from its identification of the schemes of Mega Records with the U.S. government, instead attributing the most evil aspects of this scheme to the private grudges of Fiona, who wants to get even for having been mocked as a teenager because of a lisp. But this diversion of responsibility is hardly necessary. Any potential political message in the film is undermined by its campy silliness, and the film even identifies itself as part of the scheme by flashing messages on the screen to the effect that "*Josie and the Pussycats* is the Best Movie Ever!" The film also has fun with its own obvious attempt to cash in on the recent popularity of the screen adaptation of the 1970s television series *Charlie's Angels* by announcing, when the Pussycats become stars, that they will be the subject of a new movie starring Drew Barrymore, Cameron Diaz, and Lucy Liu, the stars of *Charlie's Angels* (2000). In any case, the real point of *Josie and the Pussycats* is that America's young people are *not* being manipulated into blind consumption and that they are far too smart and savvy to be so easily duped. The joke in this extremely jokey film is not on the young Americans who constituted its principal theatrical audience but on those who would be naïve enough to believe that these young people could be manipulated into buying things they do not want by the messages conveyed to them in popular culture.

Thus, the excessively obvious accusation of the commodification of popular music in *Josie in the Pussycats* ultimately serves to mock such critiques, once again illustrating the extent to which it is difficult for any political analysis to be taken seriously in the early twenty-first century.

One might compare here the much more serious political and social commentary that is embedded in Robert Altman's *Nashville* (1975), another film that uses a segment of the music industry as a sort of microcosm of American society as a whole, as a way of tracking the decline in seriousness in American political films over the last quarter of the twentieth century.[2]

The particular involvement of *Josie and the Pussycats* with television potentially suggests that TV may be a major culprit in this decline and the closely related decline in the ability of Americans to distinguish between fiction and reality. By reducing everything, including the news, to a form of entertainment, television completes the aestheticization of reality that Walter Benjamin saw as a central strategy of the Nazi regime in Germany, but in a way that is distinctly postmodern. In addition, Brian McHale argues in *Postmodernist Fiction* that a common technique used by postmodern writers involves the blurring of boundaries between different levels of reality, as when fictional characters enter the worlds of their authors or vice versa. McHale sees this technique as emanating from a general decrease in faith that there is a real distinction between fiction and reality or that there is such a thing as a stable and concrete reality apart from human construction. In addition, one can see this blurring of the separation between fiction and reality as part of a more general withering of boundaries (between genres, between high and low culture, and so on) that is typical of postmodern culture.

The tendency of postmodern films to be based on the world of cinema rather than the "real" world, as discussed in the previous chapter, is very much a part of this phenomenon. But recent films have drawn their material from other fictional sources as well, and often in ways that specifically address the postmodern blurring of the distinction between fiction and reality. As early as 1973, for example, Philippe de Broca's *Le Magnifique* featured a writer of espionage fiction (played by Jean-Paul Belmondo) whose own life becomes intertwined with the lives of his fictional creations. More recently, Marc Forster's *Stranger than Fiction* (2006) hopelessly entangles fiction and reality as protagonist Harold Crick (Will Ferrell) discovers that he is a character in a book being written by novelist Kay Eiffel (Emma Thompson), then attempts to convince Eiffel not to kill him off in the end, as is her usual practice. In *Tune in Tomorrow* (1990), the increasingly preposterous (and anti-Albanian) plots of a radio soap opera in 1950s New Orleans become entangled with real life.[3] And in films such as Ralph Bakshi's *Cool World* (1992) and Henry Selick's *Monkeybone* (2001), the boundary between the world of reality and that of cartoons proves permeable—while the latter throws in a significant amount of nightmare imagery that is reminiscent of the work of David Lynch, especially in *Eraserhead* (1977). Both *Cool World* and *Monkeybone* followed the postmodern technological breakthrough of Robert Zemeckis's *Who Framed Roger Rabbit?* (1988), which allowed the seamless mixing of cartoon and live action, though Zemeckis's film itself probably uses the technology more effectively.[4]

In *Cool World*, the time-honored science-fiction theme of parallel universes is used to portray the parallel worlds of "noids" (real people) and "doodles" (cartoons). The principal plot involves the efforts of Holli Would (Kim Basinger), an ultrasexy doodle, to perform a typical feat of postmodern crossing of ontological boundaries by moving into the real world so she can become a real woman and, among other things, experience real sex. Her attempt, however, upsets the balance between the two universes and nearly destroys them both, until the efforts of cartoonist Jack Deebs (Gabriel Byrne) and police detective Frank Harris (Brad Pitt) manage to return her to the cartoon universe, aka Cool World, and restore the balance.

This pedestrian plot is not exactly riveting, though the film does contain a few interesting images and notions. For one thing, the constantly gyrating and spectacularly voluptuous Holli Would, who doesn't actually look all that different from Basinger, potentially calls attention to the almost cartoonish visions of feminine sexuality that have been conveyed in Hollywood movies, especially given Holli's suggestive name and the fact that Marilyn Monroe is her declared idol and role model. In addition, Cool World is itself a sort of postmodern fantasy, entirely timeless, with no sense of historical change. For example, Harris had been accidentally transported there from the real world in 1945, but still remains the same age in 1992, when the main events of the film occur. Nothing else in Cool World seems to have changed since 1945 either; this cartoon universe is not just frozen in time, but frozen in approximately the mid- to late 1940s (at about the time film noir was reaching its peak), as can be seen from its noirish look. Moreover, the time frame of Cool World is appropriately fixed at about the time when postmodernism, with its ahistorical worldview, was beginning to emerge as a powerful current in American culture, though the film certainly gives no indication that it is intentionally trying to comment on postmodernism as a cultural phenomenon.

In *Monkeybone* (based on the graphic novel *Dark Town* by Kaja Blackley), the crossing of the boundary between different levels of reality has a straightforward explanation: cartoonist Stu Miley is plunged into a nightmare realm emanating from his own unconscious mind after an

auto accident leaves him in a coma. Miley's experiences in this underworld make for some lively graphics, though the film ultimately descends into a rather predictable resolution as the cartoon world spills
back into reality and Miley is forced to defeat his own cartoon creation
(the mischievous Monkeybone) for possession of his own body and for
the hand of the beautiful Dr. Julie McElroy (Bridget Fonda), Miley's
would-be fiancée.

Of all media other than film itself, television has been the most
important source of cinematic material, including explorations of the
postmodern blurring of reality boundaries. Indeed, a key example of this
is the disappearing separation between film and television as distinct
media. In the 1950s, when television first emerged as an important medium, it was largely perceived by the movie industry as a threat, and
early representations of television in film, whether serious (as in Elia
Kazan's *A Face in the Crowd*, 1957) or comic (as in Frank Tashlin's *Will
Success Spoil Rock Hunter?*, 1957), were unremittingly negative. By the
1980s, however, the television and film industries were thoroughly integrated, both dominated by the same large corporate entities. For example, MTV is owned by the giant media conglomerate Viacom, which
also owns CBS and part of the CW broadcast network, as well as a
whole string of other cable networks, including BET, Comedy Central,
VH1, CMT (Country Music Television), Nickelodeon, and Spike TV,
plus the cable movie channels Showtime, the Movie Channel, Flix, and
part of the Sundance Channel. Meanwhile, both MTV and Nickelodeon
have their own film production units, while Viacom also owns Para-
mount and Dreamworks, two of the leading movie studios.

Television, by the 1980s, was no longer a rival of the film industry:
it was just another income stream, although it might be more accurate
to say that the film industry is now a subsidiary of the television industry, for which it produces large amounts of content. In the current
media environment, even the most successful films will be seen by far
more viewers in various television formats than in theaters, with television outlets such as pay-per-view, subscription movie channels, and
commercial broadcast and cable networks, now receiving important sup-
plementation from recorded formats, especially DVD. In addition, many
films go straight to video and are never even seen in theaters, while
some "films" are shot in digital video to begin with, including such key
examples of postmodern filmmaking as Mike Figgis's *Timecode* and
Robert Rodriguez's *Sin City* (2005). Finally, British art film director
Peter Greenaway has achieved some of his most impressive visual effects
in pictures such as *Prospero's Books* (1991) by combining film and video

in a single composition. In short, the line of demarcation between film and television is now hazy at best, yet film, though often criticized as a bad influence on America's youth, has, by and large, been able to escape the sweeping indictments with which so many critics have declared American television programming universally awful. Indeed, one of the truly impressive achievements of American cinema is that it has managed to maintain a certain aesthetic reputation after decades in which television has not only dominated American cultural production but has, in fact, been the principal means through which audiences are exposed to film itself.

One reason film continues to have a loftier critical reputation than television is surely that cinema, like literature, continues to be judged, in important ways, by its finest and most successful works, while all television programming tends to be tossed into the same critical hopper. However, part of the difference between the critical reputations of television and film surely has to do with the fact that, well beyond the 1950s, many movies have continued to be critical of television as a debased medium, even as the film and television businesses were gradually merging.

Sidney Lumet's *Network* (1976), for example, is bitterly critical of the tendency of television to turn news into entertainment (a trend that would become even more pronounced with the advent of twenty-four-hour cable news networks in later years). One of the signature films of the 1970s, *Network* is not overtly postmodern; indeed, it attempts a serious critique of the tendencies of postmodernist culture, especially as embodied in the tendency of television to reinforce the postmodern conversion of reality into a series of spectacles. *Network*, in fact, is a scathing cynical commentary on the venal, corrupt, and thoroughly commodified nature of American culture in the postmodern era of late capitalism. It focuses on the cheerful willingness of television network executives to stoop to any level of exploitation in the interest of higher ratings—and thus higher profits for their corporate bosses. At the same time, the film clearly indicates that the operations of this unscrupulous network are symptomatic of larger forces at work in the global capitalist system. As one corporate mogul tells newsman Howard Beale (Peter Finch) after the latter complains on the air about a deal between his network's corporate ownership and Arab oil interests, we now live amid the "multinational dominion of dollars" in which "there is no America. There is no democracy. There is only IBM and ITT and AT&T, and DuPont, Dow, Union Carbide, and Exxon." "The world," he tells Beale, "is a business," in which only profit matters and in which nations and ideologies are irrelevant.

Network is a powerful denunciation of the dehumanizing consequences of late capitalism and of the complicity of the media and popular culture in that phenomenon. Yet the film was produced by a large
corporate studio (MGM) and was a major critical and commercial hit,
winning four Oscars and being nominated for six others. This demonstrates, however inadvertently, the ability of capitalism to turn a profit
even from the criticism of itself—just as Beale's initial rants against the
system causes his ratings to soar.

The failure of *Network* to find a point of view outside the capitalist
system from which to critique capitalism might also be described as a
failure to escape the gravitational pull of the postmodernist cultural system that surrounded it. For a contrasting strategy, one might consider
David Cronenberg's *Videodrome* (1983), a film that is just as critical of
the sinister potential of television but that is itself avowedly postmodern.
Videodrome features a relatively rough-hewn look, which in this case
reinforces its subject matter—the B-grade programming of a small, independent cable channel in a North American city (possibly, but not necessarily, Toronto, where it was filmed). The movie also features some of
Cronenberg's most horrifying images of the invasion of the human body
by technology, in this case by television. Of course, television, like film,
is both a technological and a cultural force, and it is clear that the critical examination of television in *Videodrome* can also be taken as a commentary on the film industry, though this commentary is ambivalent
and a bit difficult to decode.

Max Renn (James Woods), the protagonist of *Videodrome*, is the
president of Channel 83, a small and struggling channel whose programming focuses largely on sensational sex and violence (or the combination of the two) in an effort to carve out a niche viewership. In this
sense, it is tempting to read Renn as a stand-in for Cronenberg himself,
yet Renn is quite insistent in his refusal to produce original programming, relying instead on acquiring programming produced by others.
Indeed, the plot of the film revolves around Renn's attempts to acquire
a tawdry S&M-based production called "Videodrome" for his cable
channel. This attempt lures him into a dark world of conspiracy and
perversion in which it turns out that Spectacular Optics, a global conglomerate, is planning to use the "Videodrome" program to send signals
that will tamper with the minds of the public, reversing the "rot" that is
making them "soft" and thus dangerously vulnerable to attacks by the
rest of the world, which has been toughened by poverty and hardship.

Exposed to these signals himself, Renn becomes a programmed
murderer, somewhat in the mode of Raymond Shaw (Laurence Harvey)

in John Frankenheimer's Cold War classic *The Manchurian Candidate* (1962), a film that also gestures toward television as a potential tool for brainwashing. Renn experiences a series of bizarre hallucinations, and viewers follow him in his descent toward a condition of psychic confusion in which it ultimately becomes impossible to distinguish between reality and illusion. This condition makes Renn a sort of allegorical extension of the postmodern predicament as a whole, while many of his hallucinations dramatize popular fears and anxieties of the postmodern condition. These illusions largely involve the abject invasion of Renn's body by technology, as when his right hand becomes fused with the gun he uses as a murder weapon or when a huge vulva-like opening appears in his stomach, allowing the insertion of items such as videotapes, making him a sort of human VCR. Then again, this film implies that we are all becoming human VCRs, playing out the programming we have received from television.

By the 1990s, developments in the American media had made the media critique of films such as *Network* seem prescient. In Gus Van Sant's *To Die For* (1995), television news has been thoroughly converted into show business, and television journalists are big-time media stars. Here, protagonist and aspiring television journalist Suzanne Stone (Nicole Kidman) explains to a class of high schoolers that many of America's leading television personalities got their starts precisely by seeing themselves on television in store displays. The film then details her relentless attempts to become just such a television personality, dreaming not of becoming a fine journalist, but merely of being famous, a talking head in the idiot box.

Suzanne is a creature of the media who has led a life sheltered from reality. In her case, the shelter is provided by her affluent suburban WASP family, but her immersion in television produces an even more empty personality. Suzanne is relentlessly superficial, absolutely chilling in the amoral, ruthless single-mindedness with which she pursues her goals. Beautiful in a plastic, Barbie-doll sort of way (and similarly not too bright), Suzanne dreams of a career in the "professional media." She has, in fact, spent her whole life preparing for this career, watching her television media heroes in rapt fascination, crafting a look, sound, and personality for herself based on what she sees on television. She thinks entirely in superficial stereotypes and speaks only in clichés, with perfect grammar and a slightly artificial-sounding Midwestern accent. This effect was no doubt enhanced by the fact that Kidman did, in fact, have to fake the accent in place of her own Australian one, but it works perfectly in conjunction with her overly well-coiffed hair and perfectly tailored (but somewhat tasteless) wardrobe to project the self-conscious artificiality of her entire identity.

Mirroring its own themes, *To Die For* is itself presented in mediated form, telling its story in retrospect, largely through interviews with the main characters. The narrative itself begins as Suzanne, having graduated from community college but so far unable to land a media job, meets and marries Larry Maretto (Matt Dillon), the son of a well-off, but uncultured, Italian restaurant owner (Dan Hedaya). Larry is devoted to Suzanne, so the marriage seems promising. The problem is that Suzanne is also devoted to Suzanne, particularly to the pursuit of her career. Thus, while they are on their honeymoon in Florida, she slips away to a TV convention at a hotel in town, where she meets (and sleeps with) a big-shot TV journalist. Inspired by this meeting, she renews the pursuit of her career, landing a job as a girl Friday at a local cable station back home in Little Hope, New Hampshire. She soon parlays this job into a position as the station's weather girl.

Suzanne treats this modest gig as if "she were reporting on D-day," at the same time constantly proposing new projects that will give her more on-air exposure (and thus more opportunities to advance to a bigger job in a larger market). Larry, meanwhile, begins to suggest ways in which she might work with him in the family restaurant, and she soon begins to regard him as a possible impediment to her career. Divorce, however, is not an option for Suzanne, because "the word *failure* is not in my vocabulary." Her viewing of television, though, has taught her that any problem can be solved by resolute action, so she quickly conceives a plan to get rid of Larry with the help of a simple-minded local teenager, Jimmy Emmett (Joaquin Phoenix), whose mind is also saturated with media images and who dreams of being like rocker Jim Morrison. Suzanne seduces Jimmy, then convinces him and his friends to murder her husband. They do so on the couple's first wedding anniversary, while Suzanne is on-air doing the weather and sending anniversary greetings to her beloved husband, thus establishing an alibi.

Not surprisingly, the bumbling teenagers leave a glaring trail of clues and are all soon arrested, as is Suzanne. Jimmy attempts to justify his behavior by suggesting that he felt the whole time that he was acting with no free will, like some zombie from a horror movie. Nonetheless, he is convicted of murder and sentenced to life plus thirty years, "if I live that long." There are, however, signs that the absolutely remorseless Suzanne might be able to beat the rap, especially after she invents an entirely fictitious story relating Larry's killing to his serious cocaine habit. Not to fear, though. *To Die For* is based on the same media images as is Suzanne herself, so the elder Maretto simply calls on his connections in the Italian underworld to have her rubbed out. Live by the media stereotype, die by the media stereotype.

To Die For is relentless in its depiction of the saturation of contemporary American society by television-generated media images, refusing to pretend that it can somehow stand outside the phenomenon, commenting on it from some God's-eye view beyond contamination. It is unwavering in its portrayal of Suzanne's complete lack of morals or conscience, never giving her even a whisper of sympathetic depth. Thus, its representation of Suzanne threatens to make her seem monstrous and pathological, detracting from the impact of the film as a critique of American society as a whole. However, the film also refuses to present us with admirable characters who somehow escape the influence of the media. Larry's sister, Janice Maretto (Ileana Douglas) seems vaguely sympathetic, but she, too, aspires to a career in show business as a professional ice-skater. She symbolically ends the film skating happily on the frozen river in which Suzanne's murdered body has been encased in ice. Probably the most sympathetic character in the film is Lydia Mertz (Alison Folland), an unattractive teenage girl made miserable by her inability to live up to media images of feminine beauty. In this situation, it may be understandable that the glamorous Suzanne is her idol, but then, in a display of her own lack of depth, Lydia escapes sentencing for her own involvement in the murder of Larry by helping the police in an attempt to gather evidence against Suzanne. Moreover, Lydia ends the film by embarking on her own media career (of sorts), preparing to hit the TV talk show circuit to discuss her involvement with the now notorious Suzanne, who is famous at last.

A film such as Barry Levinson's *Wag the Dog* (1997) can be taken as a sort of sequel to *Network* that tracks the continuing decline of the American media over the intervening two decades. Levinson's film also makes clear the ways in which the influence of television has, by the 1990s, invaded the political process. At the same time, it blurs the boundary between film and television (as historical reality had already done) by featuring a Hollywood film producer who helps to develop images for television. Much like *Network*, *Wag the Dog* is, at first glance, an exaggerated satire of the operations of the media. On closer examination, however, it may be disturbingly realistic. Meanwhile, unlike the rather bitter *Network*, it takes an essentially comic approach that seems to treat the phenomena it satirizes as inevitable.[5]

In the film, the unnamed president of the United States is in the midst of a reelection campaign when a teenage "Firefly Girl" (something like a slightly older version of a Girl Scout) accuses him of sexually assaulting her in the Oval Office. Whether or not the charge is true seems irrelevant. Instead of attempting to refute the charge, the president's handlers concentrate on coming up with a way to divert media attention away from the burgeoning sex scandal, at least for the eleven days remaining until the election—while the president himself basically just tries to keep a low profile. Realizing they need extra help for a job this big, the president's campaign team, headed by Winifred Ames (Anne Heche), decides to call in "fixer" Conrad Brean (Robert De Niro), an expert at dealing with precisely such crises. Brean, citing as his inspiration the Reagan administration's 1983 invasion of Grenada within twenty-four hours of the bombing deaths of 240 U.S. marines in Beirut, decides that only a war could provide a diversion big enough for their needs. However, the postmodern times being what they are, he sees no need for a real war. Instead, he hires Hollywood producer Stanley Motss (Dustin Hoffman) to orchestrate a simulated war that will exist only in the media's images of it. After all, Brean points out to Motss as he sells him the idea, "War is show business," and people respond far more to the images and slogans of a war than to the war itself.

Motss whips up a few key scenes (complete with patriotic musical accompaniment) to feed to the media to convince them that the United States is now fighting a war in Albania, chosen largely for its obscurity (though the choice would appear oddly appropriate given the heightened importance of Albania to the U.S. military involvement in the Balkans only two years after the film was released). In the key scene, a young woman (Kirsten Dunst) is shown fleeing a burning village, carrying a kitten in her arms—with the village, the flames, and even the kitten being provided via computer-generated images. The strategy initially works, and the media begins to focus on the war rather than the sex scandal. In response, the president's opponent is able, within days, to get information from the CIA to the effect that the war has already ended. Needing to extend the diversion a few days more, Motss and Brean come up with the idea that a lone, heroic soldier has been left behind enemy lines, then focus their media blitz on the supposed attempts to rescue the soldier. Afraid they might actually have to produce him for the media, they tab Sgt. William Schumann (Woody Harrelson) for the role, choosing him from the Pentagon's personnel files largely because his surname allows them to generate a media campaign around his last name, nicknaming him "Old Shoe" and noting that he has been left behind like that item. Unfortunately, they find out only later that Schumann is a dangerous psychotic who has spent the last twelve years in a military prison for raping a nun.

One misfortune leads to another. Brean, Motss, and Ames board a small plane with Schumann to take him to Washington, only to have the plane crash in a rural area. Schumann is then shot and killed by an irate storekeeper after he attempts to sexually assault the man's daughter. But never fear, a quick spin to the media campaign converts Schumann into a fallen hero killed in battle, generating a wave of sympathy that sweeps the president back into office in the election. Then Motss, enraged that the president's own lame media campaign (consisting of little more than repetition of the cliché "Don't Change Horses in Midstream") is given credit for his reelection, decides to go public so he can get credit for what he has done. However, before he can do so, Motss is found dead (supposedly from natural causes), with the obvious implication that he has been killed by the president's operatives.

This chilling ending provides a closing reminder that the highly amusing escapades we have just seen have a decidedly dark side. For one thing, the film delivers a disturbing message about the intervention of the media in the political process. At one point, Ames expresses contempt for television and is asked what she has against the medium. Her reply, that it has "destroyed the political process," can be taken as the central statement of the film, and events since 1997 have only served to reinforce the point. Indeed, while *Wag the Dog* is something of a farce, real-world events since its release make it appear closer and closer to reality. This is especially the case after the 2003 U.S. invasion of Iraq, based on inaccurate (possibly falsified) intelligence about the existence of weapons of mass destruction in Iraq. This invasion, like the whole "war on terrorism" of which it was supposed to be a part, was as much a media campaign as a military one, and fears of a global terrorism crisis (promoted by extensive media hype, especially on the Fox News network) were central to the success of George W. Bush's own "Don't Change Horses in Midstream" reelection campaign in 2004. Throw in the fact that the supposed U.S. invasion of Albania in *Wag the Dog* is justified on the basis of the claim that the country has long been a harbor for terrorists, and the film begins to appear more and more prophetic.

Of all the media critiques produced in the 1990s, Oliver Stone's *Natural Born Killers* (1994) may be the finest film and the most powerful political statement. It may, in fact, be the director's masterpiece, despite the fact that it triggered a firestorm of negative criticism especially among those who saw it as precisely the sort of gory media spectacle that it was meant to criticize. Here, Stone pulls out all the stops, employing all the resources of American popular culture to produce a scathing

indictment of that culture. This is a high-risk effort, and the film was
excoriated as debased, obscene, and immoral, especially by right-wing
Republicans and conservative Christians. It was, for example, singled out
by Bob Dole in his 1996 presidential campaign as an example of the
negative influence of Hollywood films because of what Dole characterized as the movie's celebration of grotesque violence. But Dole, who at
the same time endorsed the equally violent films of fellow Republican
Arnold Schwarzenegger as wholesome entertainment, admitted that he
had not actually seen *Natural Born Killers*, thus epitomizing the extent
to which the picture's critics so often spoke out of ignorance. The film
does indeed include a great deal of horrifying violence, but (unlike
Schwarzenegger's films) it does not endorse violence as a solution to
life's problems. In *Natural Born Killers*, the horror is directed at the violence and at the celebration of violence in American popular culture. Its
condemnation of the latter is especially powerful—or would have been if
the film's attempt to parody postmodern culture had not been taken
instead by so many critics as a paradigm of that culture.

Natural Born Killers focuses on young lovers Mickey and Mallory
Knox (Woody Harrelson and Juliette Lewis) as they work their way
across the American Southwest (down the suggestively numbered Highway 666) on a three-week crime and murder spree. In this sense, the
film is the culmination of a cinematic tradition that includes such predecessors as *You Only Live Once* (1937), *They Live by Night* (1948), *Bonnie
and Clyde* (1967), *Badlands* (1973), and *Kalifornia* (1993). It was also
followed by such films as Gregg Araki's *The Doom Generation* (1995),
which treats much of the same material as *Natural Born Killers*, but with
a darkly comic twist. In a very real sense, *Natural Born Killers* is a sort
of self-critical summa of American popular culture as a whole. The film
is composed of a dizzying array of fragments, quick-cutting MTV-style
from color to black-and-white, from film to video, and among different
film stocks, creating a highly disorienting look and feel that greatly
enhances the thematic content. This visual fragmentation, of course,
mirrors the fragmentation of contemporary American culture. Furthermore, it is supplemented by generic fragmentation; the film is essentially
constructed from bits and pieces of parodies of various popular genres,
including not only crime and police films but westerns, sitcoms, cartoons, television commercials, and tabloid journalism. Scenes from a
variety of earlier movies and television shows often literally play in the
background of scenes in *Natural Born Killers*, thus identifying the film's
predecessors, while also indicating that contemporary American reality
exists only within the context of media images.

Natural Born Killers makes especially good use of popular music, employing a soundtrack that brilliantly enhances the impact of various scenes. The haunting apocalyptic ballads of Leonard Cohen are particularly effective in this sense. One of the major strategies employed in the soundtrack involves a careful mixture of contemporary violent rock and rap music with traditional saccharine products from earlier years (such as Patsy Cline's "Back in Baby's Arms"), clearly suggesting that these various musical forms arise from similar impulses in American culture, despite their apparent differences. The film makes similar suggestions through its allusions to 1950s television programs that idealize American life (such as *Leave It to Beaver* and *I Love Lucy*). In particular, such idealized sitcoms are skewered in one of the film's most striking set pieces, the presentation of the initial meeting and courtship of Mickey and Mallory via a parodic television sitcom (entitled "I Love Mallory," complete with laugh tracks), in which the two young people meet, fall in love, then murder her grossly abusive father (Rodney Dangerfield) and wimpy mother (Edie McClurg) before setting off on their crime spree.

Crucial to this spree is the extensive media coverage it attracts, making cult heroes of the murderous Knoxes. As part of this, notorious television tabloid journalist Wayne Gale (Robert Downey Jr.) makes Mickey and Mallory the focal point of his program, *American Maniacs*, which specializes in mass murders and other sensational crimes. Jack Scagnetti (Tom Sizemore), the police detective who devotes himself to the pursuit of the couple, is a media star (and murderer), and one of the most controversial aspects of the film is its tendency to suggest that the dark impulses that drive the Knoxes are so endemic in American society that they also underlie the activities of the police and prison officials who serve as the film's representatives of official authority.

Eventually, Mickey and Mallory are captured and incarcerated, at which point *Natural Born Killers* becomes a prison film, depicting conditions in the prison, run by deranged warden Dwight McClusky (Tommy Lee Jones) as an especially brutal form of the viciousness that pervades all of American society. McClusky, in fact, plots with Scagnetti to murder the Knoxes in prison, feeling that their demonic presence is somehow stirring the other inmates to violence. Meanwhile, Gale brings his camera crew to the prison for an exclusive live interview with Mickey, to be conducted and broadcast immediately following the Super Bowl.

In the midst of the interview, a riot erupts in the prison. Mickey overpowers his captors and takes Gale and a prison guard hostage. They go to Mallory's cell, where Scagnetti is attempting to rape her before killing her. Scagnetti is killed instead, and the couple, with the aid of the other inmates, manages to escape from the prison (on live television), still holding Gale as a hostage. McClusky, overtaken by the prisoners he has tormented for so long, is torn to pieces. (Stone was forced to remove a scene of the prisoners displaying McClusky's head on a spike, one of many cuts required to reduce the film's rating from NC-17 to R.) Free in the woods, the Knoxes make a final statement for Gale's camera, then turn the camera on their hostage, videotaping as they blow him to bits with shotguns. The film then cuts to a brilliant final scene in which Mickey and a pregnant Mallory drive in a camper van with their two children, thus further linking the murderous pair with ordinary middle Americans, suggesting that they are a product of, not an aberration from, the mainstream ideology of contemporary America.

If movies such as *Wag the Dog* and *Natural Born Killers* suggested the complicity of the media (especially television) in the corrosion of the boundary between fiction and reality in the postmodern world of the 1990s, another film from the same period, Robert Redford's *Quiz Show* (1994), about the television quiz show corruption scandal of the 1950s, reminds us that the media were already corrupt even in those halcyon days. Redford's film appropriately begins with the theme music of "Mack the Knife," a song from Bertolt Brecht's *Threepenny Opera*, a play that characterizes capitalism as a form of legalized crime. *Quiz Show* then pursues this capitalism-as-crime theme by exploring the quiz show scandals, in the process narrating not only the destruction of American values by capitalist greed but also the role of the media, particularly television, in this destruction. Indeed, the film's central message seems to be that television has corrupted American values not only by offering easy opportunities for the unscrupulous but also by creating a population of viewers who are inured to deceit. Meanwhile, as congressional investigator Richard Goodwin (Rob Morrow) remarks after realizing that the investigations in which he has participated will never touch the real corporate powers behind the quiz show scandals, "I thought we were gonna get television. The truth is, television is gonna get us."

"Us" here presumably means the American people, but this ominous warning might also be taken to indicate the Hollywood film industry, whose efforts in the 1950s to dismiss television as a debased and subartistic form did not prevent the eventual integration of the two media, at least at the level of corporate ownership. Moreover, given these forms of corporate integration, it should come as no surprise that television became a major source of source material for film by the end of the 1980s.

Actually, movies based on television series date back at least to 1966, when Hanna-Barbera Productions topped off the prime-time run of *The Flintstones* with the theatrical release of *The Man Called Flint-stone*. But the late 1980s saw the beginnings of a veritable explosion of such crossover films, many of them drawing on memories of earlier successful television series in the nostalgic mode that Fredric Jameson sees as being central to postmodernist culture as a whole. These nostalgia films include *Dragnet* (1987), *The Addams Family* (1991), *The Fugitive* (1993), *The Brady Bunch Movie* (1995), and *The Avengers* (1998), however varied their treatments of these series would appear to be. For example, *The Fugitive* plays it "straight," treating a popular crime drama from the 1960s essentially seriously, "remaking" it with a big budget look and more spectacular special effects. *Dragnet*, on the other hand, pokes a great deal of fun at the excessive seriousness of its deadpan 1950s original, giving audiences of the late 1980s a pat on the back for presumably being more sophisticated than audiences of the 1950s. In both cases, however, the films leave the original series essentially untouched, forgoing any sort of genuine dialogue in favor of pure nostalgia. The campiness of *The Addams Family*, *The Avengers*, and *The Brady Bunch Movie* might appear to be more truly parodic—except that the original series were campy to start with, something that might also be noted of the sequence of three *Naked Gun* films (1988–1994), all starring Leslie Nielsen, who had also starred in the short-lived 1982 television series *Police Squad!* on which the films were based.

Nielsen also starred in *Wrongfully Accused* (1998), a spoof of *The Fugitive*, while the *Naked Gun* comedies were made by many of the same principals who had been involved in the earlier *Airplane!* (1980), which lampooned such earlier airborne suspense thrillers as *Zero Hour!* (1957) and *Airport* (1970), while deriving much of its humor from send-ups of individual scenes from any number of earlier films. This group of spoof films—which includes the above campy television crossovers and would later include the *Scary Movie* sequence of horror-film spoofs—are indicative of the self-conscious (and self-consciously silly) turn taken by pastiche films in the 1980s. Indeed, in addition to Jameson's suggestion of pastiche as a particularly postmodern form of blank parody, one should probably add the spoof as another mode of parody that fails to engage in any real dialogue with its source.

Other films based on television series involve even less dialogue and indeed function merely as extended-length episodes of the original series, some of them having appeared in theaters while the series were still on the air. These include *Beavis and Butt-head Do America* (1996), *The X-Files: Fight the Future* (1998), and *South Park: Bigger, Longer, and Uncut* (1999), all tellingly based on television series that are themselves paradigms of the postmodern. *Twilight Zone: The Movie* (1983), meanwhile, was simply a collection of nostalgic remakes of classic episodes of that legendary series, while Joss Whedon's excellent *Serenity* (2005) wraps up a few loose ends left over from the premature cancellation of the Fox TV series *Firefly*.

Worthy of special mention in this category is the extensive sequence of films that extend the first two *Star Trek* television series. Partly inspired by the then-recent commercial and technical success of *Star Wars* (1977), Robert Wise's *Star Trek: The Motion Picture* (1979) was an attempt to update the *Star Trek* franchise for a new generation of fans, building upon recent dramatic advances in special-effects technology. With nearly three times the budget of *Star Wars* and with special effects wizards such as Douglas Trumbull and John Dykstra on board, *Star Trek* is indeed an impressive-looking film, even if it is not really groundbreaking in the way *Star Wars* had been. It is grander than *Star Wars* (and intended for a more sophisticated audience), but the plot is a bit weak, and the interpersonal relationships (especially among Capt. James T. Kirk, Spock, and Dr. Leonard McCoy) that had provided so much of the energy of the original television series never really quite come off in the film. Still, the built-in audience from fans of the series made the first *Star Trek* film a substantial commercial success, leading to the longest series of sequels in science-fiction film history. For most fans (and critics), *Star Trek: The Wrath of Khan* (1982) was a great improvement over the first film, returning more to the spirit of the original series. *Star Trek III: The Search for Spock* (1984), *Star Trek IV: The Voyage Home* (1986), *Star Trek V: The Final Frontier* (1989), and *Star Trek VI: The Undiscovered Country* (1991) found fans as well (and made better use of the evolving relationship among Kirk, Spock, and McCoy), though the aging original cast was beginning to creak a bit by the last film. *Star Trek: Generations* (1994) handed the mantle over to the younger cast of television's *Star Trek: The Next Generation*, who continued the film series in *Star Trek: First Contact* (1996), *Star Trek: Insurrection* (1998), and *Star Trek: Nemesis* (2002).

Another entire class of postmodernist films might be described almost as "spin-offs" of television series. The long-running *Saturday Night Live* (which began airing in 1975) is especially important here. Numerous film stars got their first widespread exposure on this weekly sketch comedy, while any number of its characters and brief skits provided the basis for subsequent feature films, including *The Blues Brothers* (1980, plus a 1998 sequel, *Blues Brothers 2000*), *Mr. Bill's Real Life Adventures* (1986), *Coneheads* (1993), *It's Pat* (1994), *Stuart Saves His*

Family (1995), *A Night at the Roxbury* (1998), *Office Space* (1999), *Superstar* (1999), and *The Ladies Man* (2000). *The Blues Brothers*, with its emphasis on the musical performances of its title characters (played by John Belushi and Dan Ackroyd), also points toward the centrality of various forms of popular music as a source of material in postmodernist film. Blues music is the key here, but the most important musical inspiration for such films has derived from rock and roll, including the crucial role played by such music in *Josie and the Pussycats*, as well as the very successful *Saturday Night Live* spin-offs *Wayne's World* (1992) and *Wayne's World 2* (1993).

Wayne's World not only derives from television but is literally about television. It features a local public-access television talk show (of the same title) that is produced by Wayne Campbell (Mike Myers) and Garth Algar (Dana Carvey) from the basement of Wayne's parents' home in Aurora, Illinois. The minimal plot involves the efforts of an oily Chicago television producer, Benjamin Oliver (Rob Lowe), to get the rights to the show and then commercialize it in order to sell advertising. As such, the film contains some feeble criticism of the television industry and of the larger phenomenon of commodification in American society, but its generally silly, self-parodic tone tends to undermine any such criticism as a mere joke. The film's jokiness also extends to its frequent pastiches of television series and other movies, as when Wayne and Garth reenact the opening sequence of *Laverne and Shirley* upon arriving in Milwaukee, where that series was set. *Wayne's World* involves a number of other postmodern reflexive gestures, as well, for example, when the characters step out of the narrative frame to address the camera directly or when the audience is presented with three alternative endings. Such seemingly Brechtian moves call attention to the fictionality of the narrative and potentially highlight the fictional basis of any number of systems of presumed truth and authority. However, unlike the plays of Brecht, the film does not present utopian alternatives but instead playfully revels in its own fictionality, thereby essentially endorsing the dishonesty of the social system of which it is a part.

Many of the allusions in *Wayne's World* are enhanced through music, as in the playing of the well-known themes from *Laverne and Shirley* and *Mission: Impossible* during the pastiches of those series. Many of the references are directly to music, and the film's best-known scene is one in which Wayne and Garth, along with two friends, lip-synch to Queen's "Bohemian Rhapsody" while driving in their antiquated Pacer. The film's subplot involves music as well, as Garth's girlfriend Cassandra (Tia Carrere) is attempting to make it as a rock singer, while (itself a typical postmodern gesture) Oliver tries to use his show-business connections to steal her away from Wayne. Music plays an even more central role in *Wayne's World 2*, the main plot of which involves the efforts of Wayne and Garth to stage a rock festival so that Wayne can prevent Cassandra from being lured away to the bright lights of Los Angeles by slick record producer Bobby Cahn (Christopher Walken). *Wayne's World 2* also features many of the same postmodern-ist gestures as its predecessor, including embedded pastiches of television series and films, most notably a long sequence that reenacts the wedding scene from *The Graduate* (1967).

In addition to the silliness of such television-to-big-screen crossovers, several recent rather silly films have spoofed broader television phenom-ena, rather than individual programs. For example, Michael Hoffman's *Soapdish* (1991), a lackluster comedy with an A-list cast, gently lampoons the ridiculousness of television soap operas (a pretty easy target) while at the same time suggesting that the lives of the actors and others involved in the soap featured in the movie are gradually becoming much like the seemingly extreme matter of the program in which they are involved. By extension, one could see the film as suggesting that numerous contempo-rary ills are due to the unfortunate influence of soap operas and other unrealistic television programming, but this relatively lighthearted farce never really seems interested in such commentary. Tom Mankiewicz's *Delirious* (also 1991) is even more lighthearted in lampooning the world of soap opera—and more postmodern in the way its protagonist, belea-guered soap opera producer and writer Jack Gable (John Candy) actually spends most of the film in the world of his soap opera. While there, he not only interacts with that world but is also able to rescript it in his attempt to emerge triumphant and win the heart of the beautiful (but bitchy) Rachel Hedison (played by real-life soap-opera goddess Emma Samms). Ulti-mately, however, in a motif that dates back to Buster Keaton's *Sherlock, Jr.* (1924), it's all a fantasy: Gable is dreaming while unconscious from a blow to the head.

Similarly, Neil LaBute's *Nurse Betty* (2000) features Renée Zellweger as Betty Sizemore, a soap opera buff who confuses the world of her favorite soap with reality after she goes into traumatic shock from see-ing her husband murdered by two hit men. By attributing this collapse of distinctions between different levels of reality to Betty's psychological condition, *Nurse Betty* is not particularly postmodern. It is, however, postmodern in its mixture of genres. Betty's interaction with the soap world is almost purely comic; her pursuit by the hit men after they real-ize she is a witness to the killing of her husband derives largely from the world of film noir. In the end, however, comedy prevails. The two hit men are killed by police, while Betty goes on to become a soap opera star in her own right.

Peter Hyams's somewhat muddled *Stay Tuned* (1992) addresses the role of television in postmodern boundary crossing in a particularly direct way. Here, a troubled suburban couple, the Knables (played by John Ritter and Pam Dawber), are unwittingly pulled via a Faustian deal into a hellish television world, hopping from one channel (and genre) to another and finding themselves imperiled at every turn. Predictably, they emerge unscathed. Indeed, Roy Knable's heroism in saving his wife Helen restores both his sense of manhood and their marriage. Meanwhile, Roy is cured of his former television addiction and now finds that he has more time for his family and for real life. Banal, clichéd, and sentimental though it may be, *Stay Tuned* nevertheless displays a very postmodern sense of the permeability of the boundaries between different levels of reality, while also suggesting the culpability of television in creating this unstable sense of reality and providing an image of channel-surfing as the quintessential postmodern experience. At the same time, like so many recent films about television, *Stay Tuned* is essentially a lightweight farce with little critical force.

On the other hand, a number of small-screen-to-big-screen crossovers have been high-budget films from major Hollywood directors. For example, two of the most commercially successful films by postmodern pastiche-master Brian De Palma—*The Untouchables* (1987) and *Mission: Impossible* (1996)—are both adapted from television series. Both of these lack the campy self-consciousness of a film such as *The Brady Bunch Movie*—that they are, in fact, movies based on well-known television series. Thus, *The Untouchables* is essentially a straightforward gangster film that just happens to bear a vague intertextual relationship to the television series of the same title. Meanwhile, *Mission: Impossible* includes some of the twists and turns and clever con game–like schemes that distinguished the television series, but ultimately becomes largely an action-thriller, employing high-tech special effects and outrageous over-the-top action sequences that go well beyond anything ever seen in the series. Still, these films can rightly be considered postmodern in the way they build upon multiple generic models, reaching outside the cinematic traditions in which they participate to acknowledge the importance of television as a constitutive force in the American cultural consciousness.

The Untouchables is also postmodern in its treatment of history, even though, unlike many postmodern films, it seems to locate itself in a very specific time and place. It is, in fact, a film with multiple historical referents. Set in 1930 Chicago, the picture is a richly imagined period piece, copiously detailed with clothing, home furnishings, weapons, and (especially) automobiles appropriate to the time. But it is almost too richly imagined, looking more like a late-1980s fantasy of 1930 than 1930 itself. This is a sanitized movie-set Chicago, with no garbage, no dirt, no poverty, and no sign at all of the Depression. It is, in short, an example of the postmodern nostalgia films cited by Jameson.

Streetwise Irish beat cop Jimmy Malone (Sean Connery) is the closest *The Untouchables* comes to representing a working-class character, but even Malone lives a comfortable life in a large and well-appointed corner apartment. Otherwise, an array of middle-class lawmen (led by Kevin Costner as Eliot Ness) do battle against mob kingpin Al Capone (Robert De Niro), whose unrealistically lavish lifestyle serves as a fantasy of capitalist wealth, but whose brutality ensures that the line between good guys and bad guys remains clear. Meanwhile, the very casting of De Niro, whatever his talents as an actor, in the role gives Capone an almost cartoonish quality, making him less a convincing villain than a pastiche of all those other Italian mobsters played by De Niro, while at the same time reminding those in the know that De Niro began his career as a film actor in such rather undistinguished early De Palma films as *Greetings* (1968), *The Wedding Party* (1969), and *Hi, Mom!* (1970).

In the same way, the casting of major movie stars such as Costner and Connery (both playing characters they have essentially played many times before) also calls attention to the fictionality of the film, making it much more a cinematic spectacle of the late 1980s than a realistic historical representation of 1930. Of course, if the characters of De Niro, Costner, and Connery seem derived more from other movie characters than from historical reality, the entire film is ultimately derived from the popular television series that ran on ABC from 1959 to 1963, with Robert Stack as Ness. The film is, in a very real sense "about" the television series and thus about the late 1950s and early 1960s. It thus becomes a postmodern simulacrum, a copy of an "original" that was itself already a copy. Little wonder that the representation of 1930 seems unrealistic, given the double mediation at work in this representation.

Mission: Impossible, at first glance, seems to lack this historical dimension, given that it appears to be set in the present time. Nevertheless, the film inevitably evokes the original Cold War context of the series, which ran from 1966 to 1973 on CBS. This relationship between time frames is made even more peculiar (and postmodern) in that Jim Phelps, the leader of the Impossible Missions Force on television, occupies the same position in the film, and furthermore does not seem to have aged a day, even though he is played by a different actor (Jon Voight in the film, versus Peter Graves). After all, Phelps is a fictional character, so there is no reason (other than an attempt to maintain historical realism) why he cannot freely float among different periods in history.

On the other hand, while Phelps might not have changed much between 1973 and 1996, the world has changed a great deal, leaving little room for Cold Warriors such as Phelps to operate. Indeed, the film turns the series on its head by making Phelps the villain: with the Cold War over, the once simple good-versus-evil oppositions on which the series was based no longer hold sway, leaving nothing but every-man-for-himself individualism. Under these circumstances, Phelps feels that he owes no loyalty to anyone but himself, so he turns his considerable talents to a nefarious plot to make himself rich. Standing in the way, however, is a new protagonist, Ethan Hunt, played by Tom Cruise, still another highly recognizable movie star.

With no evil Russians on the horizon, the American agents of *Mission: Impossible* are reduced to battling each other. The film thus potentially comments on the confusing complexities of the post–Cold War world, looking back nostalgically on the Cold War era as a time of stable verities and meaningful morals. On the other hand, it also suggests that the Cold War might have been a dirty business and that those, such as Phelps, who carried it out might not necessarily have been very nice people. Ultimately, however, the film is entirely neutral in its treatment of the Cold War. It is a film ostensibly without politics or ideology, pitting a likeable good guy against a reprehensible bad guy simply for the purpose of putting the plot into action and creating opportunities for spectacular violence and special effects.

This neutrality is typical of the "blank" representation of the past in postmodernist art. It is also typical of De Palma's films as a whole, which are at their most postmodern in their appeal to a wide variety of intertextual sources without engaging those sources in any sort of genuine dialogue, critical or otherwise. If *Mission: Impossible* is in many ways nostalgic for the Cold War, *The Untouchables* is also openly nostalgic, toward both its source in the 1950s and even its setting in the 1930s, presumably a simpler time when it was possible for true heroes to emerge in battles against true villains.

A relatively serious recent movie about television is Gary Ross's *Pleasantville* (1998), although this film is, at first glance, antinostalgic, ostensibly serving as a sort of rejoinder to previous nostalgic representations of the 1950s. *Pleasantville* once again focuses on remembered images from fifties culture (this time the idyllic 1950s family sitcom, à la *Leave It to Beaver* or *The Donna Reed Show*), rather than on the historical reality of the period. Here, however, the 1950s are portrayed as a gray (literally) and oppressive world of stagnant conformism, contrasted to the color, abundance, and possibility that seem to inform the film's version of its own 1990s.

Pleasantville is postmodern in a number of ways. For one thing, it openly acknowledges the extent to which our memories of the 1950s are constituted through media representations, especially on television. For another, it foregrounds the process of representation through its symbolic use of black-and-white to represent the spiritual poverty of the conformist past and brilliant color to represent the richness of the human potential that is being thwarted by this conformism. Finally, it crosses ontological boundaries, blurring the distinction between "reality" and representation by having its central characters begin the film in the "reality" of the 1990s (which is really only the film's *representation* of that reality), then literally projecting them into the world of a 1950s television sitcom.

Pleasantville makes no pretensions to realism, openly presenting itself as a fable or fairy tale, as evidenced by an opening title that reads, "Once upon a time...." The main protagonist, David Wagner (Tobey Maguire), is an unhappy high school nerd who is fascinated by reruns of the fifties sitcom *Pleasantville* because it seems to project a perfect world in which life is so much simpler and easier than his life in the nineties, where his own troubled family situation mirrors the seeming chaos of a social world characterized by violence, venereal disease, and economic uncertainty. Then, by the unlikely expedient of a godlike TV repairman (played by Don Knotts, himself a major figure of TV nostalgia) who arrives and gives David a magical remote control, David and twin sister Jennifer (Reese Witherspoon) are propelled into the TV world of the town of Pleasantville. There, they assume the roles of Bud and Mary Sue, the son and daughter of George and Betty Parker (William H. Macy and Joan Allen), thus constituting the central family in the sitcom.

The perfect world of Pleasantville turns out to be less than paradise. Its peace has been bought at the price of total stagnation and complete ignorance of the outside world. For example, all of the books in the town library are blank on the inside, signaling the unavailability of ideas or points of view that are not already mainstream to the community. Everyone in the town shares exactly the same values and ideas, and everyone lives a repetitive life of scripted routine, any deviation from which is viewed with horror. Not surprisingly, the new Bud and Mary Sue quickly introduce disruptive elements into the peacefully conformist world of Pleasantville, especially after the sexually liberated Mary Sue introduces one of the local boys to sex, which had previously not existed in the town, triggering a wave of sexual activity, especially among the local teenagers.

This outburst of sexuality is part of a broadening of experience that is indicated in the film by the gradual appearance of color in the black-and-white world of the sitcom. Central here is the character of Bill Johnson (Jeff Daniels), owner of the local soda shop, who finds his artistic temperament stimulated by Bud's encouragement and begins to paint a series of brilliantly colored paintings with which he decorates his shop.[6] Meanwhile, content begins to appear in the books in the library, bringing even more new ideas to the community. The local authorities react with indignant horror, while a mob of threatened locals attacks and wrecks the soda shop, destroying the paintings. They then attack the library and burn the books in a bonfire. The town elders back the mob, and a new code of even more conformist behavior is quickly enacted: sex, books, colorful paint, and rock 'n' roll music are banned from the town. Those who have been infected by new ideas (and thus now appear in color) become outcasts in obviously racial terms, banned from various spots by signs reading "No Coloreds."

Bud and Johnson protest by painting a colorful mural on the side of the police station, leading to their arrest, the first ever in Pleasantville. Bud's rousing oration at the subsequent trial wins their release, while also converting the entire town (and its population) to full color and even opening the town to the outside world. Bud then returns home to resume his life as David, but now much wiser for his recent experience, which has taught him to value the messiness of the 1990s. Granted, Mary Sue (as Jennifer a party girl with disastrous grades in school) opts to stay behind in Pleasantville, where she has discovered the world of books and even won admission to college. But this plot element does not really detract from the film's preference for the nineties over the fifties. After all, the 1950s world in which Mary Sue stays has already been transformed by its absorption of ideas from the 1990s. It has, in fact, become the sixties, with sex, books, and rock 'n' roll primly substituted for sex, drugs, and rock 'n' roll. Indeed, while the film's soundtrack uses 1950s rock-and-roll classics by such artists as Buddy Holly and Elvis Presley to signal the sensuous awakening of the citizens of Pleasantville, it ends with the Beatles' "Across the Universe," very much a song of the

1960s—except here performed by Fiona Apple, a well-known artist of the 1990s. Apple's lovely (and very modern-sounding) rendition of the song is, in fact, one of the highlights of the soundtrack, as if to emphasize the compatibility between the sixties and the nineties.

In short, *Pleasantville* contrasts the gray conformism of the 1950s not just with the 1990s but also with the colorful variety of the time from the 1960s onward, essentially portrayed as a homogenous period. Meanwhile, the liberation of 1950s Pleasantville is staged very much in terms of sexuality (especially women's sexuality, figured in the liberation of Betty Parker from her kitchen) and race ("coloreds" are no longer discriminated against), thus repeating the terms of the sexual revolution and the civil rights and women's movements of the sixties. But this liberation is a consumerist one as well: citizens of the town are now free to buy various colorful items (including color television sets) that had not previously been available in the town. *Pleasantville* in this way directly enacts the vision of recent American cultural history suggested by Thomas Frank, who notes that the counterculture of the 1960s consistently opposed itself to the stagnant conformism of the 1950s, but in a way that was thoroughly in line with the ethos of consumer capitalism. For Frank, in fact, the counterculture of the 1960s was largely a creation of Madison Avenue, intended more to open markets than to open minds. Furthermore, Frank notes that a consistent marketing strategy of the consumer capitalism of the 1990s has been to link that decade to the 1960s counterculture, thus allowing a reinvigoration of the consumerist energies that informed the calls for cultural pluralism in the earlier decade (233–34).

Frank suggests that the apparent liberation of the 1960s actually extended the penetration of capitalism into every aspect of American life, allowing capitalist ideas to exercise an unprecedented hold on individual minds. This view makes *Pleasantville*'s nostalgic vision of the 1960s highly problematic, but then nostalgia always deals with fantasy rather than reality, and it is certainly the case that fantasies of liberation from the restrictions of the 1950s have been central to our imaginary construction of the 1960s ever since the decade itself. Moreover, this shift from the fifties to the sixties indicates the easy way in which postmodern nostalgic reminiscences of the past can slide around in history.

Postmodern nostalgia is always based more on a perceived lack of something in present times rather than on any specific perceived abundance in the past. Thus, *Pleasantville*'s seeming rejection of nostalgia for the fifties merely displaces that nostalgia to the sixties, while its repudiation of the "non-changist" model of history initially supported by the authorities in Pleasantville only goes so far as to suggest a change that occurred from the 1950s to the 1960s, without suggesting that any further change has occurred or is desirable.[7] The 1960s are thus synonymous with the 1990s, and the film's nostalgia for the sixties is an example of precisely the "nostalgia for the present" that Jameson sees as central to many works of postmodern culture.

Contemporaneous with *Pleasantville*, Peter Weir's *The Truman Show* (1998) suggests that more recent television (and not just the unrealistic sitcoms of the 1950s) can have a sinister side. Weir's film details the seemingly normal life of thirty-year-old Truman Burbank (Jim Carrey), an insurance salesman in the idyllic island community of Seahaven Island. Burbank's world, however, is a sham. It is, in fact, a gigantic television studio constructed by an entertainment corporation that adopted Truman at birth, then placed him in this community so that his entire life could be broadcast to a global audience, twenty-four hours a day, seven days a week. All of the other residents of Seahaven Island are hired actors. Truman alone is not in on the scheme, the point being that, however artificial this world, at least Truman himself will be authentic, giving the audience the dose of realism that they supposedly crave.

The show, in fact, is a huge success with devoted fans all over the world. In the course of the film, however, Truman himself begins to suspect that there is something wrong with his world. Eventually, he attempts to escape, ultimately reaching the boundaries of the studio. Christof (Ed Harris), the show's creator and director, attempts to convince Truman to stay inside, telling him that he will find the world outside the studio no more authentic than the one inside: "There is no more truth out there than in the world I created for you." Nevertheless, Truman opts for the real world and exits the studio, thus bringing the program (and the film) to an end.

The Truman Show addresses, in a fairly obvious way, a number of issues that are crucial to the phenomenon of postmodernism. Most obviously, it suggests the mediatization of reality in the postmodern era, Truman functioning in this sense as a sort of Everyman whose life is not unique but merely typical of life in the postmodern world, where we all encounter a reality that is thoroughly constituted by the media and its images. Indeed, the program clearly derives its popularity from the fact that audiences identify so directly and completely with Truman, whose plight dramatizes their own (probably unarticulated) sense of living in a media-dominated world whose machinations they do not understand. In this sense, the obvious progenitor of *The Truman Show* is, appropriately enough, a television program: the 1960s British series

The Prisoner. However, *The Prisoner* continually and overtly indicates
that the artificial community in which its protagonist is imprisoned is
not fundamentally different from the equally restrictive world outside
the community.[8] The television program that is the subject of Weir's
film, however, allows audiences to feel that *their* world is real—which
may account for the fact that it is hugely popular, while *The Prisoner*
was a commercial flop.

Indeed, the *Truman* television program functions very much in the
manner of Disneyland and other amusement parks, as discussed by Jean
Baudrillard, who argues that such parks act to encourage the general
population to accept the reality of a consumer capitalist social world that
is itself "hyperreal," saturated with images and simulations:

> Disneyland is there to conceal the fact that it is the "real" country, all of
> "real" America, which *is* Disneyland (just as prisons are there to conceal
> the fact that it is the social in its entirety, in its banal omnipresence,
> which is carceral). Disneyland is presented as imaginary in order to make
> us all believe that the rest is real, when in fact all of Los Angeles and the
> America surrounding it are no longer real, but of the order of the hyper-
> real and of simulation. (172)

Christof's arguments to Truman about the artificiality of the outside
world at the end of *The Truman Show* might have come directly from
Baudrillard. However, Christof, despite the casting of the likeable Harris
in the role, is presented as a rather sinister figure with whom we are not
encouraged to agree. Indeed, the film stops far short of a Baudrillard's
vision of the hyperreality of modern consumer society by making it appear
that, Christof's protestations notwithstanding, Truman has in fact
escaped into reality at the end of the film. Truman Burbank thereby
becomes just another in a long line of individualist heroes in American
film, and the film's plot just another example of the standard formula:
hero encounters obstacles, hero overcomes obstacles, hero triumphs.
Granted, we are left without complete closure and the success of Truman's
new life in the world at large remains unassured, but that is largely the
point. He has now escaped into a world of freedom (and uncertainty),
where his every move is no longer scripted by others. We can imagine, of
course, that he will soon appear on the talk show circuit and that his life
outside his television program will consist of a never-ending series of still
more programs, but the film again stops short of exploring this possibility.

In the final analysis, *The Truman Show* is not so much an exploration of the saturation of our contemporary reality by media images as a

rather banal critique of the venality of television networks that are willing to stoop to any level, including the manipulation of the lives of real people, in search of better ratings and higher advertising revenues. Thus, the film is careful to indicate the extent to which Truman's reality is engineered to create numerous opportunities for product-placement advertising, as the show, being continuous, has no overt commercial interruptions. But this is an idea as old as *Will Success Spoil Rock Hunter?*, a film that, more than forty years earlier, already mocked the commercial orientation of television programming. This announcement of the economic motivation of TV is hardly news, nor is it particularly threatening to commercial television networks, as can be seen by the explosion of "reality" programming that appeared on American television shortly after the release of *The Truman Show*, almost as if the film provided inspiration to programmers, rather than chastening them.

Ron Howard's *Edtv*, released a year after *The Truman Show*, also addresses the phenomenon of reality-based programming by featuring a protagonist whose life becomes the subject of an around-the-clock live television broadcast. Otherwise, however, the two films have little in common. *Edtv* is a sort of screwball comedy in which ordinary guy Ed Pekurny (Matthew McConaughey) has agreed to let the cameras of a cable network follow him through his life, a concept that one can easily imagine actually appearing on television. The show soon becomes a big hit, Ed becomes a major celebrity, and his entire life is dramatically altered. This fact, of course, only increases the popularity of the show, allowing audiences to fantasize that, if an ordinary (maybe even subordinary) guy like Ed can become rich and famous almost overnight, then the same might someday happen to them. Again, however, the film does not really explore the questions it raises about the media and fame, but simply focuses on Ed's (successful, of course) attempts to get out of his contract with the network so that he can return to a normal life and live happily ever after with true love Shari (Jenna Elfman).

In *Edtv*, the blurring of the boundary between fiction and reality is intensified by the fact that television transforms the reality of Ed's life into a media-induced fiction. In Hal Ashby's *Being There* (1979), the protagonist's entire life is conditioned by watching television. In the film, Peter Sellers plays Chance, a middle-aged, simple-minded gardener who works on the estate of a rich employer, the "Old Man." He may, in fact, be the employer's son, though that possibility is never verified. Instead, all we know is that Chance has lived his whole life on the enclosed grounds of the estate and has never, in fact, left those grounds. Chance has never learned to read or write (and may in fact lack the intelligence to do so), so all of his knowledge of the outside world comes from television, which he watches incessantly, but indiscriminately, flipping at random among children's cartoons, movies, game shows, commercials, concerts, and news programs, viewing all with an equal enthusiasm and superficiality. Soon after the film begins, the employer dies and lawyers arrive to close up the house. Chance is thus ejected into the outside world, issuing forth in a daze into the shabby urban neighborhood that surrounds the estate.

Because Chance has worked primarily as a gardener on the estate, the resonances of the story of the fall from the Garden of Eden are fairly clear here, though his suggestive name suggests a variety of other allegorical readings as well. Among other things, his sojourn into the outer world seems marked by an amazing sequence of good luck, which eventually finds him ensconced in the palatial estate of aging tycoon Benjamin Rand (Melvyn Douglas). Having no genuine social skills, Chance merely responds to prompts in a manner programmed by his viewing of television. However, his pithy remarks (which can always be interpreted by his interlocutors in a manner flattering to themselves) are consistently mistaken for laconic profundity, while his tendency to see everything through the optic of his experience as a gardener is taken for metaphorical insight into society and the human condition.

Chance quickly becomes a trusted associate of old Rand and a much-desired object of sexual fascination on the part of Rand's lonely wife, Eve (Shirley MacLaine), who attempts (with Rand's blessing) to lure Chance into a sexual liaison, much as the original Eve had tempted the original Adam from his innocence. Chance, however, cannot be tempted, apparently because his arrested intellectual and emotional development has left him trapped in a childhood world devoid of sexual desire. Through Rand, Chance meets the president of the United States, who is much impressed by Chance's earthy wisdom. Soon Chance becomes a darling of the media, a guest on television talk shows, even the heir apparent to the presidency. As the film ends, a group of political cronies, acting as Rand's pallbearers, discuss Chance's suitability as a presidential candidate while carrying the coffin to be entombed. Chance himself wanders away from the burial and ends the film walking, Christ-like, across the waters of a lake.

This ending allows for multiple interpretations, but it seems to be that it most obviously comments on the way in which these political power brokers, along with the media, hope to convert Chance into a superhuman figure, largely in order to further their own ambitions for political power or simply to attract audiences. That a public hero can be manufactured in such a calculated way is telling, as is the fact that Chance, in particular, would be chosen for this role. There is, in the film, no implication whatsoever that Chance's simple-mindedness conceals a deeper form of wisdom. His stupidity and vacuity are clearly genuine. He is essentially an empty vessel, a blank slate, which makes him a perfect candidate for public office: with no ideas or opinions of his own, he is less likely to get into trouble or to conflict with the image produced for him by his backers.

In many ways, Chance is reminiscent of figures from the literary past, such as Emma Bovary, whose response to literature is mediated by her immersion in romantic novels. However, Chance is an actual idiot who literally cannot tell the difference between television and reality, as is evidenced in a scene in which he attempts to do away with would-be muggers by simply turning them off with his remote control.[9] In Gustave Flaubert's novel, Madame Bovary's confusion is much more subtle. Moreover, her unrealistic and romantic attitudes lead to her downfall, while it is the cunning and conniving Homais who succeeds. In *Being There,* Chance's profound disengagement from reality makes him a rousing success, suggesting that reality itself has by now been so pervaded by the processed medium of television that his inability to distinguish between reality and television is, in a way, an advantage. Meanwhile, the way in which the media and the general public respond to his empty platitudes provides a damning commentary on what it takes to succeed as a public figure in a media-dominated America.

The most problematic (and perhaps tantalizing) aspect of *Being There* is its appeal to mythological precedents, such as the fall from the Garden of Eden or Christ's walking on water, motifs that cry out for allegorical readings while providing no clear allegorical referents. Indeed, amid the thoroughly routinized and rationalized environment of late capitalism, such allegorical gestures cannot really function. Instead, such fragmentary supernatural references function as bits and pieces of historical memory of a time when it was possible for such magical motifs to function more fully. *Being There* implies that, in the contemporary world of America, magic has been replaced by the media, with television now playing the role once played by religion and the supernatural.

Of course, the rationalization of the capitalist world is an old phenomenon, described in detail by Max Weber at the beginning of the twentieth century and already gestured toward by German philosopher G. W. F. Hegel early in the nineteenth century. Thus, Chance's descent into the world after the death of the Old Man potentially makes him a figure not just of the fall from the Garden of Eden but of mankind set adrift in the world after the death of God. His predicament at large in the world is, in fact, quite reminiscent of the "transcendental homelessness" described by Georg Lukács in his early study of the novel. In *The Theory of the Novel*, Lukács envisions the epic as the genre of a stable world underwritten by theological certainties that provide a sense of stability and wholeness. The novel, on the other hand, is the genre of a modern, secularized world in which mankind has been set adrift, bereft of such certainties but still longing for them. "The novel," he writes, "is the epic of an age in which the extensive totality of life is no longer directly given, in which the immanence of meaning in life has become a problem, yet which still thinks in terms of totality" (56). Similarly, individuals in the modern world described by Lukács have lost their once stable and secure sense of their own identities. He sees the individualism of the novel as an expression of the striving of the individual to recover this identity.

Being There, on the other hand, details a postmodern world in which it is no longer possible even to *think* in terms of totality or stable identity. Chance cannot strive to recover his true identity because he is a genuinely hollow man; he need not look within himself because there's no *there* there. He is all surface, a creature of television. However, in this sense, he is a perfect mirror of the world around him, which is so thoroughly saturated by media-generated images that there is no longer a baseline reality that lies beneath it all. Thus, if *Madame Bovary* is in this sense a highly representative novel that details one step in the historical disintegration of both social and individual totality, then *Being There* marks a further stage in the same process. Chance's more radical disengagement from reality indicates not his personal pathology but a profound historical change.

Disengagement from reality is, after all, a central subjective experience of the postmodern era. It is thus not surprising that some of the most successful films of the postmodern era have belonged to genres that are specifically distanced from contemporary reality. Science-fiction films have been particularly successful at the box office in recent decades, and films such as the *Star Trek* sequence, *Serenity*, and *The X-Files* largely go beyond their television predecessors by making use of the better special effects that can be produced by the bigger budgets of the movies relative to individual television episodes. Meanwhile, the centrality of special effects to science-fiction film is itself something of a postmodern phenomenon in that it allows those pictures to produce fictional representations of settings, situations, and events that have never existed in reality. The films thus have much in common with Baudrillard's notion of the postmodern simulacrum, and it should therefore come as no surprise that some of the films that have been most pivotal to discussions of postmodernism in film have been science-fiction entries such as Ridley Scott's *Alien* (1979) and *Blade Runner* (1982) and James Cameron's *The Terminator* (1984). Meanwhile, Kerry Conran's *Sky Captain and the World of Tomorrow* (2004) is a quintessentially postmodern film. Not only does it look nostalgically back to the 1930s, but it also employs new techniques of computer-generated imagery (CGI) in which practically everything in the film except the human actors themselves (and even one of the actors) is the product of computer imaging.

There is clearly a close relationship between the heavy use of CGI in such films and the generation of simulated worlds in video games, themselves crucial postmodern phenomena. Indeed, one important recent development in postmodern cinema involves films based on video games (while many popular movies are themselves accompanied by video game tie-ins). Thus, films such as *Mortal Kombat* (1995) and *Lara Croft: Tomb Raider* (2001) are based on highly popular video games, while Paul W. S. Anderson's *Resident Evil* (2002) and Alexander Witt's *Resident Evil: Apocalypse* (2004) are particularly interesting and successful examples of video-game-to-film adaptations.

Computer simulation is also important in a series of films in which the technology allowed comic books to come to life. Many of the latter were semi-SF superhero films, a trend that actually began with Richard Donner's *Superman* (1978), which made little use of CGI, though its most recent sequel, Bryan Singer's *Superman Returns* (2006) uses CGI extensively. Particularly successful examples of films adapted from superhero comics include Sam Raimi's *Spider-Man* (2002) and *Spider-Man 2* (2004), Singer's *X-Men* (2000) and *X2* (2003), and Brett Rattner's *X-Men: The Last Stand* (2006).

As the example of *Monkeybone* shows, a variety of other films have also been developed from comic books and graphic novels. One of the most intriguing (and perhaps the most postmodern) of these films is Robert Rodriguez's *Sin City* (2005), based on a series of graphic novels by Frank Miller, who was so heavily involved in the making of the film that Rodriguez insisted that Miller be credited as the film's codirector. *Sin City* is particularly distinctive for the way it attempts to emulate the visual style of Miller's novels, so that in a very real sense, it is not a traditional adaptation so much as a representation of the graphic novels—and thus even at a further remove from reality than the already over-the-top novels.

Key postmodernist filmmaker David Cronenberg has also made a graphic-novel adaptation in *A History of Violence* (2005), based on a graphic novel written by John Wagner and drawn by Vince Locke. The film, like the novel, is a sort of noir thriller, though Cronenberg's version is additionally spiced with atmospheric elements that clearly recall the movie western, creating a postmodern intergeneric mix that is missing in the graphic novel. Like both of the classic genres on which it centrally draws, the film is punctuated by moments of extreme physical violence. However, except for the opening scene, all of this violence is perpetrated against villains (from a high school bully to a mob kingpin), thus inviting audience approval. In this case, however, the violence is presented in classic Cronenberg fashion through a graphic emphasis on the damage done to human bodies, thus complicating the audience reaction to what might otherwise be thrilling moments in the film. Interestingly, however, the most abject examples of the destruction of the human body that appear in the original graphic novel do not appear at all in the film.

A History of Violence stars Viggo Mortensen as Tom Stall, a devoted family man who runs a diner in the small town of Millbrook, Indiana, which here takes on almost mythic dimensions as the embodiment of small-town America. As opposed to the small towns of David Lynch, whose ideal surfaces mask dark, sinister cores, Millbrook really is what it appears to be: a quiet, peaceful town inhabited by hard-working solid citizens. However, Stall, like so many of the protagonists of films noirs, has a dark past, which eventually catches up with him after he gains media attention by violently killing two thugs who were attempting to rob his diner. Unknown even to wife Edy (Maria Bello), Stall was formerly Joey Cusack, a mobster whose brother Richie (William Hurt) is now a kingpin in the Philadelphia mob. When mobsters from Philadelphia come to Millbrook to fetch Stall/Cusack back to the city to settle some accounts, the violent side of America finally makes itself felt in Millbrook. Stall ultimately kills all the gangsters involved (including Richie), then returns to his home and family, though it is not at all clear as the film ends that they will be able to resume their formerly idyllic existence.

Far more than a crime thriller, *A History of Violence* interrogates numerous elements of the mythology of America. Indeed, if one reads Cusack/Stall as a sort of national allegory, then his own story can be taken as a marker of the way in which the United States as a nation strives for the ideal future but remains haunted by its violent past, while periodically returning to violence in the present. The film, however, is not really so much about American history as it is about cinematic representations of the American national identity, especially in the western and the film noir. Probably the two most American of all genres, these two film genres explore, perhaps more than any other cultural form, both the promise and the darkness of the history and mythology of America. Cronenberg's revisiting of these genres might thus be taken as a dialogue with America itself, though this dialogue is really with cinematic representations of America.

A History of Violence is at its most postmodern in its sense of its own belatedness, its self-conscious awareness that it is not only an adaptation of an earlier work but is traversing ground that has often been traveled in other films. Thus, Cronenberg, despite his reputation as a sort of rogue auteur, ends up demonstrating just how difficult it is to be truly "original" in the postmodern era. His work thus brings us back to Jameson's concern about the lack of genuine individual artistic style among postmodern artists in whatever medium, despite the fact that so many postmodern film directors, including Cronenberg, are widely regarded as making distinctive, even eccentric, motion pictures. Indeed, a consideration of the work of such directors provides an opportunity to sum up many of the characteristics of postmodern film that have been discussed in the earlier chapters of this volume.

Conclusion

CREATIVITY, ORIGINALITY, AND POSTMODERN FILM

For Fredric Jameson, one of the principal characteristics of late (i.e., postmodern) capitalism is the extension of capitalist economic control not only to new parts of the globe but also to new aspects of life, even in the capitalist West. One of these aspects is art itself, which now becomes a mere subcategory of commodity production in general. However, this commodification of aesthetic production does not lead, as one might initially expect, to the output of banal, interchangeable, cookie-cutter artworks devoid of innovation and ingenuity. After all, capitalism—especially late capitalism—is nothing if not innovative and ingenious. Indeed, as Jameson notes, postmodern aesthetic production joins a larger system of commodity production in which "the frantic economic urgency of producing fresh waves of ever more novel-seeming goods (from clothing to airplanes), at ever greater rates of turnover, now assigns an increasingly essential structural function and position to aesthetic innovation and experimentation" (*Postmodernism*, 4–5).

One should, therefore, expect a great deal of artistic creativity in postmodern art, even in forms (such as film) that are dominated by economics in particularly obvious ways. The films discussed in this volume—made by such illustrious directors as Robert Altman, Woody Allen, Brian De Palma, Joel and Ethan Coen, Quentin Tarantino, Tim Burton, David Lynch, and David Cronenberg—certainly indicate that creativity is alive and well in the world of postmodern film, however weak that film might be in terms of political critique. At the same time, Jameson's reading of postmodernism, at least, would suggest that this creativity is of a different sort altogether from that found in modernist art. For Jameson, one of the key underpinnings of modernist artistic production is the belief that artists should strive to develop unique individual styles that are the direct expressions of their own inner selves—thus evading the very conscription within the system of commodity production that is emblematic of postmodern art. In his view, however, the intense psychic pressures of life under late capitalism shatter the psyche itself, destabilizing the once-solid core of individual identity and rendering it ineffective as a source of aesthetic expression. As a result, postmodern artists, however ingenious and inventive their works might be, are unable to establish and maintain a distinctive and easily identifiable personal style in the modernist sense. Instead, postmodern artists "have nowhere to turn but to the past: the imitation of dead styles, speech through all the masks and voices stored up in the imaginary museum of a now global culture" (*Postmodernism*, 17–18). Postmodern artistic creativity, then, resides not in the production of unique individual styles but in the clever appropriation and assembly of the styles of others, while individual films themselves have an assembled, fragmentary quality.

What all of this really amounts to, according to Jameson, is that modernist artists were able to think beyond the bounds of the capitalist system that was still congealing around them and to point, in their art, toward the utopian possibilities of alternative systems and ways of life. Postmodernist artists, on the other hand, live and work in a world in which capitalist modernization is essentially complete and in which the ability to imagine genuine alternatives to capitalism has been seriously curtailed. In addition, the audiences for postmodern art—who can entirely appropriately be described as the consumers of this art—have a diminished ability to recognize and appreciate any utopian suggestions that, however faint and feeble, might still be present in the art they consume.

Of course, the application of Jameson's suggestion of the loss of distinctive individual styles in postmodern art is complicated in the case of film by the difficulty of attributing any film to the work and vision of any one artist. While auteur theory (epitomized in the United States by the work of Andrew Sarris) has attempted to treat film directors as the individual creators of films, much recent work in film studies has moved away from this approach, instead emphasizing the collective nature of the process of filmmaking. For one thing, the thinking goes, actors, writers, and others make substantial creative contributions to films. For another, the extremely expensive nature of filmmaking means that those who finance films have a great deal invested in them and therefore tend to expect to have some input into the creative process as well. This was especially the case in the heyday of the Hollywood studio system, when, as Thomas Schatz has effectively demonstrated, film style was often much more a product of the tastes and inclinations of specific studios than of individual directors.

In this sense, of course, directors of the postmodern era often have more control over the creative process than did their predecessors in the studio era, because studios now lack the clout to control the filmmaking process as thoroughly as they once did. One thinks particularly of someone like John Sayles, who has staunchly maintained independent control of his work as a filmmaker, both scripting and financing his own films. Yet Sayles is known more for his politically engaged subject matter than for any sort of distinctive cinematic style, and he is in any case perhaps the least postmodern of contemporary film directors. Except for occasional moments (such as the inconclusive ending of his 1999 film *Limbo*), Sayles employs a relatively conventional, realistic narrative style, even as the engaged subject matter of his films differs dramatically from that of typical Hollywood fare. Even a film such as *Lone Star* (1996), with its fragmented, nonlinear plot, is not very postmodern in that the pieces ultimately fit smoothly together.[1]

Sayles thus serves as a sort of counterexample in the world of contemporary Hollywood film, while the established directors mentioned above—along with such less mainstream directors as Todd Solondz, Gregg Araki, and Mike Figgis, as well as such up-and-coming "Hollywood" directors as Alejandro González Iñárritu, Christopher Nolan, Don Roos, and Paul Thomas Anderson—indicate the wide variety of filmmaking styles that can still be considered postmodern. This variety in no way contradicts Jameson's vision of postmodernism as a cultural dominant under late capitalism, and indeed the way in which very different directors nevertheless show postmodern inclinations in their work tends to verify Jameson's central proposal that postmodernism is the cultural logic of late capitalism, the variety of postmodern film merely demonstrating the multiplicity of late capitalism itself.

At the same time, this very multiplicity means that capitalism does not establish the terms upon which art is produced in a mode of strict determination. That is, while virtually all art (and certainly all big-budget art, such as commercial film) produced in our contemporary era tends to reproduce and propagate the ideology of late capitalism, there are always cracks and fissures through which alternative ideologies can potentially shine through. The continued existence of directors such as Sayles, who is hardly postmodern at all, demonstrates the incomplete nature of capitalist cultural hegemony in the postmodern era, while there are moments in the work of even the most postmodern of directors—such as Tarantino, Burton, Lynch, and Cronenberg—that potentially challenge the cynical, ahistorical, and emotionally flat worldview of late capitalism. Postmodern film thus contains glimmers of utopian possibility even as it largely embodies and ratifies the anti-utopian orientation of late capitalist thought. Given the economic realities of the business of filmmaking, an explosion of radical utopian energy in commercial film hardly seems in the cards at this point in time. It thus remains for astute viewers to focus on the progressive potential inherent in the films we have and to read them in enlightening and liberating ways, toward a day when true enlightenment and liberation might become a concrete possibility.

Appendix: Films Cited

The Addams Family. Dir. Barry Sonnenfeld, 1991.
Airplane! Dir. Jim Abrahams, David Zucker, and Jerry Zucker, 1980.
Airport. Dir. George Seaton, 1970.
Alien. Dir. Ridley Scott, 1979.
American Beauty. Dir. Sam Mendes, 1999.
American Graffiti. Dir. George Lucas, 1973.
Amores perros. Dir. Alejandro González Iñárritu, 2000.
The Asphalt Jungle. Dir. John Huston, 1950.
Au revoir, les enfants. Dir. Louis Malle, 1987.
Austin Powers, International Man of Mystery. Dir. Jay Roach, 1997.
An Autumn Afternoon. Dir. Yasujiro Oku, 1962.
The Avengers. Dir. Jeremiah S. Chechik, 1998.
Babel. Dir. Alejandro González Iñárritu, 2006.
Back to the Future. Dir. Robert Zemeckis, 1985.
The Bad and the Beautiful. Dir. Vincente Minnelli, 1952.
Badlands. Dir. Terrence Malick, 1973.
La Bamba. Dir. Luis Valdez, 1987.
Barton Fink. Dir. Joel and Ethan Coen, 1991.
Batman. Dir. Tim Burton, 1989.
Batman Returns. Dir. Tim Burton, 1992.
Beavis and Butt-head Do America. Dir. Mike Judge and Yvette Kaplan, 1996.
Beetlejuice. Dir. Tim Burton, 1988.
Being John Malkovich. Dir. Spike Jonze, 1999.
Being There. Dir. Hal Ashby, 1979.
The Bicycle Thief. Dir. Vittorio de Sica, 1948.
The Birds. Dir. Alfred Hitchcock, 1963.
The Black Dahlia. Dir. Brian De Palma, 2006.
The Blackboard Jungle. Dir. Richard Brooks, 1955.

Blade Runner. Dir. Ridley Scott, 1982.

The Blob. Dir. Irwin S. Yeaworth Jr., 1958.

Blood Simple. Dir. Joel and Ethan Coen, 1984.

Blow Out. Dir. Brian De Palma, 1981.

Blowup. Dir. Michelangelo Antonioni, 1966.

Blue Velvet. Dir. David Lynch, 1986.

The Blues Brothers. Dir. John Landis, 1980.

Blues Brothers 2000. Dir. John Landis, 1998.

Bob le flambeur. Dir. Jean-Pierre Melville, 1955.

Body Double. Dir. Brian De Palma, 1984.

Body Heat. Dir. Lawrence Kasdan, 1981.

Bonnie and Clyde. Dir. Arthur Penn, 1967.

Bounce. Dir. Don Roos, 2000.

The Brady Bunch Movie. Dir. Betty Thomas, 1995.

Bram Stoker's Dracula. Dir. Francis Ford Coppola, 1992.

Breathless. Dir. Jean-Luc Godard, 1959.

Broadway Danny Rose. Dir. Woody Allen, 1984.

The Brood. Dir. David Cronenberg, 1979.

The Buddy Holly Story. Dir. Steve Rash, 1978.

Buffalo Bill and the Indians. Dir. Robert Altman, 1976.

Cape of Good Hope. Dir. Mark Bamford, 2004.

Carnival of Souls. Dir. Herk Harvey, 1962.

Carrie. Dir. Brian De Palma, 1976.

Cecil B. Demented. Dir. John Waters, 2000.

Charlie and the Chocolate Factory. Dir. Tim Burton, 2005.

Charlie's Angels. Dir. McG, 2000.

Chinatown. Dir. Roman Polanski, 1974.

Click. Dir. Frank Coraci, 2006.

Coneheads. Dir. Steve Barron, 1993.

The Conversation. Dir. Francis Ford Coppola, 1974.

Cool World. Dir. Ralph Bakshi, 1992.

The Corpse Bride. Dir. Tim Burton and Mike Johnson, 2005.

Crash. Dir. David Cronenberg, 1996.

Crash. Dir. Paul Haggis, 2004.

Cry-Baby. Dir. John Waters, 1990.

Dancer in the Dark. Dir. Lars von Trier, 2000.

Dark City. Dir. Alex Proyas, 1998.

Dead Ringers. Dir. David Cronenberg, 1988.

The Dead Zone. Dir. David Cronenberg, 1983.

Detour. Dir. Edgar G. Ulmer, 1945.

Delirious. Dir. Tom Mankiewicz, 1991.

Dick Tracy. Dir. Warren Beatty, 1990.

Dirty Harry. Dir. Don Siegel, 1971.

Diva. Dir. Jean-Jacques Beineix, 1981.

D.O.A. Dir. Rudolph Maté, 1950.

The Doom Generation. Dir. Gregg Araki, 1995.

Donnie Darko. Dir. Richard Kelly, 2001.

Double Indemnity. Dir. Billy Wilder, 1944.

Dragnet. Dir. Tom Mankiewicz, 1987.

Dressed to Kill. Dir. Brian De Palma, 1980.

Du refifi chez les hommes. Dir. Jules Dassin, 1955.

Duck Soup. Dir. Leo McCarey, 1933.

Dune. Dir. David Lynch, 1984.

Ed Wood. Dir. Tim Burton, 1994.

Eddie and the Cruisers. Dir. Martin Davidson, 1983.

Edtv. Dir. Ron Howard, 1999.

Edward Scissorhands. Dir. Tim Burton, 1990.

8½. Dir. Federico Fellini, 1963.

The Elephant Man. Dir. David Lynch, 1980.

Eraserhead. Dir. David Lynch, 1977.

E.T. the Extra-Terrestrial. Dir. Steven Spielberg, 1982.

eXistenZ. Dir. David Cronenberg, 1999.

The Exorcist. Dir. William Friedkin, 1973.

A Face in the Crowd. Dir. Elia Kazan, 1957.

Fargo. Dir. Joel and Ethan Coen, 1996.

Fear and Loathing in Las Vegas. Dir. Terry Gilliam, 1998.

Fifteen Minutes. Dir. John Herzfeld, 2001.

Fight Club. Dir. David Fincher, 1999.

The Fly. Dir. David Cronenberg, 1986.

Follow the Fleet. Dir. Mark Sandrich, 1936.

Forrest Gump. Dir. Robert Zemeckis, 1994.

Frankenstein. Dir. James Whale, 1931.

Frankenweenie. Dir. Tim Burton, 1984.

From Hell. Dir. Albert and Allen Hughes, 2001.

The Fugitive. Dir. Andrew Davis, 1993.

The Fury. Dir. Brian De Palma, 1978.

Gilda. Dir. Charles Vidor, 1946.

Glen or Glenda. Dir. Edward D. Wood Jr., 1953.

Go. Dir. Doug Liman, 1999.

The Godfather: Part II. Dir. Francis Ford Coppola, 1974.

The Graduate. Dir. Mike Nichols, 1967.

Grease. Dir. Randal Kleiser, 1978.

Greetings. Dir. Brian De Palma, 1968.

Hairspray. Dir. John Waters, 1988.

Hannah and Her Sisters. Dir. Woody Allen, 1986.

Happiness. Dir. Todd Solondz, 1998.

Happy Endings. Dir. Don Roos, 2005.

Hi, Mom! Dir. Brian De Palma, 1970.

High Noon. Dir. Fred Zinnemann, 1952.

A History of Violence. Dir. David Cronenberg, 2005.

Hold Your Man. Dir. Sam Wood, 1933.

Hotel. Dir. Mike Figgis, 2003.

I Am a Fugitive from a Chain Gang. Dir. Mervyn LeRoy, 1932.

Intolerable Cruelty. Dir. Joel and Ethan Coen, 2003.

Invaders from Mars. Dir. William Cameron Menzies, 1953.

It Happened One Night. Dir. Frank Capra, 1934.

It's a Wonderful Life. Dir. Frank Capra, 1946.

It's Pat. Dir. Adam Bernstein, 1994.

Jackie Brown. Dir. Quentin Tarantino, 1997.

Johnny Mnemonic. Dir. Robert Longo, 1995.

Josie and the Pussycats. Dir. Harry Elfont and Deborah Kaplan, 2001.

Jules et Jim. Dir. François Truffaut, 1961.

Kalifornia. Dir. Dominic Sena, 1993.

Kansas City. Dir. Robert Altman, 1996.

Kill Bill: Vol. 1. Dir. Quentin Tarantino, 2003.

Kill Bill: Vol. 2. Dir. Quentin Tarantino, 2004.

The Killing. Dir. Stanley Kubrick, 1956.

Kiss Me Deadly. Dir. Robert Aldrich, 1955.

A Knight's Tale. Dir. Brian Helgeland, 2001.

L.A. Confidential. Dir. Curtis Hanson, 1997.

The Ladies Man. Dir. Reginald Hudlin, 2000.

Ladykillers. Dir. Joel and Ethan Coen, 2004.

Lara Croft: Tomb Raider. Dir. Simon West, 2001.

The Last Picture Show. Dir. Peter Bogdanovich, 1971.

Limbo. Dir. John Sayles, 1999.

Little Caesar. Dir. Mervyn LeRoy, 1931.

Living in Oblivion. Dir. Tom DiCillo, 1995.

Lock, Stock, and Two Smoking Barrels. Dir. Guy Ritchie, 1998.

Lola rennt. Dir. Tom Tykwer, 1998.

Lone Star. Dir. John Sayles, 1996.

The Long Goodbye. Dir. Robert Altman, 1973.

Lost Highway. Dir. David Lynch, 1997.

Lucky Number Slevin. Dir. Paul McGuigan, 2006.

Mad City. Dir. Costa-Gavras, 1997.

Le Magnifique. Dir. Philippe de Broca, 1973.

Magnolia. Dir. P. T. Anderson, 1999.

The Man Called Flintstone. Dir. Joseph Barbera and William Hanna, 1966.

The Man Who Wasn't There. Dir. Joel and Ethan Coen, 2001.

The Manchurian Candidate. Dir. John Frankenheimer, 1962.

Manhattan. Dir. Woody Allen, 1979.

Marie Antoinette. Dir. Sofia Coppola, 2006.

Marnie. Dir. Alfred Hitchcock, 1964.

Mars Attacks! Dir. Tim Burton, 1996.

M*A*S*H. Dir. Robert Altman, 1970.

The Matrix. Dir. Andy and Larry Wachowski, 1999.

McCabe and Mrs. Miller. Dir. Robert Altman, 1971.

Mean Streets. Dir. Martin Scorsese, 1973.

Memento. Dir. Christopher Nolan, 2000.

A Midsummer Night's Sex Comedy. Dir. Woody Allen, 1982.

Miller's Crossing. Dir. Joel and Ethan Coen, 1990.

Mission: Impossible. Dir. Brian De Palma, 1996.

Mr. Bill's Real Life Adventures. Dir. Jim Drake, 1986.

Monkeybone. Dir. Henry Selick, 2001.

Monty Python and the Holy Grail. Dir. Terry Gilliam and Terry Jones, 1975.

Mortal Kombat. Dir. Paul W. S. Anderson, 1995.

Moulin Rouge. Dir. John Huston, 1952.

Moulin Rouge! Dir. Baz Luhrmann, 2001.

Mulholland Drive. Dir. David Lynch, 2001.

Murder, My Sweet. Dir. Edward Dmytryk, 1944.

Naked Gun: From the Files of Police Squad! Dir. David Zucker, 1988.

Naked Gun 2½: The Smell of Fear. Dir. David Zucker, 1991.

Naked Gun 33⅓: The Final Insult. Dir. Peter Segal, 1994.

Naked Lunch. Dir. David Cronenberg, 1991.

Nashville. Dir. Robert Altman, 1975.

Natural Born Killers. Dir. Oliver Stone, 1994.

Network. Dir. Sidney Lumet, 1976.

A Night at the Roxbury. Dir. John Fortenberry, 1998.

Night of the Living Dead. Dir. George A. Romero, 1968.

The Nightmare before Christmas. Dir. Henry Selick, 1993.

Nurse Betty. Dir. Neil LaBute, 2000.

O Brother, Where Art Thou? Dir. Joel and Ethan Coen, 2000.

Obsession. Dir. Brian De Palma, 1976.

Ocean's Eleven. Dir. Lewis Milestone, 1960.

Office Space. Dir. Mike Judge, 1999.

Once upon a Time in America. Dir. Sergio Leone, 1984.

The Opposite of Sex. Dir. Don Roos, 1998.

Out of Sight. Dir. Steven Soderbergh, 1998.

Pee-wee's Big Adventure. Dir. Tim Burton, 1985.

Peggy Sue Got Married. Dir. Francis Ford Coppola, 1986.

Pennies from Heaven. Dir. Herbert Ross, 1981.

Phantom of the Paradise. Dir. Brian De Palma, 1974.

Plan 9 from Outer Space. Dir. Edward D. Wood Jr., 1959.

Planet of the Apes. Dir. Franklin Schaffner, 1968.

Planet of the Apes. Dir. Tim Burton, 2001.

The Player. Dir. Robert Altman, 1992.

Pleasantville. Dir. Gary Ross, 1998.

Popeye. Dir. Robert Altman, 1980.

The Prairie Home Companion. Dir. Robert Altman, 2006.

The Prestige. Dir. Christopher Nolan, 2006.

Prêt-à-Porter (Ready to Wear). Dir. Robert Altman, 1994.

Prospero's Books. Dir. Peter Greenaway, 1991.

Psycho. Dir. Alfred Hitchcock, 1960.

Psycho. Dir. Gus Van Sant, 1998.

Public Enemy. Dir. William Wellman, 1931.

Pulp Fiction. Dir. Quentin Tarantino, 1994.

The Purple Rose of Cairo. Dir. Woody Allen, 1985.

Quiz Show. Dir. Robert Redford, 1994.

Rabid. Dir. David Cronenberg, 1977.

Radio Days. Dir. Woody Allen, 1987.

Raising Cain. Dir. Brian De Palma, 1992.

Rear Window. Dir. Alfred Hitchcock, 1954.

Rebel without a Cause. Dir. Nicholas Ray, 1955.

Red River. Dir. Howard Hawks, 1948.

Requiem for a Dream. Dir. Darren Aronofsky, 2000.

Reservoir Dogs. Dir. Quentin Tarantino, 1992.

Resident Evil. Dir. Paul W. S. Anderson, 2002.

Resident Evil: Apocalypse. Dir. Alexander Witt, 2004.

Revolver. Dir. Guy Ritchie, 2005.

Robert Altman's Jazz '34: Remembrances of Kansas City Swing. Dir. Robert Altman, 1996.

The Rocky Horror Picture Show. Dir. Jim Sharman, 1975.

Romeo Must Die. Dir. Andrzej Bartkowiak, 2000.

Rope. Dir. Alfred Hitchcock, 1948.

Rumble Fish. Dir. Francis Ford Coppola, 1983.

A Scanner Darkly. Dir. Richard Linklater, 2006.

Scanners. Dir. David Cronenberg, 1981.

Scarface. Dir. Howard Hawks, 1932.

Scary Movie. Dir. Keenen Ivory Wayans, 2000.

Scary Movie 2. Dir. Keenen Ivory Wayans, 2001.

Scary Movie 3. Dir. David Zucker, 2003.

Scary Movie 4. Dir. David Zucker, 2006.

The Searchers. Dir. John Ford, 1956.

Serenity. Dir. Joss Whedon, 2005.

The Seventh Seal. Dir. Ingmar Bergman, 1957.

Sherlock, Jr. Dir. Buster Keaton, 1924.

Shivers. Dir. David Cronenberg, 1975.

Short Cuts. Dir. Robert Altman, 1993.

Sin City. Dir. Robert Rodriguez and Frank Miller, 2005.

Sisters. Dir. Brian De Palma, 1973.

Sky Captain and the World of Tomorrow. Dir. Kerry Conran, 2004.

Sleepy Hollow. Dir. Tim Burton, 1999.
Sliding Doors. Dir. Peter Howitt, 1998.
Smiles of a Summer Night. Dir. Ingmar Bergman, 1955.
Snatch. Dir. Guy Ritchie, 2000.
Soapdish. Dir. Michael Hoffman, 1991.
The Sound of Music. Dir. Robert Wise, 1965.
South Park: Bigger, Longer, and Uncut. Dir. Trey Parker, 1999.
Spider-Man. Dir. Sam Raimi, 2002.
Spider-Man 2. Dir. Sam Raimi, 2004.
Star Trek: First Contact. Dir. Jonathan Frakes, 1996.
Star Trek: Generations. Dir. David Carson, 1994.
Star Trek: Insurrection. Dir. Jonathan Frakes, 1998.
Star Trek: Nemesis. Dir. Stuart Baird, 2002.
Star Trek: The Motion Picture. Dir. Robert Wise, 1979.
Star Trek II: The Wrath of Khan. Dir. Nicholas Meyer, 1982.
Star Trek III: The Search for Spock. Dir. Leonard Nimoy, 1984.
Star Trek IV: The Voyage Home. Dir. Leonard Nimoy, 1986.
Star Trek V: The Final Frontier. Dir. William Shatner, 1989.
Star Trek VI: The Undiscovered Country. Dir. Nicholas Meyer, 1991.
Star Wars. Dir. George Lucas, 1977.
Stardust Memories. Dir. Woody Allen, 1980.
State and Main. Dir. David Mamet, 2000.
Stay Tuned. Dir. Peter Hyams, 1992.
Storytelling. Dir. Todd Solondz, 2001.
Strange Days. Dir. Kathryn Bigelow, 1995.
Stranger than Fiction. Dir. Marc Forster, 2006.
Straw Dogs. Dir. Sam Peckinpah, 1971.
Strictly Ballroom. Dir. Baz Luhrmann, 1992.
Stuart Saves His Family. Dir. Harold Ramis, 1995.
Sullivan's Travels. Dir. Preston Sturges, 1941.
Sunset Boulevard. Dir. Billy Wilder, 1950.
Superman. Dir. Richard Donner, 1978.
Superman Returns. Dir. Bryan Singer, 2006.
Superstar. Dir. Bruce McCulloch, 1999.
Sweet and Lowdown. Dir. Woody Allen, 1999.
Swimming with Sharks. Dir. George Huang, 1994.
Syriana. Dir. Stephen Gaghan, 2005.
The Terminator. Dir. James Cameron, 1984.
They Live by Night. Dir. Nicholas Ray, 1948.
The Thirteenth Floor. Dir. Josef Rusnak, 1999.
Three Faces of Eve. Dir. Nunnally Johnson, 1957.
Three Kings. Dir. David O. Russell, 1999.
Timecode. Dir. Mike Figgis, 2000.
The Tin Drum. Dir. Volker Schlöndorff, 1979.

To Die For. Dir. Gus Van Sant, 1995.

Top Hat. Dir. Mark Sandrich, 1935.

Touch of Evil. Dir. Orson Welles, 1958.

Traffic. Dir. Steven Soderbergh, 2000.

True Romance. Dir. Tony Scott, 1993.

The Truman Show. Dir. Peter Weir, 1998.

Tune in Tomorrow. Dir. John Amiel, 1990.

21 Grams. Dir. Alejandro González Iñárritu, 2003.

Twilight Zone: The Movie. Dir. Joe Dante et al., 1983.

The Untouchables. Dir. Brian De Palma, 1987.

Vertigo. Dir. Alfred Hitchcock, 1958.

Videodrome. Dir. David Cronenberg, 1983.

Vincent. Dir. Tim Burton, 1982.

Virtuosity. Dir. Brett Leonard, 1995.

Wag the Dog. Dir. Barry Levinson, 1997.

Waking Life. Dir. Richard Linklater, 2001.

The War of the Worlds. Dir. Byron Haskin, 1953.

Wayne's World. Dir. Penelope Spheeris, 1992.

Wayne's World 2. Dir. Stephen Surjik, 1993.

The Wedding Party. Dir. Brian De Palma, 1969.

Who Framed Roger Rabbit? Dir. Robert Zemeckis, 1988.

Wild at Heart. Dir. David Lynch, 1990.

Will Success Spoil Rock Hunter? Dir. Frank Tashlin, 1957.

William Shakespeare's Romeo and Juliet. Dir. Baz Luhrmann, 1996.

Willy Wonka and the Chocolate Factory. Dir. Mel Stuart, 1971.

The Wizard of Oz. Dir. Victor Fleming, 1939.

Wrongfully Accused. Dir. Pat Proft, 1998.

X2. Dir. Bryan Singer, 2003.

The X-Files: Fight the Future. Dir. Rob Bowman, 1998.

X-Men. Dir. Bryan Singer, 2000.

X-Men: The Last Stand. Dir. Brett Ratner, 2006.

Ying hung boon sik ("A better tomorrow"). Dir. John Woo, 1986.

You Only Live Once. Dir. Fritz Lang, 1937.

Zelig. Dir. Woody Allen, 1983.

Zero Hour! Dir. Hall Bartlett, 1957.

NOTES

INTRODUCTION

1. For a discussion of nostalgia in *Twin Peaks*, see my *Strange TV*.

CHAPTER 1

1. For another version of this garden-of-forking-paths motif, see Peter Howitt's *Sliding Doors* (1998).
2. The DVD release of the film contains both the first and the fifteenth takes of the film, thus showing the net distance traveled by the various improvisations.
3. On the other hand, Jameson sometimes expands this coverage to include other forms of "marginal" culture, as when he suggests that "the only authentic cultural production today has seemed to be that which can draw on the collective experience of marginal pockets of the social life of the world system: black literature and blues, British working-class rock, women's literature, gay literature, the *roman québecois*, the literature of the Third World" (*Signatures*, 23).
4. As Alan Jones notes, the plot and scenario of *Edward Scissorhands* closely follow those of Heinrich Hoffman's 1845 story "Struwwelpeter," though Burton has professed that he was unfamiliar with that story while making the film (14).
5. Burton had apparently conceived the image of a man with scissors for hands years earlier, thus the construction of the somewhat unlikely scenario that brings such a man into existence.
6. Similar frames are spliced into *Fight Club* itself, generally involving a large, semi-erect penis, which reinforces the phallic nature of the fight club motif.

7. The film does not address the fact that simply blowing up a few buildings could never achieve this effect, as modern data systems include numerous redundancies and are distributed over extensive networks.

8. For a convenient summary of some of these criticisms, see Peter and Will Brooker's "Pulpmodernism." The Brookers, however, ultimately defend Tarantino's world as a richly constructed intertextual realm that can point toward positive modes of interaction with the highly textual world of postmodern reality.

9. For a real "drug movie," see Terry Gilliam's *Fear and Loathing in Las Vegas* (1998), which presents characters (based on gonzo journalist Hunter S. Thompson and his attorney) who thumb their noses at bourgeois propriety by going through their lives in a drug-induced haze. However, this motif merely serves to suggest the ultimate ideological bankruptcy of the 1960s oppositional political movements with which these characters are vaguely associated.

CHAPTER 2

1. See Geoffrey O'Brien for a rousing review of the pulp-fiction phenomenon of the 1950s.

2. *Strictly Ballroom* (1992), *William Shakespeare's Romeo and Juliet* (1996), and *Moulin Rouge!* all begin with the opening of a red stage curtain, emphasizing their theatricality and overt, self-conscious fictionality.

3. John Huston's 1952 film also titled *Moulin Rouge* (but without the exclamation point) focuses on Toulouse-Lautrec (José Ferrer) as the central character. Here, the diminutive painter is presented somewhat more realistically, though his presentation is still strongly tinted with Hollywood clichés.

4. The music of Hank Williams is similarly held up as a more authentic alternative to 1950s rock and roll (especially as represented by Presley) in Dennis Potter's 1993 BBC miniseries *Lipstick on Your Collar*. See my discussion of this series in *Strange TV*.

5. The 1987 biopic *La Bamba* focuses on the life of rocker Valens, who was killed, at age seventeen, in the same crash as Holly, along with Texas DJ J. P. Richardson, aka the "Big Bopper."

6. Again, the rerelease of *Grease* can be taken as a sort of Travolta nostalgia, and it is surely the case that the reemergence of Travolta as a major star after *Pulp Fiction* contributed greatly to the commercial viability of the *Grease* rerelease.

7. Note that this first class of baby boomers would have graduated from college, the year Mike Nichols's *The Graduate* scored big with its portrayal of a new college graduate disillusioned by the world awaiting him after college.

8. For a valuable discussion of the treatment of the 1950s in American advertising of the 1960s, see Thomas Frank's *The Conquest of Cool*.

9. The exception, in terms of characters, is female lead Verna Bernbaum (Marcia Gay Harden), who seems to derive from the *femme fatale* tradition of film noir.

10. There is, of course, an element of the simulacrum in any acting performance in a fictional film. However, Penn's performance in *Sweet and Lowdown* is particularly postmodern because of the mock documentary way in which the fictional Ray is presented as if he were a real historical personage, blurring the boundary between fiction and reality.

11. On this issue, see Hutcheon (422–23).

12. In this sense, *O Brother* resembles both *The Last Picture Show* and Altman's *Nashville* (1975), which suggests the way in which, by the 1970s, consumer capitalism had conscripted country music as a profit-making enterprise, separating it from its earlier and more authentic roots in Southern folk culture.

13. In finding a progressive potential in certain forms of nostalgia, Baxendale and Pawling draw directly upon Dyer's work on the utopian energies of Hollywood film in the 1930s. See also E. P. Thompson's argument that nostalgic appeals to the past can have a progressive potential under certain circumstances.

14. Though finding the film inferior to the miniseries, Peter Stead notes the smoothness with which the British miniseries translated into an American film, largely because much of the music in the miniseries was already American to begin with. The film project thus illustrates "the extent to which Potter had been influenced by American culture and conceived his original English story in the American idiom" (100).

CHAPTER 3

1. Note that Depp plays a similar detective figure in the Hughes brothers' *From Hell* (2001), which centers on the story of Jack the Ripper as told in the Alan Moore graphic novel of the same title. Here, however, the serial killer is envisioned as a harbinger of a new, ominous, and violent century, while Victorian England itself is depicted via dark and disturbing images that are reminiscent of Burton's Gotham City.

2. Most criticism on the Pee-wee Herman phenomenon has focused on his ambiguous gender. See, for example, Winning.

3. The Hardy films themselves represent examples of notoriously bad (if extremely popular) Hollywood products. But see Robert Ray's *The Avant-Garde Finds Andy Hardy* for a spirited argument that a sufficiently creative film critic might find much of value in the Hardy series.

4. Compare John Herzfeld's *Fifteen Minutes* (2001), also featuring De Niro, in which two Eastern European gangsters go on a crime spree in New York, videotaping their own crimes in an attempt to achieve the fame they have learned to believe is available in America. They hope then to use their notoriety to get into careers in filmmaking.

5. See my extensive discussion of Joyce's dialogue with Homer in *Joyce, Bakhtin, and the Literary Tradition* (17–43).

CHAPTER 4

1. See, for example, Kaplan.
2. See my book *From Box Office to Ballot Box* for a more detailed consideration of this phenomenon.
3. *Tune in Tomorrow* is based on Mario Vargas Llosa's Peruvian novel *Aunt Julia and the Scriptwriter* (1977), a work whose own postmodern aspects are discussed in my book *Vargas Llosa among the Postmodernists*.
4. A similar postmodern impulse underlies the blurring of the boundary between live action and animation in Richard Linklater's *Waking Life* (2001) and *A Scanner Darkly* (2006).
5. For a 1990s film more in the mood of *Network*, see Costa-Gavras's *Mad City* (1997), in which opportunistic media coverage turns a potentially minor situation into a genuine tragedy.
6. Among other things, the casting of Daniels provides an intertextual link to Woody Allen's *The Purple Rose of Cairo* (1985), in which Daniels plays a character in a black-and-white film who steps down off the screen and enters the real world, reversing the ontological movement of the Wagner twins in *Pleasantville*.
7. Indeed, "Across the Universe," apparently a musical marker of the new world of the 1960s, includes the repeated refrain "Nothing's gonna change my world."
8. See my discussion of this aspect of the program in *Strange TV* (97–120).
9. The remote control, of course, is crucial to the experience of channel-surfing and thus might be considered the central piece of postmodern technology. For another take on the motif of controlling the real world via a TV remote (surely a exemplary postmodern fantasy), see Frank Coraci's *Click* (2006), in which the Angel of Death (Christopher Walken) conveys to architect Michael Newman (Adam Sandler) a truly universal remote that lets him control—with near-disastrous results—not just his television, but the world at large.

CONCLUSION

1. One might contrast here something like Richard Kelly's *Donnie Darko* (2001), in which the convoluted plot is impossible to assemble into a coherent whole.

BIBLIOGRAPHY

Appignanesi, Richard. *Introducing Postmodernism*. 3rd ed. Lanham, MD: Totem Books, 2005.

Baron, Cynthia. "*The Player*'s Parody of Hollywood: A Different Kind of Suture." In *Postmodernism in the Cinema*, ed. Cristina Degli-Esposti, 21–43. New York: Berghahn Books, 1998.

Baudrillard, Jean. *Selected Writings*. Ed. Mark Poster. Stanford, CA: Stanford University Press, 1988.

Baxendale, John, and Chris Pawling. *Narrating the Thirties: A Decade in the Making, 1930 to the Present*. New York: St. Martin's, 1996.

Beard, William. *The Artist as Monster: The Cinema of David Cronenberg*. Toronto: University of Toronto Press, 2001.

Belton, John. American Cinema/American Culture. 2nd ed. Boston: McGraw-Hill, 2005.

Benjamin, Walter. "The Work of Art in the Age of Mechanical Reproduction." *Illuminations*. Trans. Harry Zohn, 219–51. New York: Harcourt, Brace, and World, 1955.

Bergan, Ronald. *The Coen Brothers*. New York: Thunder's Mouth, 2000.

Booker, M. Keith. *From Box Office to Ballot Box: The American Political Film*. Westport, CT: Praeger, 2007.

———. *Joyce, Bakhtin, and the Literary Tradition: Toward a Comparative Cultural Poetics*. Ann Arbor: University of Michigan Press, 1996.

———. *Monsters, Mushroom Clouds, and the Cold War: American Science Fiction and the Roots of Postmodernism, 1946–1964*. Westport, CT: Greenwood, 2001.

———. *Strange TV: Innovative Television Series from* The Twilight Zone *to* The X-Files. Westport, CT: Greenwood, 2002.

———. *Vargas Llosa among the Postmodernists*. Gainesville: University Press of Florida, 1994.

Brecht, Bertolt. *The Threepenny Opera*. Trans. Desmond Vesey and Eric Bentley. New York: Grove Weidenfeld, 1964.

Brie, Steve. "'Yesterday Once More': Thoughts on the Relationship between Popular Music, Audience and Authorial Intention in Dennis Potter's *Pennies from Heaven, The Singing Detective,* and *Lipstick on Your Collar.*" In *The Passion of Dennis Potter: International Collected Essays,* ed. Vernon W. Gras and John R. Cook, 205–17. New York: St. Martin's, 2000.

Brooker, Peter, and Will Brooker, eds. *Postmodern After-Images: A Reader in Film, Television, and Video.* London: Arnold, 1997.

———. "Pulpmodernism: Tarantino's Affirmative Action." In *Postmodern After-Images,* ed. Brooker and Brooker, 89–100.

Bürger, Peter. *Theory of the Avant-garde.* Trans. Michael Shaw. Minneapolis: University of Minnesota Press, 1984.

Butler, Christopher. *After the Wake: An Essay on the Contemporary Avant-Garde.* Oxford: Clarendon, 1980.

Chumo II, Peter N. "'The Next Best Thing to a Time Machine': Quentin Tarantino's *Pulp Fiction.*" *Post Script* 15, no. 3 (1996): 16–28.

Creeber, Glen. *Dennis Potter: Between Two Worlds.* London: Macmillan, 1998.

Debord, Guy. *The Society of the Spectacle* [1967]. Trans. Donald Nicholson-Smith. Cambridge, MA: Zone Books, 1995.

Degli-Esposti, Cristina, ed. *Postmodernism in the Cinema.* New York: Berghahn Books, 1998.

Denzin, Norman K. *Images of Postmodern Society: Social Theory and Contemporary Cinema.* London: Sage, 1995.

Dworkin, Susan. *Double De Palma: A Film Study with Brian De Palma.* New York: Newmarket, 1984.

Dyer, Richard. "Entertainment and Utopia." In *Genre: The Musical,* ed. Rick Altman, 175–89. London: Routledge and Kegan Paul, 1981.

Ebert, Roger. *"Fight Club."* http://www.suntimes.com/ebert/ebert_reviews/1999/10/101502.html.

Flinn, Caryl. *Strains of Utopia: Gender, Nostalgia, and Hollywood Film Music.* Princeton, NJ: Princeton University Press, 1992.

Frank, Thomas. *The Conquest of Cool: Business Culture, Counterculture, and the Rise of Hip Consumerism.* Chicago: University of Chicago Press, 1997.

Gitlin, Todd. *Inside Prime Time.* Berkeley: University of California Press, 2000.

Haen, Theo d'. "Postmodernism in American Fiction and Art." In *Approaching Postmodernism,* ed. Douwe Fokkema and Hans Bertens, 211–31. Amsterdam: John Benjamins, 1986.

Hanke, Ken. *Tim Burton: An Unauthorized Biography of the Filmmaker.* Los Angeles: Renaissance Books, 2000.

Hart, Kevin. *Postmodernism: A Beginner's Guide.* Oxford: Oneworld, 2004.

Harvey, David. *The Condition of Postmodernity: An Enquiry into the Origins of Cultural Change.* Oxford: Blackwell, 1990.

Hirsch, Foster. *Love, Sex, Death, and the Meaning of Life: The Films of Woody Allen*. Cambridge, MA: Da Capo, 2001.

Hutcheon, Linda. *A Poetics of Postmodernism: History, Theory, Fiction*. New York: Routledge, 1988.

Hutchinson, George. *The Harlem Renaissance in Black and White*. Cambridge, MA: Belknap/Harvard University Press, 1995.

Huyssen, Andreas. *After the Great Divide: Modernism, Mass Culture, Postmodernism*. Bloomington: Indiana University Press, 1986.

Jameson, Fredric. *The Geopolitical Aesthetic: Cinema and Space in the World System*. Bloomington: Indiana University Press, 1992.

———. *The Political Unconscious: Narrative as a Socially Symbolic Act*. Ithaca, NY: Cornell University Press, 1981.

———. *Postmodernism; or, The Cultural Logic of Late Capitalism*. Durham, NC: Duke University Press, 1991.

———. "Postmodernism and Consumer Society." In *The Anti-Aesthetic: Essays on Postmodern Culture*, ed. Hal Foster, 111–25. Port Townsend, WA: Bay Press, 1983.

———. *Signatures of the Visible*. New York: Routledge, 1992.

———. "Third-World Literature in the Era of Multinational Capitalism." *Social Text* 15 (1986): 65–88.

Jones, Alan. "Tim Burton's *Edward Scissorhands*." *Cinefantastique* 25, no. 5 (1994): 12–19.

Kaplan, E. Anne. *Rocking around the Clock: Music Television, Post Modernism, and Consumer Culture*. New York: Routledge, 1987.

Kucich, John, and Dianne F. Sadoff, eds. *Victorian Afterlife: Postmodern Culture Rewrites the Nineteenth Century*. Minneapolis: University of Minnesota Press, 2000.

Le Cain, Maximilian. "In Dreams: A Review of *Muholland Drive*." In *Senses of Cinema: An Online Film Journal Devoted to the Serious and Eclectic Discussion of Cinema* 19 (March–April 2002). http://www.sensesofcinema.com/contents/01/19/mulholland_dreams.html.

Levine, Josh. *The Coen Brothers: The Story of Two American Filmmakers*. Toronto: ECW Press, 2000.

Lipman, Amanda. Review of *Pulp Fiction*. *Sight and Sound* 4, no. 11 (November 1994): 50–51.

Lukács, Georg. *The Historical Novel*. Trans. Hannah Mitchell and Stanley Mitchell. Lincoln: University of Nebraska Press, 1983.

———. *The Theory of the Novel*. Trans. Anna Bostock. Cambridge, MA: MI Press, 1971.

Lyotard, Jean-François. *The Postmodern Condition: A Report on Knowledge*. Trans. Geoff Bennington and Brian Massumi. Minneapolis: University of Minnesota Press, 1984.

Mandel, Ernest. *Late Capitalism*. Trans. Joris De Bres. London: NLB; Atlantic Highlands, NJ: Humanities Press, 1975.

McHale, Brian. *Postmodernist Fiction*. New York: Methuen, 1987.

Mottram, James. *The Coen Brothers: The Life of the Mind*. Dulles, VA: Brassey's, 2000.

O'Brien, Geoffrey. *Hardboiled America: Lurid Paperbacks and the Masters of Noir*. 1981. Expanded ed. New York: Da Capo, 1997.

Pérez Soler, Bernardo, and Edward Lawrenson. "Pup Fiction." *Sight and Sound* 11, no. 5 (May 2001): 28–30.

Powell, James M., and Joe Lee. *Postmodernism for Beginners*. London: Readers and Writers, 1998.

Quart, Alissa. "Networked." *Film Comment* 41, no. 4 (2005): 48–51.

Ray, Robert. *The Avant-Garde Finds Andy Hardy*. Cambridge, MA: Harvard University Press, 1995.

Rogers, J. A. "Jazz at Home." *The New Negro: Voices of the Harlem Renaissance*. Alaine Locke, ed. 216–24. New York: Simon and Schuster, 1997.

Salisbury, Mark, ed. *Burton on Burton*. Rev. ed. London: Faber and Faber, 2000.

Sarris, Andrew. *The American Cinema: Directors and Directions, 1929–1968*. 1968. New ed. New York: Da Capo, 1996.

Schatz, Thomas. *The Genius of the System: Hollywood Filmmaking in the Studio Era*. New York: Henry Holt, 1988.

Smith, Jeff. *The Sounds of Commerce: Marketing Popular Film Music*. New York: Columbia University Press, 1998.

Stam, Robert. *Subversive Pleasures: Bakhtin, Cultural Criticism, and Film*. Baltimore: Johns Hopkins University Press, 1989.

Stead, Peter. *Dennis Potter*. Bridgend, Mid Glamorgan, UK: Seren Books, 1993.

Thompson, E. P. *The Making of the English Working Class*. 1963. New York: Vintage/Random House, 1966.

Walsh, David. "Shouting but not Saying Much—*Requiem for a Dream*." World Socialist Web Site. 2000. http://wsws.org/articles/2000/nov2000/requ-n29.shtml.

Weber, Max. *The Protestant Ethic and the Spirit of Capitalism*. 1904–1905. Trans. Talcott Parsons. 1930. London: Routledge, 1995.

Williams, Raymond. *The Country and the City*. New York: Oxford University Press, 1975.

Winning, Rob. "Pee Wee Herman Un-Mascs Our Cultural Myths about Masculinity." *Journal of American Culture* 11, no. 2 (1988): 57–63.

Woods, Tim. *Beginning Postmodernism*. Manchester, England: Manchester University Press, 1999.

INDEX

About the Author

M. KEITH BOOKER is Professor of English at the University of Arkansas. He is the author of numerous articles and books on modern literature, literary theory, television, and film including *Monsters, Mushroom Clouds, and the Cold War* (2001), *Strange TV: Innovative Television Series from "The Twilight Zone" to "The X-Files"* (2002), *Science Fiction Television* (2004), *Alternate Americas: Science Fiction Film and American Culture* (2006), *Drawn to Television: Prime-Time Animation from The Flintstones to Family Guy* (2006), and *From Box Office to Ballot Box: The American Political Film* (2007).